The Green Revolution Reconsidered

Other Books Published in Cooperation with The International Food Policy Research Institute

Agricultural Change and Rural Poverty: Variations on a Theme by Dharm Narain
Edited by John W. Mellor and Gunvant M. Desai

Crop Insurance for Agricultural Development: Issues and Experience
Edited by Peter B. R. Hazell, Carlos Pomareda, and Alberto Valdés

Accelerating Food Production in Sub-Saharan Africa
Edited by John W. Mellor, Christopher L. Delgado, and Malcolm J. Blackie

Agricultural Price Policy for Developing Countries
Edited by John W. Mellor and Raisuddin Ahmed

Food Subsidies in Developing Countries: Costs, Benefits, and Policy Options
Edited by Per Pinstrup-Andersen

Variability in Grain Yields: Implications for Agricultural Research and Policy in Developing Countries
Edited by Jock R. Anderson and Peter B. R. Hazell

Seasonal Variability in Third World Agriculture: The Consequences for Food Security
Edited by David E. Sahn

The Green Revolution Reconsidered

The Impact of High-Yielding Rice Varieties in South India

PETER B. R. HAZELL
C. RAMASAMY

with contributions by

P. K. Aiyasamy, Neal Bliven, Barbara Harriss, John Harriss, Mauricio Jaramillo, Per Pinstrup-Andersen, V. Rajagopalan, and Sudhir Wanmali

Published for the International Food Policy Research Institute

THE JOHNS HOPKINS UNIVERSITY PRESS
Baltimore and London

The Johns Hopkins University Press
701 West 40th Street
Baltimore, Maryland 21211-2190
The Johns Hopkins Press Ltd., London

(∞)The paper used in this book meets the minimum requirements of American National Standard for Information Sciences—Permanence of Paper for Printed Library Materials, ANSI Z39.48-1984.

Library of Congress Cataloging-in-Publication Data

Hazell, P. B. R.
The Green Revolution reconsidered: the impact of high-yielding rice varieties in South India / Peter B.R. Hazell, C. Ramasamy: with contributions by P.K. Aiyasamy . . . [et al.].
p. cm.
"Published for the International Food Policy Research Institute."
Includes bibliographical references and index.
ISBN 0–8018–4185–2
1. Green Revolution—India—North Arcot. 2. Rice—India—North Arcot. 3. Farmers—India—North Arcot. 4. Rural poor—India—North Arcot. I. Ramasamy, C., 1947– . II. Aiyasamy, P. K. III. International Food Policy Research Institute. IV. Title.
HD2075.N56G74 1991.
330.954′8205—dc20 90–26234

Contents

PART II: THE INDIRECT EFFECTS

Tables and Figures

Tables

Figures

Preface

THE "GREEN REVOLUTION"—a term used for rapid increases in wheat and rice yields in developing countries brought about by improved varieties combined with the expanded use of fertilizers and other chemical inputs—has had an important impact on incomes and food supplies in many developing countries. It has also spawned a lively controversy over its impact on the poor, with some critics claiming that inequality, and perhaps even absolute poverty, has increased in rural areas as a consequence of the green revolution.

Given the importance of future rounds of yield-increasing technologies for fostering economic development and feeding growing populations in most developing countries, it is imperative that the economic and social forces released by these technologies be better understood so that they can be harnessed to achieve the twin goals of growth and equity. To this end, the International Food Policy Research Institute (IFPRI) embarked, in the early 1980s, on a series of in-depth case studies of the impact of technological change in agriculture. This study of the North Arcot district in South India is the first in that series, and it was undertaken in close collaboration with the Tamil Nadu Agricultural University (TNAU) at Coimbatore. A companion study has also been undertaken in the Eastern Province of Zambia.

A unique feature of these studies lies in the emphasis given to the growth linkage effects of agricultural growth on the rural nonfarm economy. Inspired by the earlier work of John Mellor and associates at Cornell University, it was hypothesized that the rural poor may obtain significant indirect benefits from agricultural growth because of increases in income-earning opportunities that arise in the local nonfarm economy. Moreover, this potential has not been adequately addressed in previous studies of the green revolution.

Initial funding for this study was generously provided by the Ford Foundation, New Delhi, and the Overseas Development Administration of the United Kingdom. The project ran into financial distress when a severe drought in the study region undermined the value of the household surveys conducted in 1982/83, and the need arose to repeat the surveys in the following year. The funds required to complete the study were provided by the Swiss Development Cooperation and Humanitarian Aid as part of its support of the companion study in Zambia. The Swiss Development Cooperation and Humanitarian Aid also funded a workshop held at Ootacamund, Tamil Nadu, in February 1986 at which preliminary results from the study were presented to an international group of scholars and Indian government officials. The final product benefited enormously from the open and frank discussions held at that workshop.

Many individuals have contributed to the successful completion of this study. We are grateful to them all. A special note of thanks is due B. H. Farmer, Robert Chambers, Nanjamma Chinnappa, and John and Barbara Harriss, who, as members of the Cambridge and Madras universities team that surveyed the North Arcot region in 1973/74, not only made their earlier data fully available to us for comparative analysis but also assisted greatly in the design and implementation of our own surveys to enhance their comparability with the 1973/74 survey.

Mr. A. Venkataraman and Professor V. Rajagopalan first directed our attention to the North Arcot region and, as successive vice-chancellors of Tamil Nadu Agricultural University (TNAU), were instrumental in forging and sustaining the administrative arrangements that made this study possible. Nor could the surveys have been undertaken without the enthusiastic assistance of Professor P. K. Aiyasamy (then head of the Department of Agricultural Economics at TNAU), in designing the survey instruments and in recruiting and training the field team. Professor Sundaresan, head of the Poultry Research and Development Centre, also provided vital support to the field team at its Vellore base, and Dr. Radhakrishnan, Management Information Services, Madras, supervised the entry and processing of the survey data. But the real heroes of the survey were the enumerators who, despite the unusually harsh conditions of the 1982/83 drought, diligently served at their posts and maintained high professional standards. They are as follows: S. Akbar Batcha, A. Alagesan, M. Arumugam, S. R. Asokan, M. Bhoopalan, M. Chandrasekaran, M. Dhamodharan, K. Dasarathan, V. Gunasekaran, P. Jayabalan, G. Jayaraman, U. Jayaraman, D. Kandaswamy, K. Mani, S. Marudhachalam, S. Radhakrishnan, and V. Subramanian.

Finally, we are grateful to Jock Anderson, Randy Barker, Robert Chambers, Dana Dalrymple, B. H. Farmer, Marco Ferroni, Barbara and John Harriss, and Michael Lipton for comments on parts of earlier drafts of this study, though we absolve them of responsibility for the final product.

The Green Revolution Reconsidered

CHAPTER 1

Introduction

Peter B. R. Hazell and C. Ramasamy

AGRICULTURAL TECHNOLOGIES OF the "green revolution" type have brought substantial direct benefits to many developing countries. Prominent among these has been increased food output, sometimes even in excess of the increasing food demands of a growing population. This has enabled food prices to decline in some countries, while in others prices have not risen as fast as they would have without the green revolution.

One of the attractions of the green revolution technologies is that they are, in principle, scale neutral, and can raise yields and incomes for both small- and large-scale farmers. Yet a number of early studies of the impact of the green revolution concluded that the rural poor did not receive a fair share of the benefits generated. It was argued that large farmers were the main adopters of the new technology, and smaller farmers were either unaffected or adversely affected because the green revolution resulted in lower product prices, higher input prices, efforts by large farmers to increase rents or force tenants off the land, and attempts by larger farmers to increase landholdings by purchasing smaller farms, thus forcing those farmers into landlessness. It was also argued that the green revolution encouraged unnecessary mechanization, with a resulting reduction in rural employment (Cleaver 1972; Griffin 1974). The net result, as argued by some, was a rapid increase in the inequality of income and asset distribution, and a worsening of absolute poverty in areas affected by the green revolution (e.g., Griffin 1972, 1974; Fraenkel 1976; Harriss 1977; Hewitt de Alacantara 1976; ILO 1977; Pearse 1980).

These conclusions have not proved valid when subjected to the scrutiny of more recent evidence (Blyn 1983; Pinstrup-Andersen and Hazell 1985; Lipton 1989). Ahluwalia (1985) provides evidence that the incidence of rural poverty in India declined almost steadily between 1967/68 and 1977/78. This is contrary to the earlier findings of Griffin and Ghose (1979), who analyzed comparable data for the period 1960/61 to 1973/74. Ahluwalia (1977, 1985) and Rao (1985) found that the incidence of rural poverty is negatively related to agricultural output levels per head.

Bell, Hazell, and Slade (1982) provide evidence that agricultural technology can help alleviate absolute rural poverty. They studied the combined impact of an irrigation project and high-yielding varieties (HYVs) of rice in the Muda River region of Malaysia over the period 1967–74. The average per capita income of the population living in the project area increased by 70 percent when measured in constant prices. Landowning households gained relatively most, but landless paddy workers also increased their real per capita incomes by 97 percent, despite a wholesale shift to tractor mechanization for land preparation (Bell, Hazell, and Slade 1982, Table 7.7).

Using farm-level data from a number of Asian countries, Barker and Herdt (1978) found that while small farmers reported greater difficulty in obtaining some inputs, such as credit and fertilizers, differences in the rate of adoption of new varieties between small and large farmers were not significant, even in villages with marked inequality in land distribution. In a study of the impact of the green revolution in the Indian Punjab, Blyn (1983) concluded that (1) real income from family resources increased relatively more for families with smaller holdings, thereby reducing inequality, and (2) the total employment of hired labor increased while real wages remained constant, and this led to a clear gain for labor.

Why did the earlier studies err? Pinstrup-Andersen and Hazell (1985) offer four possible reasons. First, the studies were conducted too soon after the release of the green revolution technologies. While it was true that early adopters were primarily larger farmers, the studies failed to recognize that small farmers would follow quickly once they observed the success of their larger-scale brethren. (See, for example, Byerlee and Harrington 1983; Chaudhry 1982; Pinstrup-Andersen 1982; Blyn 1983; Herdt and Capule 1983; and Prahladachar 1983.) This pattern may also have been reinforced—perhaps as a result of the initial criticisms—by the later release of plant varieties that were better suited to small-farm needs than the initial HYVs (Lipton 1989), and by improvements in the provision of services—especially credit, input supplies, marketing, and extension—for small farmers (Griffin 1988).

Second, the benefits to the poor, as consumers of rice and wheat, through lower prices were largely overlooked. Empirical evidence of consumer gains from technological change in developing-country agriculture is plentiful (e.g., Akino and Hayami 1975; Mellor 1975; Evenson and Flores 1978; Scobie and Posada 1978; Pinstrup-Andersen 1979;

and Scobie 1979). The consumer gains come about because food prices are lower than they would have been in the absence of the production increases induced by technological change. Population growth, import substitution, export growth, and domestic price policies can dampen the price reduction. In fact, price and foreign trade policies have been used extensively to strike a more desirable balance between the harmful effects of price decreases on farmers and future food production, and the beneficial effects on consumers. Since the green revolution generates an economic surplus by more efficient use of resources and reduced unit costs, consumer gains need not imply producer losses. Both may gain.

Third, little or no attention was given to indirect growth linkages of the green revolution with the rural nonfarm economy and the resulting impact on the incomes of the poor. Johnston and Kilby (1975), Mellor (1976), and Mellor and Johnston (1984) have argued that agricultural growth focused on small- and medium-sized farms generates rapid, equitable, and geographically dispersed growth because of substantial labor-intensive linkages with the rural nonfarm economy.

Accumulating empirical evidence from Asia confirms that these indirect effects are nearly as important for rural areas as the direct effects of technological change (Gibb 1974; Bell, Hazell, and Slade 1982; Haggblade and Hazell 1989). The indirect benefits, however, are not restricted to the poor. They also increase the earnings of skilled workers as well as providing lucrative returns to capital and managerial skills. In the Muda study, for example, Bell, Hazell, and Slade found that the indirect benefits of the project were skewed in favor of the nonfarm households in the region, many of which were already relatively well off. They also found that even among agricultural households, the landed households fared better than the landless. The point to be made is that although the indirect effects of agricultural growth are unlikely to improve the relative distribution of income within rural areas, they can still have wide-reaching effects in alleviating absolute poverty.

Fourth, the impact of the green revolution was frequently confused with the impact of population growth, or with institutional arrangements, agricultural policies, and labor-saving mechanization. Such confusion leads to incorrect identification of the causes of rural poverty, and thus to inappropriate recommendations for action to reduce such poverty. It also leads to a failure to appreciate the extent to which poverty and malnutrition would have been worse today without the additional food bestowed by the green revolution.

It also seems likely that too much was concluded from a limited number of case studies. Given the vastness of the South Asian subcontinent and the diversity of natural and social environments that it contains, as Farmer (1986) observes, "It is *prima facie* not to be expected that 'the new technology' would operate in the same way or have the same social and economic effects all over South Asia, or even all over any one of its countries."

To understand more fully both the short- and long-term impacts of technological change on rural welfare, and in order to assist in the design of appropriate technologies, policies, and institutional change to enhance the poverty-reducing role of technological change, the International Food Policy Research Institute and the Tamil Nadu Agricultural University (IFPRI-TNAU) collaborated in an in-depth study of the changes induced by technological change in a rice-growing region in South India.

The selected area in the North Arcot district offered several advantages. First, it is an important rice-growing region that has benefited from the high-yielding varieties developed in the late 1960s. As in many other green revolution areas, there has also been an accompanying increase in irrigation and the use of other modern inputs, especially fertilizers. Paddy yields grew at nearly 3 percent per year over the period 1950/51 to 1984/85, with most of the increase occurring since the late 1960s. These gains are modest compared with the more dramatic changes observed in Punjab and Haryana, but the North Arcot region usefully typifies the more common experience of other rice-growing areas in India.

Second, the region is dominated by small-scale farms; in 1983 the average farm size was 1.2 hectares. Given also that about one-third of the rural households are landless agricultural laborers, the equity issue is an important one for the region.

Third, the region is removed from any major urban or industrial center, and so agricultural growth is the main driving force in the local economy. This facilitates analysis of the growth linkage effects of agricultural growth on the nonfarm economy.

Last, but by no means least, the region was studied in 1973/74 by a team from Cambridge and Madras universities (Farmer 1977). This study involved the collection of monthly household survey data for one year covering detailed aspects of farm management, employment, sources of income, household assets, food consumption, and expenditure patterns. The household survey included farm and nonfarm households in the rural areas. In addition, a survey of employment and trade in one of the local towns was conducted.

An important finding of the Cambridge and Madras universities study was that only about 13 percent of the paddy area was planted to HYVs despite official statistics claiming that 39 percent of the area was so planted (Chinnappa 1977). However, in a postscript study based on a return visit in 1976, John Harriss (1977) found that HYVs had by then been adopted much more widely. This is also supported by available statistics on rice production for North Arcot. Consequently, by conducting a similar set of surveys 10 years later, it was hoped to learn much about the impact of the HYVs over a crucial period of technological change.

The book is organized in two parts. In Part 1, Chapter 2 provides essential background information on the study region and its economy, the changes in agricultural technology and output that occurred over the period of study, and the surveys and the database used in the research. Two features of the IFPRI-TNAU surveys described in Chapter 2 deserve special mention. First, although the individual households selected in the Cambridge and Madras universities and IFPRI-TNAU rural surveys were necessarily different, both surveys were conducted in the same 11 villages. These villages were originally selected as a representative sample for the study region. Second, the IFPRI-TNAU surveys were initially undertaken in 1982/83, but because this turned out to be a severe drought year, the survey was repeated in 1983/84 using a subsample of households from the previous year. The discussion of agricultural growth also includes an analysis of the sources of growth; this analysis is complemented by Appendix A, where formal decomposition methods are applied in an attempt to unravel the separate contributions of increases in HYVs, fertilizer, and irrigation to increasing rice production.

The remaining chapters of Part 1 (Chapters 3 to 6) are concerned with the socioeconomic changes that occurred in the 11 sample villages between the two surveys. Chapter 3 is concerned with changes in farm production, farm income, employment, wages, family income, consumption expenditure, and the distribution of land, and uses the survey data to analyze these changes at a pooled village level. In Chapter 4, an anthropologist (John Harriss) provides an independent but parallel analysis, based on his own fieldwork in 1972/73 and 1983/84. His analysis largely corroborates the findings in Chapter 3 and provides additional insights into some of the causal factors at work. Harriss also addresses the important question of whether the green revolution has tended to polarize class and political alliances, particularly between the rich and poor, that might lead to the kind of political unrest anticipated by some of the more radical critics of the green revolution.

In Chapter 5, Per Pinstrup-Andersen and Mauricio Jaramillo deal with observed changes in food consumption and nutrition among the sample households, and develop an analytical framework for measuring the nutritional impact of the green revolution.

To conclude Part 1, Chapter 6 examines aspects of the intervillage variation in the changes that have occurred. Building on earlier work by Chambers and Harriss (1977), John Harriss seeks to classify the villages according to underlying differences in their resource endowments, location, and caste and class structure, as a basis for better understanding the patterns of change induced by the green revolution.

Part 2 is concerned with the indirect benefits of agricultural growth to the region's nonfarm economy. We begin in Chapter 7 with the construction of a social accounting matrix (SAM) that provides a detailed description of the structure of the regional economy in 1982/83. The SAM, which is based largely on the IFPRI-TNAU 1982/83 surveys, features 59 production sector accounts, 134 commodity accounts, 8 factor accounts, 10 household accounts, 14 government accounts, a capital account, and a rest-of-world account. It is one of the most detailed sets of accounts that have ever been compiled for a rural region, and it provides insights into the linkages between different parts of the regional economy.

In Chapter 8, the SAM becomes the database for a model of the regional economy. This model is an extended input-output model in which production, household consumption, savings, and some government activities are endogenized; the exogenous variables are exports, investments, and remaining government activity. Once validated, the model provides estimates of the income multiplier arising in the nonfarm economy, given a unit increase in agricultural income. The model is also used to estimate what the regional economy would have been like in the early 1980s had the agricultural growth of the previous decade not occurred. The model is particularly attractive for these purposes because (1) it provides detailed results by production activity and household type, and (2) it enables the impact of agricultural growth to be separated from other autonomous sources of growth that occurred in the regional economy.

Chapter 9 provides a descriptive analysis of the changes that occurred between 1973 and 1983 in the private sector of Arni, one of the market towns located in the study region. The analysis is based on survey data that the author, Barbara Harriss, collected during her own fieldwork in 1973 and 1983. The analysis includes a description of the changes that occurred in the number and types of firms, and in firm assets, output, income, and employment. There is also an analysis of the changes in wages and total employment that occurred in Arni between 1973 and 1983, and in Arni's trading patterns in relation to the study region and the rest of the world.

If agricultural growth is to stimulate the development of the region's nonfarm economy, then the provision of many key services, such as credit, agroprocessing, marketing, health, education, transport, communication, and retail and personal services, must keep pace with the growth in demand. In Chapter 10, Sudhir Wanmali provides a detailed description of the spatial patterns of provision and use of services in the study region and how these changed during the period 1973–83. He also uses the IFPRI-TNAU household survey data to analyze the determinants of rural household demand for services, and especially the role of distance. Convenient access to services is clearly as important as their existence and cost. An important subsidiary outcome of the analysis in Chapter 10 is the support it provides for the definition of the study region as a meaningful unit of analysis for the growth linkages work reported in Chapters 7 and 8.

The book concludes with a synthesis of the research findings and a discussion of their implications for agricultural research and policy.

Part I

The Direct Effects

CHAPTER 2

North Arcot and the Green Revolution

C. Ramasamy, Peter B. R. Hazell, and P. K. Aiyasamy

The North Arcot Economy

NORTH ARCOT DISTRICT, which embraces the study region, lies in the northwest of Tamil Nadu state. It is a relatively densely populated region; in 1981 the population density was 357 persons per square kilometer of land. It is also a relatively poor region within India. For example, in 1980/81 the district's net domestic product (NDP) at factor cost was Rs 3,285 million, or Rs 750 (US$95) per capita. This compared with a national average in 1983 of US$260 per capita (World Bank 1986).

Agriculture is the predominant activity in the region, accounting for 40 percent of NDP (Table 2.1). Within the agricultural sector, paddy, groundnuts, and sugarcane are the predominant sources of income. These crops also support a downstream agroprocessing industry that is an important part of the manufacturing sector. In 1981 there were 1,825 paddy hullers, 542 groundnut decorticators, 850 oil mills, and three major sugar factories in the district. Milk production is also important, and a sizable herd of milk and draft animals helps support about 300 tanneries in the district, as well as numerous butchers and dairy-processing and retail shops.

Manufacturing accounts for 20 percent of the region's NDP (Table 2.1). Apart from agroprocessing and tanneries, the main manufacturing activities are silk and cotton textiles, an array of cottage industries, and chemical and metal manufacturing.

According to the 1981 census, the agricultural sector employed 1.16 million full-time workers, or 68 percent of the region's work force. Of these, 606,000 were cultivators and 552,000 were agricultural laborers. A further 111,000 workers were employed in household industry, and 437,000 were employed in other activities. The largest formal employer is the government. In 1981, the combined employment of central, state,

TABLE 2.1
Structure of Regional Production, North Arcot District, 1980/81

Sector	*Net Domestic Product (million Rs)*	*Percent of Total NDP*
Agriculture & allied activities	1,329.8	40.5
Manufacturing	649.2	19.8
Trade, hotels, & restaurants	406.4	12.4
Construction	188.7	5.7
Transport & storage (other than railways)	151.0	4.6
Real estate	86.2	2.6
Banking & insurance	69.5	2.1
Public administration	64.7	2.0
Electricity, gas, & water	41.1	1.3
Communications	36.5	1.1
Railways	25.2	0.8
Mining & quarrying	19.1	0.6
All other sectors	217.5	6.6
Total	3,284.9	100.0

Source: Assistant director of statistics, Vellore.

and district government, quasi-government organizations, municipalities, and block development offices was 73,000 jobs, or 5 percent of the region's full-time work force.

There are about 23 urban centers in the district with populations of 8,000 or more, and 13 of these are *taluk* headquarters. Vellore is the district capital and has a population of about 250,000. Of a total population of 4.4 million people in North Arcot district, only 1.0 million, or 23 percent, live in urban areas. The urban population increased at an average rate of 2.6 percent per year between 1971 and 1981, compared with a 1.3 percent growth rate for the rural population.

The district is blessed with a relatively good infrastructure. A dense network of roads extending over 8,800 kilometers connects all 2,049 rural villages in the district. A railway line also passes through the district and connects all the important towns. There are about 1,037 post offices and 126 telegraph offices. Almost all the villages have electricity.

Every village with a population of 300 or more has a primary school, and a high school is generally available within a radius of five miles. There are 536 hospitals, 18 blood banks, and about 300 child welfare centers. There is also a wide network of banking facilities, with 281 commercial bank branches servicing the district.

Agriculture

Paddy and groundnuts are the major crops, and these are grown primarily in the eastern part of the district. They each account for about one-third of the total cultivated area in the district. The western part of North Arcot is more diversified and produces sugarcane, bananas, horticultural crops, and coconut. Cattle provide the main source of draft power for crop production and also by-products such as milk, calves, and manure.

The district enjoys two monsoons: the southwest monsoon from June to September and the northeast monsoon from October to December. The northeast monsoon is the most important and provides about 60 percent of the total annual rainfall of 972 millimeters. In harmony with these rainfall patterns, paddy has traditionally been grown in three well-defined seasons, namely *samba*, *navarai*, and *sornavari*. The *samba* crop is the main rainy-season crop. It is sown in July or August and harvested in December or January. The *navarai* crop coincides with the dry season and depends entirely on irrigation. It stretches from December or January to May. The *sornavari* crop extends from May or June to September and encompasses the light, southwest monsoon.

Millets and sorghum are grown as rainfed crops from June–July to October–November, and as irrigated crops from February–March to June–July. The main cropping season for pulses (red gram, black gram, and green gram) is from June–July to December–January. For groundnuts, the rainfed season is from June–July to September–October, and the irrigated crop is grown between December–January and March–April. Sugarcane and bananas are planted in January and harvested in December.

Of a total gross area of about 690,000 hectares planted to crops in the district each year, 400,000 hectares (58 percent) are irrigated. The net irrigated area is about 250,000 hectares. Water is supplied by canals (7 percent of the net irrigated area), tanks (33 percent), and wells (60 percent). Unlike tubewells, the wells in North Arcot are large, open wells sunk in the regolith to tap groundwater supplies in the crystalline rock beneath. There are about 290,000 irrigation wells in the district, or one for every 1.81 hectares of net sown area. This is the highest ratio of all the districts in the state of Tamil Nadu. Rural electrification has had a strong influence on the expansion of well irrigation; of a total of 160,000 pumpsets in 1982/83, 140,000 were electric and only 20,000 were diesel powered.

Irrigation allows almost continuous cropping of the land throughout

TABLE 2.2
Annual Rainfall and Area, Yield, and Production of Paddy and Groundnuts, North Arcot District

Year	Paddy			Groundnuts			Annual Rainfall (mm)
	Area (thous ha)	Yield (kg/ha)	Production (thous t)	Area (thous ha)	Yield (kg/ha)	Production (thous t)	
1961/62	259	1,493	387	185	1,232	228	1,045
1962/63	279	1,440	402	206	1,189	245	1,351
1963/64	293	1,438	422	201	1,214	244	1,198
1964/65	305	1,570	480	198	1,020	202	993
1965/66	275	1,397	384	200	715	143	1,131
1966/67	301	1,320	397	202	960	194	1,239
1967/68	278	1,180	329	220	805	177	745
1968/69	170	1,224	208	201	796	160	741
1969/70	251	1,540	387	189	825	156	1,033
1970/71	294	2,143	631	181	1,122	203	811
1971/72	274	2,064	566	227	1,044	237	1,075
1972/73	290	1,906	554	223	812	181	1,034
1973/74	269	1,858	500	246	1,024	252	732
1974/75	233	1,729	404	228	908	207	896
1975/76	241	2,116	511	229	1,131	259	997
1976/77	276	2,073	572	226	823	186	1,283
1977/78	316	2,335	737	222	1,243	276	1,472
1978/79	295	2,179	642	210	814	171	1,192
1979/80	307	2,182	671	212	1,052	223	1,048
1980/81	136	1,844	250	200	650	130	570
1981/82	167	2,345	391	265	1,264	335	1,062
1982/83	118	2,452	290	230	1,291	297	751
1983/84	265	2,615	693	305	1,000	305	1,272
1984/85	255	2,694	687	208	1,076	224	1,076
Growth rate (%)	−1.47	2.94	1.47	0.96	0.07	1.04	n.a.
Coefficient of variation (%)	19.79	11.37	28.58	10.12	18.83	22.52	21.58
Average:							
1963/64–1965/66	291	1,468	429	200	983	196	1,107
1977/78–1979/80	306	2,232	683	215	1,036	223	1,237
Percent change	5.2	52.0	59.2	7.5	5.4	13.8	11.7

Note: The coefficients of variation were calculated after removing trend.

the year. However, since tanks and wells need adequate rain to replenish water reserves each year, they provide only limited insurance against drought. This is particularly troublesome because the region experiences wide variations in annual rainfall; coefficients of variation range from 18 to 31 percent among the 13 *taluks* in the district. During a severe drought in 1982/83, for example, the gross paddy area planted fell 40 percent below trend (Table 2.2).

Paddy production is particularly affected by variations in annual rainfall; the coefficient of variation (cv) around trend was 29 percent during the period 1961/62 to 1984/85 (Table 2.2). Yields are less affected by rainfall (cv = 11 percent) than the area planted (cv = 20 percent), suggesting that farmers adjust the area of paddy grown to fit available water reserves each year.

Groundnut production is slightly less variable than paddy; the cv around trend was 23 percent during 1961/62 to 1984/85. Unlike paddy, groundnut yields are less stable than the area planted. This is because only part of the crop is irrigated.

Small farmers are prevalent in North Arcot. In 1979 there were 574,000 holdings and the average size was 1 hectare. About 68 percent of the farms were 1 hectare or less, and about 86 percent were 2 hectares or less.

North Arcot is also dominated by owner-operated farms. Pure tenant farms are scarce, and most land-leasing arrangements involve farmers who already own some land of their own. Rents are paid in cash or kind, but they usually involve fixed rents. Sharecropping is rare.

The Green Revolution in North Arcot

Growth in Agricultural Output

Paddy and groundnuts are not only the predominant crops in the region's agriculture; they have also been the major sources of growth in agricultural output in recent decades. However, as shown in Table 2.2, to designate this growth as a revolution appears, at least at first blush, to be a bit of a misnomer; the average annual growth rates of paddy and groundnut production over the period 1961/62 to 1984/85 were only 1.47 and 1.04 percent, respectively.

This growth was obtained almost entirely from area expansion in the case of groundnuts, and while expansion can be partly attributed to increased investments in irrigation, there was very little change in groundnut technology. Indeed, the predominant varieties, TMV2 and

TMV7, which are of the bunch type, were grown throughout the period of study.

In contrast, the growth in paddy production was technologically driven; yields increased by nearly 3 percent per year between 1961/62 and 1984/85, while the area grown actually declined (by 1.5 percent per year). Most of this yield increase has occurred since the late 1960s (Figure 2.1) and can be attributed to green revolution inputs such as the high-yielding varieties (HYVs) and fertilizers (see Appendix A). But average growth rates do not adequately capture the discontinuities associated with abrupt changes. Comparison of three-year average yields for 1963/64–1965/66 and 1977/78–1979/80 (periods of relatively normal rainfall) shows that paddy yields jumped about 50 percent between these periods (Table 2.2). Paddy production also increased, by 60 percent, while the paddy area remained virtually constant. These changes are more impressive in size and, given their technological origin, can be labeled a green revolution within the spirit of the widespread usage of this term.

Changes in Paddy Technology

An analysis of the sources of growth (Appendix A) shows that nearly all the growth in the region's paddy production since 1950/51 can be attributed to varietal improvement and the more intensive use of nitrogen and irrigation water. Other changes in the region's paddy technology involved the mechanization of water lifting and the use of power sprayers and threshers.

VARIETIES. One of the reasons that the green revolution did not have a more dramatic impact in North Arcot is that there had been a long and successful tradition of improving paddy varieties at local research stations, and some of the features of HYVs that account for their higher productivity had already been incorporated into improved local varieties. For example, TKM6, which was later to become one of the parents of IR20, was developed and released in the region as far back as 1952. This variety is photoperiod insensitive and can be grown all year round. It is also a short-duration variety, with a growing period of only 110–15 days.

The first HYV, Taichung Native 1, was introduced in North Arcot in 1965 from Taiwan. As with all subsequent HYVs, the main advantages over existing improved local varieties lay in their short stiff-straw and their higher responsiveness to nitrogen, especially during the dry *navarai* season.

The early HYVs proved susceptible to major rice pests and diseases

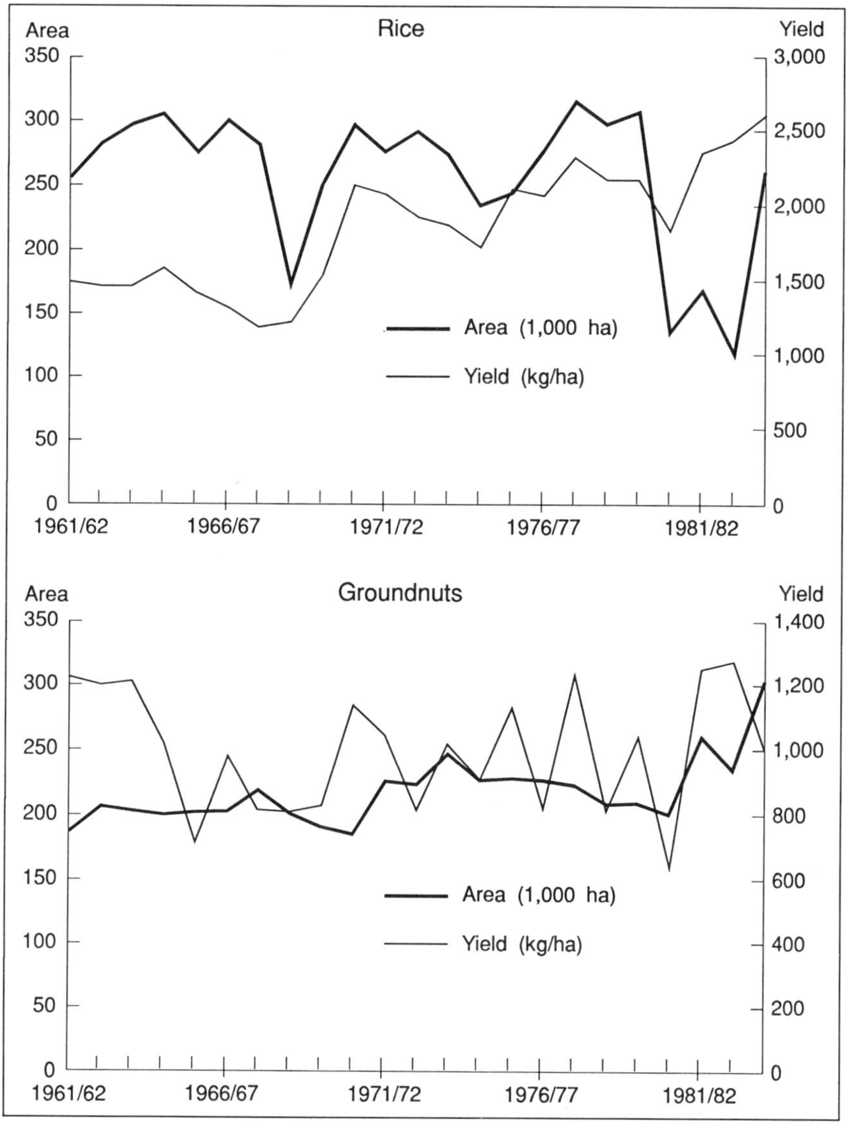

Fig. 2.1. Area and yield of rice and groundnuts.

and were not widely accepted by farmers. The major break came with the release of IR8 (developed by the International Rice Research Institute, IRRI) in the late 1960s. This was widely adopted (Table 2.3) but was subsequently displaced by other IRRI varieties such as IR20, IR36, and IR50 that were better suited to local growing conditions.

TABLE 2.3
Area Under HYV Paddy, North Arcot District

Year	*Area under Paddy (ha)*	*Area under HYVs (ha)*	*Percent of Paddy Area under HYVs*
1950/51	117,387	—	—
1960/61	251,766	—	—
1966/67	301,107	10,268	3.41
1970/71	294,428	60,917	20.69
1975/76	241,298	112,541	46.64
1980/81	135,825	121,482	89.44
1982/83	118,280	108,297	91.56
1983/84	265,015	247,206	93.28

Source: Joint director of agriculture, Vellore.

During the 1970s, national and state programs began to release HYVs of their own, many of which were based on crosses using IRRI plant material. Of the 38 paddy varieties developed and released in Tamil Nadu during the decade beginning in the mid–1970s, 23 of them had IRRI varieties in their parentage.

IRRIGATION. The adoption of HYVs coincided with a rapid expansion in the number of irrigation wells in the region, from 179,232 in 1965/66 to 301,116 in 1983/84. This increase facilitated the year-round growing of paddy and freed up land during the main rainy season (*samba*) to enable an expansion in the area of groundnuts grown (Table 2.2). The number of mechanized wells—electric and oil pumpsets—also doubled over this period, and by the early 1980s over half the wells were mechanized.

FERTILIZER. The consumption of chemical fertilizer within the region increased sixfold between 1965/66 and 1984/85, from 5,177 to 30,024 metric tons of nutrients (Fertilizer Association of India, various issues). Nitrogen consumption increased from 3,198 to 17,032 metric tons.

Data from the Cost of Cultivation of Principal Crops (CCPC) surveys conducted by TNAU for the Ministry of Agriculture show that fertilizer is used more intensively on HYVs than on improved local varieties (Tables 2.4 and 2.5). It is also used most intensively during the irrigated *navarai* season.

Nearly all paddy receives an application of basal fertilizer at transplanting, but subsequent nitrogen applications (topdressings) are done sequentially, and depend on the health of the crop, the availability of

TABLE 2.4
Costs and Returns from Improved Local Varieties of Paddy (1973/74 prices)

	1972/73	*1973/74*	*1974/75*	*1975/76*	*1976/77*	*1977/78*	*1978/79*	*1979/80*	*1980/81*	*1981/82*	*1982/83*
Yield (kg/ha)	2,042	2,267	2,941	2,763	3,148	2,537	2,364	2,793	2,368	3,364	3,009
Price (Rs/kg)	1.05	0.95	1.22	0.89	1.01	0.95	0.97	0.91	1.07	0.82	0.90
Value output (Rs/ha)	2,148	2,158	3,592	2,467	3,172	2,406	2,281	2,527	2,529	2,767	2,722
Variable costs (Rs/ha)	948	582	723	769	1,175	787	1,024	811	902	1,138	664
Seed	119	84	124	145	148	103	127	122	93	216	132
Manures	64	56	33	43	219	83	55	8	66	25	14
Fertilizers	126	99	169	233	261	159	233	157	210	325	163
Pesticides	4	—	3	8	12	13	17	—	6	13	10
Hired labor	400	297	349	290	439	358	446	464	487	389	316
Hired bullocks	46	21	21	28	44	37	38	47	21	41	17
Hired machines	168	1	11	2	11	6	92	—	3	122	11
Other	21	24	13	20	41	28	16	13	16	7	1
Gross margin (Rs/ha)	1,200	1,576	2,869	1,698	1,997	1,619	1,257	1,716	1,627	1,629	2,058
Total labor (hours/ha)	1,824	2,129	2,081	2,046	2,263	1,507	1,703	1,973	1,676	1,820	1,557

Source: Cost of Cultivation of Principal Crops data, TNAU.
Note: Costs and returns based on planted area and averaged over seasons.

TABLE 2.5
Costs and Returns from HYV Paddy (1973/74 prices)

	1972/73	*1973/74*	*1974/75*	*1975/76*	*1976/77*	*1977/78*	*1978/79*	*1979/80*	*1980/81*	*1981/82*	*1982/83*
Yield (kg/ha)	2,588	2,747	3,637	3,239	3,746	3,022	2,772	2,835	3,234	3,249	3,035
Price (Rs/kg)	1.02	0.94	1.21	1.02	1.02	1.02	1.06	0.99	1.07	0.90	1.04
Value output (Rs/ha)	2,647	2,581	4,389	3,292	3,805	3,101	2,941	2,805	3,453	2,908	3,168
Variable costs (Rs/ha)	1,179	817	845	1,067	1,986	1,175	1,240	969	1,114	1,246	1,068
Seed	113	90	103	126	203	118	133	114	89	138	139
Manures	73	66	38	88	153	116	104	90	85	50	31
Fertilizers	242	184	219	340	600	284	325	199	347	463	384
Pesticides	14	12	15	29	55	22	24	15	23	33	7
Hired labor	483	401	409	417	578	486	447	451	506	399	460
Hired bullocks	52	25	37	40	43	41	34	36	25	10	30
Hired machines	182	15	8	9	318	85	157	50	19	149	14
Other	20	24	16	18	36	23	16	14	20	4	3
Gross margin (Rs/ha)	1,468	1,764	3,544	2,225	1,819	1,926	1,701	1,836	2,339	1,662	2,100
Total labor (hours/ha)	1,969	2,338	1,955	2,226	2,295	1,891	1,816	2,092	1,787	1,692	1,899

Source: Cost of Cultivation of Principal Crops data, TNAU.
Note: Costs and returns based on planted area, and averaged over seasons.

water, and so on. For this reason there is a noticeable variation in the amounts of nitrogen used from year to year (Tables 2.4 and 2.5).

MECHANIZATION. In addition to an increase in the mechanization of water lifting, the use of power sprayers and power-operated threshers has also expanded. There were, respectively, 925 and 228 such machines in 1982, compared with zero in 1966. A new set of entrepreneurs who own these machines has emerged in the region, and they hire out their services at fixed rates.

Land preparation is, with few exceptions, still performed with labor and bullock power. However, there were 529 four-wheel tractors in the study region in 1982, compared with 114 in 1966. Their continued spread does not seem likely, given the predominance of small-scale farmers.

Mechanization has led to a modest trend decline in total labor use per hectare of paddy, for both HYVs and improved local varieties (Tables 2.4 and 2.5). But on average, HYVs use about 5 to 10 percent more labor per hectare.

Changes in the Profitability of Paddy Production

The changes that took place in paddy technology have potentially broader implications for farm incomes than the ensuing changes in per hectare costs and returns. For example, the combination of increased irrigation and the availability of quicker-maturing varieties enabled farmers to crop a larger gross area, the increase in which was not all necessarily devoted to paddy. In this section we shall be concerned only with per hectare profitability; the larger issues of changes in total farm production and incomes are taken up in Chapter 3.

YIELDS. As we saw earlier, the region's average paddy yield has grown at about 3 percent per year since the early 1960s, with a sharp jump in the 1970s (Figure 2.1). The CCPC data in Tables 2.4 and 2.5 show that the HYVs were distinctly higher yielding than the improved local varieties when first widely adopted in the early 1970s (about 20 percent higher), but their yields have not increased much since then. Moreover, the yield differential between HYVs and improved local varieties diminished over the years as local research stations incorporated additional features of the HYVs into their own genetic material.

COSTS. HYVs are more input intensive than local varieties, with total variable costs averaging about 20 to 25 percent higher per hectare (Tables 2.4 and 2.5). These higher costs are attributable to the more intensive use of fertilizers, pesticides, and hired labor. Total variable costs in constant prices show a modest trend increase over the years for both HYVs and improved local varieties.

GROSS MARGINS. While there is considerable variation between years, paddy gross margins (gross revenue less variable costs) show little trend over the years when measured in constant prices (Figure 2.2). Paddy prices barely kept pace with inflation, and the costs of production, particularly fertilizer, increased sufficiently to offset the gains from increased yields (Tables 2.4 and 2.5). The HYVs have generally proved more profitable than the improved local varieties on a per hectare basis (Figure 2.2).

Primary Data Sources

The research in this study is predominantly based on household and firm-level surveys undertaken at different points in time. In this section

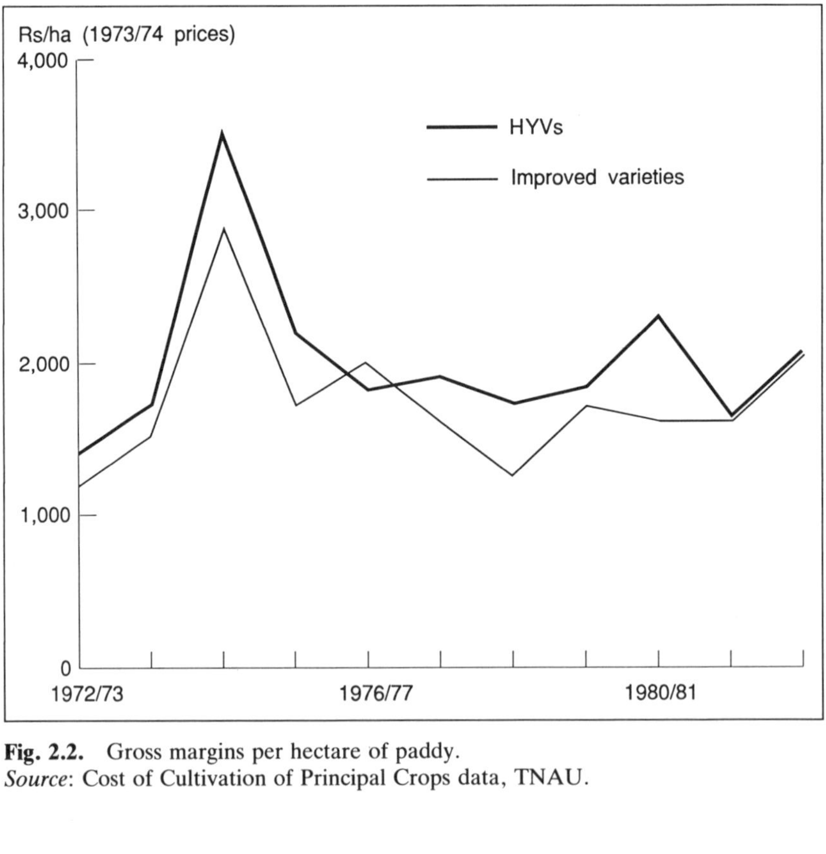

Fig. 2.2. Gross margins per hectare of paddy.
Source: Cost of Cultivation of Principal Crops data, TNAU.

we briefly review the scope of these surveys, in terms of both their geographical coverage and the kinds of variables that were monitored. Additional details about the surveys are to be found in Appendix B.

The Study Region

The study region adopted in our research is identical to the one defined by the earlier team from Cambridge and Madras universities (Farmer 1977). It consists of a contiguous area of six eastern *taluks* (Arkonam, Cheyyar, Wandiwash, Arni, Polur, and Tiruvannamalai) that lie east of the Javadi hills and south of the sandy belt along the Palar River (Figure 2.3). This area produces about three-quarters of North Arcot district's total paddy production; hence in terms of studying the impact of the green revolution, the chosen study region facilitated the efficient concentration of survey resources.

A potential drawback is that the district's headquarter town of Vellore is not included in the study region. Given that Vellore is the largest urban center in the district with a population of 250,000, its inclusion might seem essential for any analysis that purports to trace the growth linkages from agriculture. However, it turns out that the study region is well serviced by a hierarchy of smaller towns and urban villages, and the trading links with Vellore are concentrated on relatively few, higher-order goods and services (e.g., automobile repair, selected durables, and hospital treatment) that are not widely available elsewhere (Chapter 10). In essence, the study region encompasses most of the places where the day-to-day transactions of the region's households are undertaken, and as such it defines the kind of economic watershed required from a growth linkages analysis (Bell, Hazell, and Slade 1982; Hazell and Röell 1983).

Agriculturally, the study region is more specialized than North Arcot district as a whole. It is primarily a rice- and groundnut-growing area with relatively small amounts of millets, sorghum, and pulses. Its manufacturing base is also more specialized into agroprocessing and textiles. A detailed analysis of the region's economy is to be found in Chapter 7.

The Surveys

The first set of survey data available was collected by a team from Cambridge and Madras universities in 1973/74. Despite expectations, the team found that only about 13 percent of the paddy area was planted to HYVs at the time, so the survey really approximated a pre– or early–green revolution situation. A second team from IFPRI and TNAU

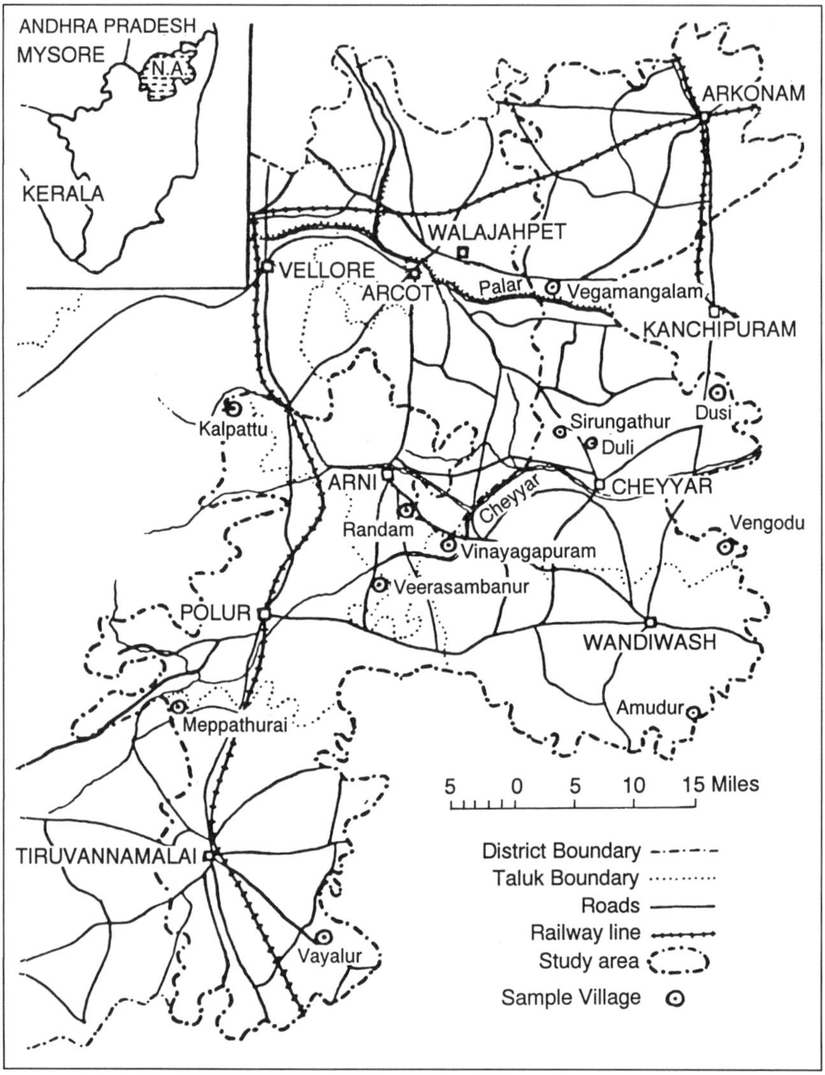

Fig. 2.3. Study villages and towns.
Source: B. H. Farmer, *Green Revolution?*, p. 8. © 1977 by The Macmillan Press Ltd.

undertook similar surveys in 1982/83, by which time over 90 percent of the paddy area was planted to HYVs. This was clearly a post–green revolution situation.

Both surveys included a representative sample of all rural households (farmers, landless farm workers, and nonagriculturalists) living in the same 11 villages. The villages were selected through sampling procedures to be representative of all the rural villages (those with populations of less than 5,000 people) in the study region (see Appendix B). These villages are Vegamangalam, Sirungathur, Duli, Vengodu, Vinayagapuram, Amudhur, Nesal (or Randam, as John Harriss prefers to call it in Chapters 4 and 6), Kalpattu, Veerasambanur, Meppathurai, and Vayalur.[1] Their locations are shown in Figure 2.3.

The Cambridge-Madras universities survey in the 11 villages had several components, each involving different samples and questionnaires (see Chambers et al. 1977). But the data used in this study were taken almost exclusively from two components. The first was a sample of 161 paddy-farm households that participated in a detailed farm management survey for three consecutive seasons ending with the 1974 *sornavari* crop. The second component was a household sample of 57 paddy farmers, 3 nonpaddy farmers, and 77 noncultivators who participated in a monthly income and expenditure survey between April 1973 and May 1974. The 57 paddy-farm households were a subsample of the 161 paddy farmers included in the farm management survey. Between them these surveys provided detailed information on most aspects of farm management, employment, sources of income, households assets, food consumption, and household expenditure patterns.

The IFPRI-TNAU survey in the rural villages covered a sample of 345 households that participated in a monthly income, expenditure, and farm management survey from March 1982 to April 1983. The sample contained 160 paddy cultivators, 25 nonpaddy cultivators, and 160 noncultivating households (of which about three-quarters were landless laborers). While the survey was conducted in the same 11 villages as the Cambridge-Madras survey, it was not possible to use the same sample of households without losing representation in the post–green revolution situation.

To enhance the comparability of the rural household data between the two surveys, the same household and variable definitions were used wherever possible. For example, a cultivator was defined as a farmer operating more than one-fourth acre and a paddy farm as a holding of one-fourth acre or larger on which paddy *was* or *could be* grown. Parts of the 1973/74 questionnaires were also used in 1982/83, although they were precoded to take advantage of interim advances in data-processing technology. Members of the earlier Cambridge-Madras universities team also provided advice and visited several of the villages while the 1982/83 survey was ongoing.

1. The Cambridge-Madras team surveyed an additional village, Dusi, which was selected purposively and not as part of the random sample. Apart from chapters 4 and 6, the Dusi data were not used in this study, and they are excluded from the description of the survey procedures and sample sizes.

A potential hazard with repeat surveys of this kind is that weather conditions, which remain largely unknown until after a survey has begun, may not prove comparable between years. If they are not, then serious problems can arise in determining how much of the observed changes in the survey data are attributable to the green revolution and how much is simply the effect of different weather conditions.

As shown in Table 2.2, annual rainfall was only 732 millimeters in 1973/74, or 35 percent below average. But because rainfall in the preceding two years had been quite normal, there were sufficient tank and groundwater reserves that aggregate paddy area and production declined only marginally. At 751 millimeters, annual rainfall was almost identical in 1982/83. However, this time the region was still recovering from the effects of a severe drought in 1980/81 and below-average rainfall in 1981/82, which together had depleted the water reserves available at the beginning of the 1982/83 agricultural year. As a result, paddy area and production fell to nearly half their normal levels in 1982/83, and the region entered a state of economic distress. In fact the situation deteriorated sufficiently that government relief schemes, such as the National Employment Program, were activated in the region during the period of survey.

Given the obvious difficulties in comparing survey data between 1973/74 and 1982/83, an additional survey was undertaken in 1983/84. This proved to be an above-average year for rainfall (1,272 mm), and paddy area and production recovered to more normal levels (Table 2.2). But available resources for the 1983/84 survey were very limited, and it proved necessary to limit the survey to those villages surveyed in the previous year that had been most affected by the drought. These villages are Duli, Vayalur, Veerasambanur, Meppathurai, and Amudhur. Not surprisingly, they are the villages with the poorest and least reliable supplies of irrigation water (see next section and Chapter 6). Within these villages, half of the 1982/83 sample of paddy cultivators and landless laborers were selected at random for resurvey, and all of the 1982/83 sample of nonpaddy cultivators and nonagriculturalists. The same monthly questionnaire was used as in 1982/83, spanning the period September 1983 to June 1984. In order to obtain information for the complete agricultural year, households were also asked to recall information for July and August when first interviewed in September.

The Cambridge-Madras universities study was less focused on agricultural growth linkages than the present study and, apart from a survey of small businesses in the single town of Arni (see Chapter 9), surveys of the nonrural economy were not undertaken in 1973/74. In contrast, a major effort to study the nonfarm economy was undertaken in 1982/83 that included a monthly income and expenditure survey of

320 urban households, a survey of 1,500 nonfarm businesses located in urban areas, and a survey of the patterns of service provision and use in all the villages in the study region that had populations of more than 750 persons (see Appendix B and Chapter 10 for details). Additionally, the monthly questionnaire for the rural household survey included details about any nonfarm business activities that the sample households undertook, and a repeat survey of small businesses in Arni was undertaken (see Chapter 9).

Characteristics of the Sampled Rural Villages

There are considerable differences among the 11 sampled villages, particularly with respect to population, land and water resources, economic activities, infrastructure, labor, and social relations in production. A detailed analysis of the intervillage variations is offered by John Harriss in Chapter 6. This section presents a very brief account of the major features of the 11 villages.

In 1982/83, the 11 villages had an average population of 959, ranging from 538 in Duli to 1,487 in Nesal. Nesal, Kalpattu, Vengodu, Vegamangalam, and Sirungathur are the largest villages, with populations in excess of 1,000. The major castes are Vanniyas, Pillai, Naidus, Mudaliars, Yadavas, and Harijans.

All the villages have a primary school, and Amudhur has a high school. Unlike the other villages, Meppathurai and Vinayagapuram do not have a bus service, but one is available within three kilometers. All the villages have electricity and, apart from Vinayagapuram, are connected by surfaced roads. A detailed account of the infrastructure facilities available in each village is to be found in Chapter 10.

As in the region generally, tanks and wells are the principal sources of irrigation in the study villages (Table 2.6). Kalpattu and Vegamangalam are unique in not having tanks. Kalpattu is surrounded by hills that recharge its wells with groundwater all year round. Because of this feature, the village is able to grow crops continuously and its cropping pattern is the most diversified; it includes paddy, banana, turmeric, sugarcane, groundnut, and horticultural crops. Vegamangalam village is supplied with water from a natural spring and also enjoys year-round irrigation. Because of good irrigation resources, Kalpattu, Vegamangalam, and Nesal are comparatively prosperous villages and are less prone to drought. Duli, Vayalur, Veerasambanur, Meppathurai, and Amudhur have the least reliable sources of irrigation water, and they were severely affected by drought in 1982/83.

The sample villages use labor from both within and outside the village. Sirungathur, Veerasambanur, Vengodu, and Amudhur are

TABLE 2.6
Irrigation Facilities in Rural Study Villages, 1982

Village	*No. of Tanks*	*No. of Wells*[a]	*No. of Pumpsets*[b]	*Average Depth of Wells*[c] *(meters)*	*Percent of Households with Access to Irrigation Wells*
Kalpattu	0	194	124	15.67	100.0
Meppathurai	1	159	69	11.00	95.0
Vayalur	1	87	37	12.18	100.0
Veerasambanur	3	130	41	12.18	82.0
Vinayagapuram	2	109	73	15.84	100.0
Nesal	3	227	161	14.21	73.7
Amudhur	2	86	59	9.32	87.5
Vengodu	3	134	75	12.81	94.1
Duli	1	38	23	12.54	58.3
Sirungathur	2	98	75	12.75	100.0
Vegamangalam	0	69	60	10.21	50.0

Source: Information collected from village-level development workers and village administrative officers.

[a]Some wells were not in use at the time of the survey.

[b]Wells without pumpsets generally have poor water supplies and the water is lifted by *mhote*.

[c]Depth of wells was determined from a random sample of nine wells in each of the villages.

labor-surplus villages, whereas Kalpattu, Nesal, and Vegamangalam are labor-deficit villages. Some sharecropping is found in Vinayagapuram and Vegamangalam, but it is unimportant in the other villages.

All the study villages have cooperative credit societies that provide crop loans. The sample villages also benefit from the presence of government-run fair-price shops, which provide rice, vegetable oils, sugar, and kerosene at subsidized prices.

Various state-run developmental programs also benefit the study villages, for example, the Noon Meal Scheme, Integrated Rural Development Programs, and Training and Visit Extension. Village *panchayats* are responsible for local water supply, road maintenance, and health programs. Milk producers' cooperative societies also function in the study villages.

CHAPTER 3

Economic Changes among Village Households

Peter B. R. Hazell, C. Ramasamy, V. Rajagopalan, P. K. Aiyasamy, and Neal Bliven

IN THIS CHAPTER we use the village household survey data to quantify the effects of the green revolution on farm production, income, and employment; the changes in family income and consumption of farm and nonfarm households; and the changes in the distribution of land. There are four problems with the data set that complicate our task.

First, 1973/74, the year of the Cambridge-Madras universities (CMU) survey, was not a true pre–green revolution year. Official government data show that about 40 percent of the paddy area was planted to high-yielding varieties (HYVs) that year. The CMU survey found a considerably lower adoption rate (13 percent of the cropped area), but most farmers were growing locally improved varieties that already had some of the key features of HYVs (see Chapter 2). In the absence of a base year in which only long-strawed, traditional varieties are grown, the prospective gains from the green revolution to be observed in the survey data are bound to be muted.

Second, our survey data for 1973/74, 1982/83, and 1983/84 are not strictly comparable as far as rainfall and irrigation water reserves are concerned. Rainfall was similar in 1973/74 and 1982/83 (about 35 percent below average), but since water reserves in the tanks and groundwater were much lower in 1982/83 because of an extended drought, the impact on paddy production was much greater (see Chapter 2). Regional paddy production was 40 percent lower in 1982/83 than in 1973/74, so it is difficult to say much about the impact of the green revolution between these two years. On the other hand, rainfall was 15 percent above average in 1983/84, and regional paddy production was 40 percent larger than in 1973/74. A simple comparison of 1973/74 and 1983/84 may overstate the effects of the green revolution between these two years.

To compound these weather-related problems, we have access to regionally representative household data only for 1973/74 and 1982/83. In 1983/84, the survey was confined to a subsample of households located in villages with the poorest water resources. These villages suffered the most during the drought of 1982/83 and, most likely, also in 1973/74. Because of their more limited access to irrigation water, they also are likely to have benefited the least from the interim changes in paddy technology. Nevertheless, comparisons between 1973/74 and 1983/84 in these "resurvey" villages provide our best basis for measuring changes in the economic welfare of the rural households.

Third, there is considerable variation in the economic conditions among the 11 sample villages. Some have only limited access to irrigation water, and supplies are unreliable (e.g., Duli). Others are blessed with generous and stable supplies of water, even in drought years (e.g., Kalpattu). This not only leads to important differences in the potential benefits obtainable from improved paddy varieties, but also determines the very economic and social fabric of the villages and the types of growth that are possible. Poorly endowed villages tend to be less equitable to begin with, and technical change is likely to induce less equitable growth there than in better-endowed villages. In this chapter we exploit the statistical representation of the sample data to analyze changes in the average welfare of different types of households at a pooled village level. We leave it to John Harriss in Chapters 4 and 6 to analyze the changes by type of village, and to relate these changes to the underlying water resource endowments.

Fourth, as shown below, the 1973/74 farm sample has a much smaller percentage of farms larger than 1 hectare in the resurvey villages than do the 1982/83 and 1983/84 samples:

	1973/74	*1982/83*	*1983/84*
Resurvey villages	25.0	63.6	66.7
Nonresurvey villages	45.9	49.5	n.a.
All villages	38.6	55.2	n.a.

These figures are not consistent with other data on changes in the farm size distribution (see Chapter 4 and later sections of this chapter). Nor are they consistent with the village listing (census) data collected by CMU in 1973 and by IFPRI-TNAU in 1982; these put the percentage of farms greater than 1 hectare at 42 and 48 percent, respectively, for the resurvey villages. Since the sampling design did not involve a stratification by farm size, the problem seems to be one of unlucky samples, a not uncommon occurrence when working with relatively small samples. But an immediate consequence is that uncorrected sample means for the resurvey villages are biased toward small farms in 1973/74 and toward large farms in 1982/83 and 1983/84. For the most part we resolve the problem by reporting separate results for small (1 hectare or less) and large (greater than 1 hectare) farms. Where pooled estimates are reported for the resurvey villages, they are weighted means using the farm size shares observed in the 1973 and 1982 village listings (i.e., large farm weights of 0.42 for the 1973/74 survey and 0.48 for the 1982/83 and 1983/84 surveys).

Of the four problems discussed above, only the first two raise unresolved difficulties for our data analysis: the lack of a true before–green revolution sample, and uncorrected differences in rainfall and water reserves between years. In Chapter 8 we develop a regional model of the study region and use it to simulate the impact of the green revolution under normal weather conditions. Because the model can correct for weather conditions, as well as simulate with– and without–green revolution situations, it enables us to overcome the major limitations of our survey data analysis. However, as with any model, its construction requires a healthy dose of assumptions about the way in which the regional economy works. We shall therefore use the survey and model results to provide a check on each other, drawing comfort from instances where the two tell a consistent story. Further checks on the reliability of our findings are provided in Chapter 4, where John Harriss uses his own independently collected data to examine changes in some of the same village and household variables.

Changes in Paddy and Groundnut Production

Our analysis of the impact of the green revolution begins with the increases in farm production. Since most farmers engage in mixed cropping, our analysis must go beyond simple changes in paddy area and yield to encompass any induced changes in the production of other crops. These changes might arise from crop substitution (e.g., more paddy at the expense of other crops, or vice versa), or from the more intensive cropping of land throughout the year (e.g., HYVs and increased irrigation permit a greater cropped area during the *navarai* season).

Table 3.1 shows the changes in paddy and groundnut production between the survey years. Paddy production declined between 1973/74 and 1982/83, by 5 percent on small paddy farms and by 33 percent on large paddy farms. This is less than the 42 percent drop recorded at the district level between these two years (Table 2.2), but differences are to be expected since (1) the survey data are based on different procedures for estimating output than those used by district officials,

TABLE 3.1
Average Cropped Area, Yield, and Production of Paddy and Groundnuts by Farm Size Group

	Area (ha)			*Yield (kg/ha)*			*Production (kg)*		
	1973/74	*1982/83*	*1983/84*	*1973/74*	*1982/83*	*1983/84*	*1973/74*	*1982/83*	*1983/84*
All villages									
Paddy									
Small farms	0.53	0.35	n.a.	2,123	3,043	n.a.	1,125	1,065	n.a.
Large farms	1.41	0.89	n.a.	2,854	3,045	n.a.	4,024	2,710	n.a.
Groundnuts									
Small farms	0.30	0.33	n.a.	1,280	897	n.a.	384	296	n.a.
Large farms	1.19	1.21	n.a.	1,495	969	n.a.	1,779	1,172	n.a.
Resurvey villages									
Paddy									
Small farms	0.55	0.31	0.64	1,773	2,826	2,777	975	876	1,777
Large farms	0.75	0.79	2.11	2,524	2,430	2,176	1,893	1,920	4,592
Groundnuts									
Small farms	0.48	0.28	0.15	1,073	782	1,760	515	219	264
Large farms	1.08	1.10	0.86	1,227	914	1,309	1,325	1,005	1,126

(2) they pertain to different 12-month periods, (3) they exclude part of the district's production, and (4) they are, of course, subject to sampling error. The decline was more muted in the resurvey villages, probably because they were more affected by the 1973/74 drought than the non-resurvey villages. The decline in paddy production was entirely due to a loss in the paddy area grown (Table 3.1). Yields were actually higher in 1982/83, despite the drought.

Groundnut production also declined between 1973/74 and 1982/83 in the sample villages, by 23 percent for small farms and by 34 percent for large farms. This decline is nearly all attributable to lower yields, since the planted area changed little. Unlike paddy, most groundnuts are not irrigated, and hence yields are more affected by variations in rainfall (see also the coefficient of variation calculations in Chapter 2).

Paddy production recovered dramatically in 1983/84, more than doubling in the resurvey villages from the low levels of the 1982/83 drought. The recovery was entirely due to an increase in the paddy area. Yields actually declined a little, probably because late rains during the 1983/84 *samba* season caused some damage to the harvest.

Groundnut production increased little between 1982/83 and 1983/84. While yields recovered after the drought, the area planted to groundnuts declined sharply on both small and large farms. This area decline was necessary to facilitate the expansion of the paddy area, as confirmed by the cropping pattern data in Table 3.2. The sharp increase in the paddy area also displaced sorghum and millets. These relatively drought-resistant crops were widely grown during 1982/83, particularly in the resurvey villages (Table 3.2).

Comparing 1973/74 with 1983/84, paddy production increased by 82 percent on small farms and by 143 percent on large farms. On large farms these increases were entirely due to an expansion of the paddy area, but on small farms they were predominantly due to yield increases. Large farms had already widely adopted the HYVs by 1973/74 (Chinnappa 1977), and their yields were already one-third higher than small-farm yields (Table 3.1). While large-farm yields were still the same in 1983/84, small farmers adopted HYVs during the interim and closed the yield gap. In fact small-farm paddy yields were actually 27 percent higher than large-farm yields in 1983/84 in the resurvey villages (Table 3.1).

Increases in the paddy crop area between 1973/74 and 1983/84 were achieved largely at the expense of groundnuts (Table 3.2). There was no accompanying increase in the cropping intensity index, which in 1983/84 stood at 1.62 for small farms and 1.32 for large farms. Part of the increase in the paddy area on large farms was also attributable to a 63 percent increase in their operated farm size. Small farms, on the

TABLE 3.2
Cropping Patterns by Farm Size Group (ha)

	Small Farms			*Large Farms*		
	1973/74	*1982/83*	*1983/84*	*1973/74*	*1982/83*	*1983/84*
All villages						
Paddy	0.53	0.35	n.a.	1.41	0.89	n.a.
Groundnuts	0.30	0.33	n.a.	1.19	1.21	n.a.
Sorghum/millets	0.05	0.06	n.a.	0.10	0.34	n.a.
Other crops	0.05	0.09	n.a.	0.05	0.54	n.a.
Total	0.93	0.83	n.a.	2.74	2.99	n.a.
Operated farm size	0.59	0.61	n.a.	2.42	2.68	n.a.
Crop intensity index	1.57	1.36	n.a.	1.13	1.11	n.a.
Resurvey villages						
Paddy	0.55	0.31	0.64	0.75	0.79	2.11
Groundnuts	0.48	0.28	0.15	1.08	1.10	0.86
Sorghum/millets	0.01	0.14	0.08	0.24	0.45	0.01
Other crops	0.03	0.06	0.02	—	0.33	0.20
Total	1.07	0.80	0.89	2.08	2.68	3.18
Operated farm size	0.64	0.66	0.55	1.48	2.59	2.41
Crop intensity index	1.67	1.21	1.62	1.41	1.04	1.32

other hand, shrank by 14 percent in size. These results pertain only to the resurvey villages and should not be extrapolated to the entire study region (see a later section in this chapter on changes in the farm size distribution).

What, then, can we conclude about the productivity effects of the green revolution between 1973/74 and 1983/84? Paddy production did increase sharply, but this seems to have been more the result of substituting paddy for groundnuts in the cropping pattern. Yields increased on small farms, and this reflects the fact that they adopted HYVs during the period studied. But most large farms had already adopted HYVs by 1973/74, hence their yield increases are not captured in the survey data. Despite the expansion of irrigation between 1973/74 and 1982/83, there is no evidence that this led to any increase in annual cropping intensity. However, our 1983/84 results are confined to the resurvey villages, and these villages participated the least in the general expansion in irrigation.

The substitution between paddy and groundnuts could also be partly driven by technological change, especially if improved paddy varieties have lower costs and this increases the relative profitability of paddy. On the other hand, part of the substitution appears to be related to weather conditions. Groundnuts need less water than paddy and hence, along with millets and sorghum, are more favored by farmers during drought years.

Irrespective of cause, the observed changes in the cropping pattern are considerable, and they have important implications for changes in farm income and employment.

Changes in Farm Income

The value of farm output (gross output) is dominated by paddy and groundnuts (Table 3.3), hence changes in their production and prices largely determine the changes in total gross output. We have already seen that paddy and groundnut production changed markedly from one survey year to another (Table 3.1). However, these changes were partially buffered by opposing price movements, as shown below (in Rs/t, constant 1973/74 prices):

	Paddy	*Groundnut*
1973/74	865	1,080
1982/83	922	1,547
1983/84	755	1,613

TABLE 3.3
Paddy Farm Incomes (1973/74 prices)

	All Villages				*Resurvey Villages*					
	1973/74		*1982/83*		*1973/74*		*1982/83*		*1983/84*	
	Small Farms	*Large Farms*	*Small Farms*	*Large Farms*	*Small Farms*	*Large Farms*	*Small Farms*	*Large Farms*	*Small Farms*	*Large Farms*
Gross output[a]										
Paddy	954	3,581	982	2,499	808	1,546	808	1,771	1,341	3,464
Groundnuts	431	1,803	458	1,812	574	994	339	1,554	426	1,816
Other crops	757	1,153	162	264	39	1,223	40	102	64	176
Livestock products	23	88	129	200	5	91	70	204	179	820
Bullock & machine rent	—	—	34	41	—	—	18	4	3	4
Total gross output	2,165	6,625	1,765	4,816	1,426	3,854	1,275	3,635	2,013	6,280
Costs										
Hired labor	235	598	176	814	213	424	84	707	276	1,331
Bullock & machine hire	27	99	33	96	23	76	8	83	20	48
Fertilizers	71	303	103	351	35	75	27	236	227	809
Other	660	1,546	222	632	429	959	110	444	385	1,208
Total costs	992	2,546	533	1,893	700	1,534	228	1,470	908	3,396
Net farm income	1,173	4,078	1,232	2,923	726	2,320	1,047	2,165	1,105	2,884

[a]Includes home-consumed foods valued at farm-gate prices.

Both paddy and groundnut production fell sharply between 1973/74 and 1982/83 (Table 3.1), but these losses were partially offset by higher prices. On the other hand, the sharp increase in paddy output between 1982/83 and 1983/84 was tempered by a drop in price, while the limited growth in groundnut output was supplemented by a price increase. As a result, changes in paddy and groundnut gross output are less dramatic than the changes in production. For example, small and large farms in the resurvey villages increased their paddy production by 103 percent and 139 percent, respectively, between 1982/83 and 1983/84, but paddy gross output increased by only two-thirds as much—by 66 and 95 percent, respectively.

Changes in farm costs also acted to buffer the changes in production (Table 3.3). Costs were lowest during the 1982/83 drought and increased substantially in 1983/84. These buffering effects led to surprisingly stable farm incomes from one year to another. In the resurvey villages, small-farm incomes were only 5 percent lower during the 1982/83 drought than in 1983/84, while large-farm incomes were 25 percent lower.

Taking 1973/74 and 1983/84 as our relevant comparison for evaluating the green revolution, Table 3.3 shows that small-farm incomes increased by 52 percent and large-farm incomes by 24 percent. The increases would have been greater but for the 13 percent decline in the paddy price and the sharp increase in labor and fertilizer costs, especially for large farms.

Changes in Employment and Wages

Total labor use in crop production declined sharply during the 1982/83 drought on both large and small farms, but it rebounded in 1983/84 (Table 3.4). Between 1973/74 and 1983/84, total crop employment in the resurvey villages increased by 15 percent on large farms but declined by 20 percent on small farms. However, since operated farm sizes also changed (Table 3.2), a more useful measure is labor use per hectare of operated land. This declined by 7 percent for small farms and by 30 percent for large farms. Similar declines occurred in the labor use per gross cropped hectare (Table 3.4). Note that the small farms use considerably more labor than large farms on an operated area basis, but they use about the same amount per hectare of gross cropped land. This simply reflects their more intensive cropping of land (Table 3.2).

Overall, these results suggest that the green revolution did little to increase total crop employment, despite the fact that HYV paddy uses about 5 to 10 percent more labor per hectare than locally improved varieties (Tables 2.4 and 2.5). Using the farm size weights discussed in

TABLE 3.4
Adult Employment per Paddy Farm in Crop Production by Type of Labor (days)

	All Villages				*Resurvey Villages*					
	1973/74		*1982/83*		*1973/74*		*1982/83*		*1983/84*	
	Small Farms	*Large Farms*	*Small Farms*	*Large Farms*	*Small Farms*	*Large Farms*	*Small Farms*	*Large Farms*	*Small Farms*	*Large Farms*
Family labor										
Male	95.4	148.5	52.2	96.7	94.4	177.4	54.1	88.5	104.8	191.9
Female	34.3	58.5	11.9	18.3	37.3	86.6	10.4	15.3	43.0	111.1
Total	129.7	207.0	64.1	115.0	131.7	264.0	64.5	103.8	147.8	303.0
Attached labor										
Male	5.6	46.6	3.0	31.1	10.8	—	—	21.7	—	68.3
Female	0.4	—	—	0.4	—	—	—	0.3	—	15.3
Total	6.0	46.6	3.0	31.5	10.8	—	—	22.0	—	83.6
Exchange labor										
Male	3.9	12.8	0.1	0.6	2.5	9.0	—	0.2	0.2	13.7
Female	17.4	37.3	0.4	3.2	7.8	24.7	—	1.7	0.3	3.3
Total	21.3	50.1	0.5	3.8	10.3	33.7	—	1.9	0.5	17.0
Hired labor										
Male	39.2	125.5	19.2	72.5	40.6	97.3	8.4	63.8	28.7	100.6
Female	98.9	234.7	57.0	215.0	89.0	170.3	33.6	154.6	48.6	143.7
Total	138.1	360.2	76.2	287.5	129.6	267.6	42.0	218.4	77.3	244.3
Total labor										
Male	144.1	333.4	74.5	200.9	148.3	283.7	62.5	174.2	133.7	374.5
Female	151.0	330.5	69.3	236.9	134.1	281.6	44.0	171.9	91.9	273.4
Total	295.1	663.9	143.8	437.8	282.4	565.3	106.5	346.1	225.6	647.9
Total labor/ha										
Operated area	500	274	236	163	441	382	161	134	410	269
Gross cropped area	317	242	173	146	264	272	133	129	253	204
Total hired labor/ha										
Operated area	234	149	125	107	203	181	64	84	141	101
Gross cropped area	148	131	92	96	121	129	53	81	87	77

the introduction to this chapter, total labor use in crop production declined by 4 percent (from 401 to 386 days) on the average paddy farm between 1973/74 and 1983/84, and by 14 percent per hectare of operated land. These changes reflect the increased mechanization of irrigation pumping and paddy threshing, changes that were not adequately offset by the substitution of paddy for groundnuts in the cropping pattern (groundnuts use about half to two-thirds as much labor per hectare).

Male and female labor were about equally employed in crop production in 1973/74 and 1982/83, but males dominated in 1983/84 (Table 3.4). Hired labor was also about as important as family labor in 1973/74, but its share in total labor use fell in 1983/84, from 47 percent to 34 percent on small farms, and from 46 to 38 percent on large farms. The total use of hired labor fell by 25 percent on the average farm, or by 11 percent if attached labor is included.

Although total crop employment did not increase between 1973/74 and 1983/84, real wage rates did (Table 3.5). Wage rates differ by sex and task, but of the more important tasks, wages for males increased by about 20 percent in real terms, while wages for females increased by only half as much. These increases are observed for both cash and kind wages. They are also generally consistent with the changes reported by John Harriss in Chapter 4.

Real wage rates could only have increased in the face of an 11 percent decline in the use of hired and attached labor on the average farm if the supply of labor had also contracted. Table 3.6 shows that, at least in the resurvey villages, this is exactly what happened. Large-farm households sharply curtailed their participation in the agricultural labor market, and their wage earnings (in constant prices) fell from Rs 228 in 1973/74 to Rs 47 in 1983/84. Given also a sharp increase in wage payments on these farms, net wage earnings (earnings less payments) fell from Rs −196 to Rs −1,284. Small-farm households met part of the increase in the labor deficit on large farms (their net wage earnings increased from Rs 176 to Rs 464), but this was insufficient to fill the gap. Taking a weighted average of small and large farms, net wage earnings fell from Rs 20 in 1973/74 to Rs −375 in 1983/84. As we shall see in the next section, the gap was filled by landless laborers and nonpaddy farmers.

As discussed by John Harriss in Chapter 4, other factors that helped to increase wages were a growing demand for labor in rural nonfarm activities; an expansion of local milk production under Operation Flood; and an outmigration of workers that helped contain the growth in the number of landless laborers.

TABLE 3.5
Agricultural Wages by Operation

	Plowing (Men)				Weeding (Women)				Harvesting (Women)			Threshing (Men)		
Village	1973/74 (Rs/day)	1982/83 (Rs/day)	Deflated 1982/83 Wage[a]	Percent Change	1973/74 (Rs/day)	1982/83 (Rs/day)	Deflated 1982/83 Wage[a]	Percent Change	1973/74 (kg/paddy/day)	1982/83 (kg/paddy/day)	Percent Change	1973/74 (kg/paddy/day)	1982/83 (kg/paddy/day)	Percent Change
Kalpattu	3.50	6.00	3.25	−7.0	1.00	2.00	1.09	9.0	5.00	5.60	12	5.00	8.50	70
Nesal	1.50	6.00	3.25	116.7	1.30	3.00	1.63	25.4	4.25	5.00	18	8.50	10.00	18
Vegamangalam	3.00	5.00	2.71	−9.7	1.00	3.00	1.63	63.0	5.60	5.60	—	5.60	5.60	—
Vinayagapuram	2.00	5.00	2.71	35.5	0.70	2.50	1.36	94.3	3.00	4.00	33	3.25	4.00	23
Sirungathur	2.50	5.00	2.71	8.4	1.00	2.00	1.09	9.0	5.60	5.60	—	5.60	5.60	—
Vayalur	2.50	5.00	2.71	8.4	1.00	2.50	1.36	36.0	3.50	4.00	14	7.00	7.00	—
Vengodu	2.00	5.00	2.71	35.5	1.50	2.00	1.09	−27.3	5.00	5.00	—	4.25	5.00	18
Meppathurai	2.80	5.00	2.71	−3.2	1.30	2.00	1.09	−16.2	4.25	5.00	18	6.25	7.00	12
Duli	2.00	6.00	3.25	62.5	1.50	3.00	1.63	8.7	5.00	5.60	12	1.40	5.60	400
Veerasambanur	0.75	5.00	2.71	261.3	1.25	2.50	1.36	8.8	4.25	4.25	—	8.50	8.50	—
Amudhur	2.00	3.00	1.63	−18.5	1.30	2.50	1.36	4.6	3.50	4.80	37	5.00	6.40	28
Average	2.23	5.10	2.76	23.8	1.17	2.45	1.33	13.7	4.45	4.95	11	5.49	6.65	21

Source: Cambridge-Madras and IFPRI-TNAU surveys.
[a]Deflated to 1973/74 prices with a rural cost-of-living index for Kunnathur village in Chingleput (*Tamil Nadu—An Economic Appraisal*, various volumes, Finance Department, Government of Tamil Nadu).

TABLE 3.6
Agricultural Wage Transactions by Size of Farm, Resurvey Villages (1973/74 Rs)

	Small Farms			*Large Farms*		
	1973/74	*1982/83*	*1983/84*	*1973/74*	*1982/83*	*1983/84*
Wage earnings	389	200	740	228	26	47
Wage payments	213	84	276	424	707	1,331
Net earnings	176	116	464	−196	−681	−1,284

Changes in Family Income

The total family income of each household type is summarized by year in Table 3.7. The detrimental impact of the 1982/83 drought is again apparent. Most households were actually worse off in 1982/83 than in 1973/74, despite the intervening changes in irrigation and paddy technology. There was less change in the resurvey villages between these two years, but family incomes in these villages were already well below average in 1973/74. The favorable rains of 1983/84 led to substantial increases in family incomes in the resurvey villages; in many cases incomes more than doubled. Clearly, the income of rural households in North Arcot is very vulnerable to fluctuations in rainfall.

Family incomes improved substantially between 1973/74 and 1983/84 in the resurvey villages. It increased by 18 percent for large paddy farms and by 90 percent for small paddy farms. The landless laborers more than doubled their income (up 125 percent), bringing their average income almost up to the level of small paddy farmers. The nonpaddy farmers and the nonagricultural households increased their incomes by about 17 and 55 percent, respectively, even though they were not directly involved in the changes that occurred in paddy technology.

These changes are more substantial than the income increases obtained from the regional model in Chapter 8 (see Table 8.4 and the accompanying discussion). When normalized for rainfall, the model predicts that the green revolution increased the incomes of farmers and landless laborers by about 30 percent and of nonagriculturalists by 20 percent. It would seem that the survey results were affected by the 1973/74 drought, especially as our 1973/74 to 1983/84 comparison is limited to the poorer and more drought-prone resurvey villages, and this has exaggerated the income increases. However, both the model and the survey are consistent in showing that (1) small farmers increased their incomes in at least the same proportion as large farmers, (2) landless laborers gained favorably compared with any other group, and (3) nonagricultural households became relatively poorer.

The details of the composition of family incomes are reported in

TABLE 3.7
Changes in Household Incomes (1973/74 Rs)

Type of Household	*All Villages*		*Resurvey Villages*		
	1973/74	*1982/83*	*1973/74*	*1982/83*	*1983/84*
Small paddy farms	2,028	1,866	1,199	1,605	2,286
	(100)	(92)	(100)	(134)	(190)
Large paddy farms	4,553	3,778	2,764	2,809	3,268
	(100)	(83)	(100)	(102)	(118)
Nonpaddy farms	1,927	1,135	1,732	845	2,032
	(100)	(59)	(100)	(49)	(117)
Landless laborers	988	807	935	912	2,102
	(100)	(82)	(100)	(98)	(225)
Nonagricultural	1,240	1,480	1,187	792	1,837
households	(100)	(119)	(100)	(67)	(155)

Note: Figures in parentheses are income indices with 1973/74 = 100.

Tables 3.8 to 3.12. Farm income accounts for only about 50–60 percent of the family income of small-paddy-farm households (Table 3.8). Wage earnings, particularly in agriculture, account for another third, though these were considerably reduced during the drought year. Increased wage earnings also accounted for 45 percent of the increase in family income between 1973/74 and 1983/84 for small paddy farms in the resurvey villages.

Large-sized paddy farms receive over 80 percent of their income from farming (Table 3.9), hence the changes in net farm income discussed earlier explain most of the changes in their family income.

Nonpaddy farmers have become more dependent on wage earnings since 1973/74 (Table 3.10). Their farm income was almost nonexistent in the resurvey villages during the 1982/83 drought. Agricultural wage earnings were the most important source of income in 1983/84, but nonfarm wage earnings were more important during the drought. Self-employment in nonfarm business activities has also become more important since 1973/74; it accounted for 18 percent of family income in 1983/84.

The landless workers are almost totally dependent on wage earnings, particularly in agriculture (Table 3.11). They suffered from the contraction in agricultural employment during the drought but, more generally, benefited substantially from the increase in the demand for hired labor that has occurred since 1973/74 (see previous sections).

The nonagricultural households have the most diverse sources of income (Table 3.12). Own nonfarm business income is most important, and although this virtually disappeared during the 1982/83 drought, it was the prime source of increase in family income between 1973/74 and 1983/84 in the resurvey villages; it increased from Rs 493 per household

TABLE 3.8
Composition of Family Income, Small Paddy Farms (1973/74 Rs)

	All Villages		*Resurvey Villages*		
Source of Income	*1973/74*	*1982/83*	*1973/74*	*1982/83*	*1983/84*
Net farm income	1,173	1,232	726	1,047	1,105
Agric. wage earnings	410	205	389	200	740
White-collar earnings	91	42	—	2	—
Other wage earnings	36	123	24	196	157
Nonfarm business income	78	159	9	60	20
Rents & money lending	4	25	—	—	162
Other unearned income	236	80	51	100	102
Total family income	2,028	1,866	1,199	1,605	2,286
Sample size	35	72	15	23	11

TABLE 3.9
Composition of Family Income, Large Paddy Farms (1973/74 Rs)

	All Villages		*Resurvey Villages*		
Source of Income	*1973/74*	*1982/83*	*1973/74*	*1982/83*	*1983/84*
Net farm income	4,078	2,923	2,320	2,165	2,884
Agric. wage earnings	180	79	228	26	47
White-collar earnings	138	251	216	239	156
Other wage earnings	28	70	—	44	—
Nonfarm business income	—	214	—	−12	—
Rents & money lending	—	51	—	3	141
Other unearned income	129	190	—	344	40
Total family income	4,553	3,778	2,764	2,809	3,268
Sample size	22	88	5	41	22

TABLE 3.10
Composition of Family Income, Nonpaddy Farmers (1973/74 Rs)

Source of Income	*All Villages* 1973/74	*All Villages* 1982/83	*Resurvey Villages* 1973/74	*Resurvey Villages* 1982/83	*Resurvey Villages* 1983/84
Net farm income	927	155	1,012	3	408
Agric. wage earnings	963	232	720	181	1,008
White-collar earnings	—	54	—	—	—
Other wage earnings	37	334	—	622	142
Nonfarm business income	—	201	—	−164	361
Rents & money lending	—	63	—	195	64
Other unearned income	—	96	—	8	49
Total family income	1,927	1,135	1,732	845	2,032
Sample size	3	28	2	9	9

TABLE 3.11
Composition of Family Income, Landless Agricultural Workers (1973/74 Rs)

Source of Income	*All Villages* 1973/74	*All Villages* 1982/83	*Resurvey Villages* 1973/74	*Resurvey Villages* 1982/83	*Resurvey Villages* 1983/84
Net farm income	32	14	18	16	11
Agric. wage earnings	809	513	809	577	1,670
White-collar earnings	23	2	—	4	17
Other wage earnings	47	171	38	209	131
Nonfarm business income	15	22	16	24	55
Rents & money lending	—	10	—	—	6
Other unearned income	62	75	54	82	212
Total family income	988	807	935	912	2,102
Sample size	50	114	19	44	23

TABLE 3.12
Composition of Family Income, Nonagricultural Households (1973/74 Rs)

Source of Income	All Villages 1973/74	All Villages 1982/83	Resurvey Villages 1973/74	Resurvey Villages 1982/83	Resurvey Villages 1983/84
Net farm income	2	34	—	27	48
Agric. wage earnings	251	141	267	33	492
White-collar earnings	309	459	332	262	—
Other wage earnings	219	379	95	382	—
Nonfarm business income	377	295	493	19	1,094
Rents & money lending	5	—	—	—	4
Other unearned income	77	172	—	69	199
Total family income	1,240	1,480	1,187	792	1,837
Sample size	27	39	5	12	10

to Rs 1,094 per household in constant 1973/74 prices. However, wage earnings, salaries from white-collar employment, and various types of unearned income (including pensions and remittances from relatives) continue to be important sources of income.

Changes in Household Consumption Expenditure

Income is not the most reliable measure of welfare, because it fluctuates widely from year to year in accordance with rainfall, changes in prices, and other random factors beyond a household's control. Households do have some capacity to buffer transitory fluctuations in income to maintain more stable levels of consumption and hence welfare. For example, in drought years they can draw down their savings, borrow, sell capital assets such as livestock, and increase their nonfarm earnings. In this sense household consumption expenditure is a more stable and direct measure of welfare.

The total consumption expenditure (in 1973/74 prices) of each household type is summarized by year in Table 3.13. Unlike the income data in Table 3.7, the consumption data show a definite improvement in the welfare of all household types between 1973/74 and 1982/83, despite the drought. These increases range between 28 and 42 percent among

TABLE 3.13
Changes in Family Expenditures (1973/74 Rs)

Type of Household	*All Villages*		*Resurvey Villages*		
	1973/74	*1982/83*	*1973/74*	*1982/83*	*1983/84*
Small paddy farms	1,379	1,833	1,143	1,726	3,044
	(100)	(133)	(100)	(151)	(266)
Large paddy farms	2,486	3,540	2,182	3,408	5,105
	(100)	(142)	(100)	(156)	(234)
Nonpaddy farms	1,443	1,846	1,163	1,373	2,679
	(100)	(128)	(100)	(118)	(230)
Landless laborers	928	1,184	846	1,244	2,553
	(100)	(128)	(100)	(147)	(302)
Nonagricultural households	1,325	1,733	1,056	1,114	2,191
	(100)	(131)	(100)	(105)	(207)

Notes: Figures in parentheses are income indices with 1973/74 = 100.
Home-produced foods are valued at retail prices.

the household types, and they are a little higher when only the resurvey villages are considered.

The real value of consumption expenditures more than doubled for all household groups in the resurvey villages between 1973/74 and 1983/84. These increases are consistently higher than the income increases reported in Table 3.7.

These results merit some explanation because there are many cases where household expenditures exceed total income, especially in the resurvey villages. Part of the problem arises because homegrown foods consumed by the household were valued at farm-gate prices when calculating income but were valued at retail prices when calculating expenditures. However, as Table 3.14 shows, the problem is not resolved when income is modified to value these home-produced foods at retail prices; the expenditure/income ratios exceed unity for all the household types in the resurvey villages in both 1982/83 and 1983/84. Even after allowing for reported net investment (purchases minus sales of livestock and machinery) and net borrowings (new loans minus debt repaid), there remains a deficit to be accounted for in nearly every case. It is possible that households were drawing down savings in response to financial distress during and immediately following the severe drought. But we also suspect that incomes may have been underreported, especially given the rather higher income estimates obtained in the regional model (Table 8.4).

The increases in total consumption expenditure between 1973/74 and 1983/84 in the resurvey villages were matched by an improvement in the mix of commodities and services purchased (Table 3.15). Although the average budget share for total foods remained relatively

TABLE 3.14
Consolidated Statement of Income, Expenditure, and Savings by Household Type, Resurvey Villages (1973/74 Rs)

	Small Paddy Farms		*Large Paddy Farms*		*Nonpaddy Farms*		*Landless*		*Nonagricultural*	
	1982/83	*1983/84*	*1982/83*	*1983/84*	*1982/83*	*1983/84*	*1982/83*	*1983/84*	*1982/83*	*1983/84*
Modified income[a] (*Y*)	1,579	2,370	2,734	3,447	851	2,150	912	2,102	792	1,837
Total expenditure (*E*)	1,726	3,044	3,408	5,105	1,373	2,679	1,244	2,553	1,114	2,191
Ratio *E/Y*	1.09	1.28	1.25	1.48	1.61	1.25	1.36	1.21	1.41	1.19
Net investment (*I*)	−187	245	579	238	−81	48	−12	6	9	10
Net borrowing (*B*)	195	300	826	384	124	−26	126	−2	51	−7
Change in savings ($Y + B - E - I$)	235	−619	−427	−1,512	−317	−603	−194	−459	−280	−371

[a]Home-grown foods consumed by the household are valued at retail prices in these modified calculations. Because the retail price of rice is heavily subsidized, this actually reduced income in some cases compared with income levels in Table 3.7.

TABLE 3.15
Average Budget Shares for Household Expenditure, Resurvey Villages (percent)

	1973/74					1982/83					1983/84				
	Small Paddy Farms	*Large Paddy Farms*	*Non-paddy Farms*	*Land-less*	*Non-agric.*	*Small Paddy Farms*	*Large Paddy Farms*	*Non-paddy Farms*	*Land-less*	*Non-agric.*	*Small Paddy Farms*	*Large Paddy Farms*	*Non-paddy farms*	*Land-less*	*Non-agric.*
Total foods	82.5	74.7	75.6	84.0	83.7	76.5	69.4	77.5	79.0	79.1	77.0	78.1	70.2	75.9	75.1
Foodgrains	63.9	53.7	59.5	65.3	65.2	50.2	42.9	46.3	50.6	44.4	33.6	37.2	30.4	33.0	33.2
Dairy & eggs	0.4	2.0	1.4	0.1	2.5	1.3	3.0	0.7	0.3	1.5	3.9	6.5	1.7	3.3	1.2
Meat & fish	1.8	2.1	1.1	2.1	1.1	1.2	1.8	4.4	3.2	2.2	5.6	5.2	8.2	7.1	5.2
Vegetables, fruits, & nuts	2.4	3.1	1.4	2.3	3.0	6.6	5.0	6.8	6.4	8.4	12.0	8.9	11.9	12.0	14.2
Oils & spices	10.5	9.3	8.9	11.3	8.7	15.2	14.1	17.6	17.5	20.0	15.5	14.6	11.8	14.7	14.4
Alcohol & tobacco	4.5	5.4	4.2	4.3	5.3	3.4	3.0	3.9	5.2	5.2	3.4	1.6	4.4	4.6	6.9
Energy	1.4	1.3	2.6	2.9	1.7	1.6	1.5	2.6	2.0	2.2	2.1	1.8	2.1	1.8	1.6
Toiletries	1.6	1.4	0.7	1.4	1.0	1.2	1.4	1.8	1.5	1.1	1.5	1.2	1.3	1.4	1.2
Durables	0.3	0.9	0.1	0.1	0.1	0.2	0.7	0.9	1.0	0.2	0.7	1.2	1.3	1.2	0.4
Clothing & footwear	4.4	7.1	4.2	3.1	3.2	3.7	4.4	2.5	2.4	4.3	3.3	4.6	3.7	2.8	2.6
Personal services	1.6	1.8	6.4	1.4	1.6	1.4	1.3	1.0	1.1	0.9	1.3	1.3	1.6	1.3	1.3
Education	0.4	0.4	—	0.1	0.6	0.4	0.8	0.5	0.3	0.3	0.1	0.4	0.3	0.2	0.3
Medical services	0.3	2.5	0.3	0.1	0.4	0.8	1.3	1.7	0.6	1.8	1.4	1.5	1.4	1.8	2.2
Transport	1.5	1.5	1.6	1.4	1.4	2.2	3.5	3.9	2.4	1.5	2.7	2.4	8.4	2.9	2.4
Entertainment	0.3	0.3	2.7	0.6	0.1	0.6	0.9	1.1	0.7	1.7	3.5	2.1	3.5	3.4	4.4
Religious & social functions	1.2	2.7	1.5	0.7	0.9	7.8	7.8	2.5	3.1	1.6	2.9	1.7	1.7	1.9	1.5
Home improvements	n.a.	n.a.	n.a.	n.a.	n.a.	0.3	4.0	0.1	0.6	—	0.1	2.0	0.1	0.7	—

constant over the years at around 75 to 80 percent, households diversified into higher-quality foods. The average budget share for foodgrains declined and the shares for livestock and horticultural products and vegetable oils and spices increased. This pattern was particularly pronounced between 1973/74 and 1983/84.

Of the nonfoods, the average budget shares for durables, medical services, transport, entertainment, and religious and social functions increased the most between 1973/74 and 1983/84.

Changes in Welfare Distribution

The evidence reviewed shows a definite improvement in the welfare of the rural households in the surveyed villages. This implies a reduction in absolute poverty, but what has happened to the relative distribution of household income and consumption expenditure? In Table 3.16 we have expressed the income and expenditure of each household type as a ratio of the corresponding income and expenditure of the landless. These within-year indices show the relative gains and losses of each household type over the years.

Whether measured by income or by consumption expenditure, the landless laborers and the nonagricultural households are the poorest groups and the large paddy farms are the richest. The data do not suggest any worsening of the interhousehold distribution of income or expenditure since 1973/74. On the contrary, the relative income and

TABLE 3.16
Indices of Interhousehold Distribution of Income and Consumption Expenditure (Landless = 100)

	All Villages		*Resurvey Villages*		
	1973/74	*1982/83*	*1973/74*	*1982/83*	*1983/84*
Income					
Small paddy farms	205 (2)	231 (2)	128 (3)	176 (2)	109 (2)
Large paddy farms	461 (1)	468 (1)	296 (1)	308 (1)	155 (1)
Nonpaddy farms	195 (3)	141 (4)	185 (2)	93 (4)	97 (4)
Landless	100 (5)	100 (5)	100 (5)	100 (3)	100 (3)
Nonagricultural	126 (4)	183 (3)	127 (4)	87 (5)	87 (5)
Expenditure					
Small paddy farms	149 (3)	155 (3)	135 (3)	139 (2)	119 (2)
Large paddy farms	267 (1)	299 (1)	258 (1)	274 (1)	200 (1)
Nonpaddy farms	155 (2)	156 (2)	137 (2)	110 (3)	105 (3)
Landless	100 (5)	100 (5)	100 (5)	100 (4)	100 (4)
Nonagricultural	143 (4)	146 (4)	125 (4)	90 (5)	86 (5)

Note: Figures in parentheses are rankings within years.

TABLE 3.17
Average Land Area Owned by Quartile, Cultivator Households (ha)

	1st Quartile			*2nd Quartile*			*3rd Quartile*			*4th Quartile*			*All Farmers*		
Village	*1973*	*1982*	*% Change*	*1973*	*1982*	*% Change*	*1973*	*1982*	*% Change*	*1973*	*1982*	*% Change*	*1973*	*1982*	*% Change*
Kalpattu	0.34	0.23	−32.50	0.59	0.47	−20.34	1.06	0.93	−12.26	2.12	1.87	−11.79	1.03	0.88	−14.56
Nesal	0.30	0.26	−13.33	0.64	0.58	−9.38	1.54	1.25	−18.83	5.23	3.50	−33.08	1.98	1.40	−29.29
Vegamangalam	0.46	0.25	−45.65	0.72	0.61	−15.28	1.01	1.11	9.90	2.08	3.07	47.60	1.12	1.28	14.29
Vinayagapuram	0.22	0.23	4.54	0.54	0.42	−22.22	0.97	0.79	−18.56	2.27	1.96	−13.66	1.00	0.86	−14.00
Sirungathur	0.30	0.31	3.33	0.52	0.53	1.92	0.86	1.01	17.44	2.32	4.37	88.36	1.02	1.55	51.96
Vayalur	0.24	0.18	−25.00	0.45	0.40	−11.11	0.74	0.93	25.68	2.12	2.43	14.62	0.99	1.00	1.01
Vengodu	0.28	0.22	−21.43	0.58	0.42	−27.59	0.96	0.80	−16.67	2.36	2.17	−8.05	1.04	0.89	−14.42
Meppathurai	0.36	0.39	8.33	0.79	0.80	1.27	1.35	1.24	−8.15	3.08	2.12	−31.17	1.48	1.14	−22.97
Duli	0.58	0.49	−15.51	1.07	1.40	30.84	1.66	2.68	61.45	3.39	5.33	57.23	1.65	2.44	47.88
Veerasambanur	0.26	0.30	15.38	0.74	0.67	−9.46	1.24	1.00	−19.35	2.19	2.03	−7.31	1.09	1.01	−7.34
Amudhur	0.16	0.14	−12.50	0.43	0.33	−23.26	0.96	0.94	−2.08	2.93	2.98	1.71	1.12	1.08	−3.57
Pooled villages	0.28	0.25	−10.71	0.63	0.53	−15.87	1.04	1.01	−2.88	2.87	2.88	0.35	1.23	1.18	−4.07

Source: Village listing data, Cambridge-Madras universities and IFPRI-TNAU surveys.

expenditure of the large farms declined between 1973/74 and 1983/84, while that of the landless laborers increased to achieve parity with the small paddy farms. The nonagricultural households slipped in their relative standing to become the poorest group in 1982/83 and 1983/84. The nonpaddy farms also became poorer than the landless when their incomes are compared, but they did a little better on consumption expenditure.

The general pattern seems to be one of a relative gain for all the households benefiting directly from changes in paddy farming, including the landless laborers, and a less than proportionate gain for the nonagricultural households. Although the indirect gains obtained through the growth of local nonfarm activity were substantial, they were insufficient to maintain the relative standing of the nonagricultural households.

Changes in Access to Land

Early critics of the green revolution feared that since the larger farmers were typically the early adopters of HYVs, then they would use their increased profits to buy out smaller farmers. There was some evidence for this phenomenon during the early stages of HYV adoption (e.g., Griffin 1972, 1974), but such observations need not reflect longer-term changes in the distribution of land, particularly if, as in North Arcot, most small farmers have since successfully adopted HYVs. Using the village census data collected by the CMU and IFPRI-TNAU teams, this section examines the changes in the ownership and operation of land over an entire decade of technological change.

Table 3.17 shows the interquartile distribution of owned land by villages for 1973 and 1982. The owned area per farm declined from 1.23 hectares to 1.18 hectares (a reduction of 4 percent) when averaged across villages. When the households in all 11 villages are pooled, it is found that the farms in the top quartile did not change in size whereas the average size went down in the bottom three quartiles. In each case the changes were modest and not statistically significant. Since the pooled sample is expected to be representative of the entire study region, it may be concluded that the changes in paddy technology and irrigation between 1973 and 1982 have not had any significant impact on the aggregate distribution of owned land.

However, Table 3.17 also shows considerable variation in the changes by village. The average farm size increased in Vegamangalam, Sirungathur, and Duli, and in each case the increase was concentrated in the larger-size quartiles. However, an exactly opposite pattern of

TABLE 3.18
Average Land Area Operated by Quartile, Cultivator Households (ha)

Village	*1st Quartile*			*2nd Quartile*			*3rd Quartile*			*4th Quartile*			*All Farmers*		
	1973	*1982*	*% Change*	*1973*	*1982*	*% Change*	*1973*	*1982*	*% Change*	*1973*	*1982*	*% Change*	*1973*	*1982*	*% Change*
Kalpattu	0.38	0.25	−34.21	0.65	0.49	−24.62	1.22	1.07	−12.30	2.43	1.87	−23.05	1.17	0.92	−21.37
Nesal	0.30	0.26	−13.33	0.66	0.62	−6.06	1.61	1.29	−19.88	5.33	3.50	−34.33	1.97	1.42	−27.92
Vegamangalam	0.42	0.28	−33.33	0.81	0.63	−22.22	1.44	1.32	−8.33	2.23	3.29	47.53	1.22	1.38	13.11
Vinayagapuram	0.23	0.23	0	0.56	0.41	−26.79	1.02	0.80	−21.57	2.33	1.96	−15.88	1.04	0.85	−18.27
Sirungathur	0.34	0.32	−5.80	0.55	0.53	−3.64	0.98	1.01	3.06	2.48	4.37	76.21	1.10	1.55	40.91
Vayalur	0.42	0.19	−54.76	0.51	0.47	−7.84	0.84	1.03	22.62	2.36	2.47	4.66	1.03	1.04	0.97
Vengodu	0.28	0.22	−21.43	0.60	0.43	−28.33	1.11	0.80	−27.93	2.40	2.20	−8.33	1.09	0.90	−17.43
Meppathurai	0.45	0.42	−6.67	0.89	0.83	−6.74	0.89	1.27	42.70	1.51	2.12	40.40	0.93	1.17	25.81
Duli	0.58	0.53	−8.62	1.07	1.40	30.84	1.68	2.70	60.71	3.36	5.51	63.99	1.67	2.53	51.50
Veerasambanur	0.26	0.30	15.38	0.74	0.61	−17.57	1.24	1.00	−19.35	2.28	2.03	−10.96	1.12	1.01	−9.82
Amudhur	0.16	0.14	−12.50	0.43	0.33	−23.26	0.96	0.94	−2.08	2.93	2.97	1.37	1.12	1.08	−3.57
Pooled villages	0.28	0.25	−10.71	0.63	0.53	−15.87	1.10	1.02	−7.27	2.93	2.89	−1.37	1.23	1.17	−4.88

Source: Village listing data, Cambridge-Madras universities and IFPRI-TNAU surveys.

change occurred in Vinayagapuram and Meppathurai; the average farm size went down, and the reduction was borne by the farms in the top quartiles.

The average farm size in the bottom quartile declined in 7 of the 11 villages. But in only three of these villages (Vegamangalam, Vayalur, and Duli) was there any significant increase in the size of the farms in the top quartile. There seems to be little support for the proposition that large farms expanded in size at the expense of small farms.

Similar patterns of change are found in the operated size of holdings (Table 3.18).

Using the Spearman rank order correlation test, it is possible to test within each quartile whether the distribution of farm sizes across villages changed between 1973 and 1982. For example, the null hypothesis for the first quartile is that the array of numbers in the first and second columns of Table 3.17 are random samples from different size distributions. Except for the top quartile, this hypothesis was soundly rejected, suggesting that differences among villages in owned and operated farm size were no different in 1982 than in 1973.

To elucidate differences among villages further, the 11 sample villages were classified into poor and rich villages on the basis of their irrigation resources. The rich villages are Kalpattu, Vegamangalam, Nesal, Vinayagapuram, and Sirungathur. The poor villages are the five resurvey villages plus Vengodu. Table 3.19 shows the average size of holding in 1973 and 1982 by quartile for the poor and rich villages.

Irrespective of whether owned or operated area is used, the average farm size in all four quartiles declined in the rich villages. The farms in the first and second quartiles lost relatively more land than average, but the farms in the top quartile lost the most land in absolute terms.

Average farm sizes also declined in the first three quartiles of the poor villages. But unlike the rich villages, the average farm size of the top quartile increased, by about 8 percent. There would seem to have been a clear worsening—albeit a modest one—in the equity of the distribution of land in the poor villages that is not evident in the rich villages. This is confirmed by the calculated Gini coefficients in Table 3.20. They declined modestly in the rich villages but increased in the poor villages. Although these differences are not statistically significant, they provide little support for the hypothesis that the green revolution—which, because of better irrigation resources, was most prevalent in the rich villages—worsened the distribution of land.

TABLE 3.19
Average Farm Sizes by Quartile for Rich and Poor Villages (ha)

	1st Quartile			*2nd Quartile*			*3rd Quartile*			*4th Quartile*			*Total*		
	1973	*1982*	*% Change*	*1973*	*1982*	*% Change*	*1973*	*1982*	*% Change*	*1973*	*1982*	*% Change*	*1973*	*1982*	*% Change*
Owned area															
Poor villages	0.25	0.23	−8.00	0.63	0.55	−12.70	1.08	1.05	−2.78	2.70	2.93	8.52	1.20	1.20	0
Rich villages	0.30	0.26	−13.30	0.64	0.52	−18.75	1.01	0.99	−2.00	2.98	2.84	−4.70	1.25	1.15	−8.00
Pooled villages	0.28	0.25	−10.71	0.63	0.53	−15.87	1.04	1.01	−2.88	2.87	2.88	0.35	1.23	1.18	−4.07
Operated area															
Poor villages	0.25	0.24	−4.00	0.64	0.55	−14.06	1.10	1.05	−4.55	2.73	2.94	7.69	1.18	1.19	0.84
Rich villages	0.30	0.26	−13.33	0.62	0.51	−17.74	1.10	1.00	−9.09	3.08	2.85	−7.47	1.27	1.15	−9.45
Pooled villages	0.28	0.25	−10.71	0.63	0.53	−15.87	1.10	1.02	−7.27	2.93	2.89	−1.37	1.23	1.17	−4.88

Source: Village listing data, Cambridge-Madras universities and IFPRI-TNAU surveys.

TABLE 3.20
Gini Coefficients for Land Area Owned and Operated

	Area Owned		*Area Operated*	
	1973	*1982*	*1973*	*1982*
Poor villages	0.652	0.665	0.639	0.658
Rich villages	0.697	0.663	0.669	0.654
Pooled villages	0.679	0.665	0.657	0.656

Source: Village listing data, Cambridge-Madras universities and IFPRI-TNAU surveys.

Conclusions

In this chapter we have used the data from the 1973/74, 1982/83, and 1983/84 surveys to evaluate some of the economic changes that took place in the sample villages. Our task has been complicated by the severe drought of 1982/83 and the incomplete village coverage of the 1983/84 resurvey. Clearly, comparisons between 1973/74 and 1982/83 must grossly underestimate the impact of the intervening changes in irrigation and paddy technology. On the other hand, comparisons between 1973/74 and 1983/84, while more acceptable in terms of the greater similarity of irrigation water reserves, are limited to a sample of the poorer villages in the region.

Within these constraints, our conclusions are that the landless laborers gained the largest proportional increase in family income (125 percent), followed by small paddy farmers, who almost doubled their incomes (90 percent). Large paddy farms gained relatively little (18 percent) because of sharp increases in their farm costs, especially the cost of fertilizers and hired labor. The nonpaddy farms—which do not have access to irrigated land—and the nonagricultural households increased their incomes by 17 and 55 percent, respectively.

The real value of consumption expenditure doubled for all the household groups analyzed between 1973/74 and 1983/84. This was accompanied by an improvement in the mix of commodities and services purchased toward more luxurious items: more livestock and horticultural products and vegetable oils at the expense of foodgrains, and more services, especially transport, entertainment, social and religious functions, and medical services. The purchase and ownership of consumer durables also increased.

These gains in absolute welfare have also been accompanied by an improvement in equity. Whether measured by income or by consumption expenditure, the relative welfare of the large paddy farms has declined, while that of the landless laborers and the small paddy farms has improved. The nonpaddy farmers and the nonagricultural households gained relatively less than the other groups because they did not gain directly from the changes that occurred in irrigation and paddy technology.

The main source of increase in farm incomes was an expansion in paddy production. Large farms, many of which had already adopted HYVs by 1973/74, increased their paddy production through an increase in the cropped area. But most of the increase was obtained from yield increases on small paddy farms. Increases in agricultural wage earnings were also important sources of income for small paddy farms, nonpaddy farms, and landless laborers.

Nonagricultural income, either from wage earnings or from a family-owned business, has become more important not only for the specialized nonagricultural households, but also for small paddy farms, nonpaddy farms, and landless laborers. To the extent that the rural nonfarm economy is driven by agricultural growth, this finding provides support for the argument that the growth linkages do benefit the poorer rural households. Moreover, since the large paddy farms obtain very little income from nonagricultural sources, it may also be concluded that the growth linkages have also contributed to an improvement in the relative distribution of income within the villages.

The results in this chapter have also highlighted the dramatic year-to-year fluctuations in incomes that occur in North Arcot. During the 1982/83 drought, many households were actually worse off than in 1973/74, despite the intervening changes in irrigation and paddy technology. Compared with 1983/84, agricultural employment was down about 50 percent during the drought, farm incomes were down 20 percent on average, and nonfarm business earnings almost disappeared. The impact of these changes was reflected by a roughly 50 percent reduction in the value of family consumption expenditure.

Finally, our analysis does not show any worsening of the distribution of land in North Arcot since the early 1970s. The number of farms increased, presumably because of population pressures, and the average size of holding shrank a little as a result. However, this decline in farm size seems to have affected small and large farms alike, and it has been largely neutral with respect to the distribution of land.

There is some evidence that the distribution of land may have worsened a little in the poorly irrigated villages, but not in the better-endowed villages. If so, this suggests that demographic pressures, combined with less favorable technological possibilities, are more damaging for equity than the green revolution per se. In this sense our results support Ricardo rather than the critics of the green revolution (Hazell and Anderson 1984).

CHAPTER 4

The Green Revolution in North Arcot: Economic Trends, Household Mobility, and the Politics of an "Awkward Class"

John Harriss

THE PRECEDING CHAPTER used village household data from the Cambridge-Madras universities and IFPRI-TNAU surveys to assess, after a decade, the growth and equity effects of the green revolution in North Arcot. A key motivation has been to test the diverging views that have emerged in the literature on the effects of the green revolution. This chapter continues with that task, but from the perspective that my own in-depth anthropological fieldwork and analysis can provide.

Methodology

As a member of the Cambridge project, I lived in and studied one village in particular in 1973–74—Nesal, to which I assigned the pseudonym Randam in my earlier writings, a practice I maintain here—though I also spent time in the other 11 villages of the survey. The results of the research form the basis of a monograph (Harriss 1982). As baseline data, therefore, I was able to use both material I collected myself and survey data (including some of the original material as well as published results).

From December 1983 to February 1984, I went back to five of the original 12 villages studied by the Cambridge project, including Dusi, and Randam, as well as three other villages—Veerasambanur, Vinayagapuram, and Duli. These were selected to represent variation in irrigation conditions and in access to urban centers (which seemed to account for much of the variation among the villages in terms of their social and economic character; see Chambers and Harriss 1977).

The author wishes to express his gratitude in particular to P. Kandhan; and to G. Jothi, T. Ganesan and S. Guhan for invaluable assistance in conducting his fieldwork in 1983–84.

Village	Access to Urban Centers	Irrigation
Randam	Good	Good
Dusi	Good	Good
Duli	Good	Poor
Vinayagapuram	Remote	Good
Veerasambanur	Remote	Poor

Dusi is like Randam in having good access to a major urban center (Kanchipuram), and, being under one of the biggest irrigation tanks in northern Tamil Nadu, it has good irrigation also, though it has very few wells and pumps. It is larger than the other villages and has the character of a small service center (with a cinema and a fair number of shops and other businesses). It is also an industrial village, with a large population of handloom weavers who work for master weavers based in Kanchipuram. The five villages together represent the range of village types distinguished by Robert Chambers and myself in our work on intervillage variation in 1973–74 (Chambers and Harriss 1977).

In Randam, I completed a fresh census of the village and collected data on the history of landholding and land transactions in each household; on employment; on the costs of production and labor use; and on credit transactions and investment. The same information was collected for stratified random samples of households in each of the other villages, the samples being drawn from the 1973 household census list drawn up by the Cambridge and Madras universities team.

Veerasambanur: One-third sample of 1973 households = 37 households − 6 emigrants = 31 with 4 instances of partitioning = 36 households in 1984
Vinayagapuram: One-fifth sample of 1973 = 35 households − 3 emigrants = 32 with 2 instances of partitioning = 36 households in 1984
Duli: One-third sample of 1973 = 31 households, with 4 cases of partitioning = 36 households in 1984
Dusi: One-tenth sample of 1973 = 47 households − 4 emigrants = 43 with 3 cases of partitioning = 47 households in 1984
Total: 155 households

Livelihoods, Labor, Employment, and Wages

Data for Randam confirm the finding in Chapter 2 that the labor requirements of paddy cultivation have probably increased since the early 1970s. Static comparisons in 1973 showed that high-yielding varieties (HYVs) required slightly more labor than the older varieties, and the area under HYVs has expanded since then. The use of tractors and mechanical threshers has not developed to the point of displacing labor. The number of tractors owned by local people (living in Randam or adjacent villages) has not increased. There was one tractor owned locally in 1973; two more were added shortly afterward; in 1983 the number was one again, but two new tractors were added in 1984. In 1983 the owners of tractor repair workshops in Arni reported that the numbers of tractors and of mechanical threshers in the region of the town had not increased since the mid–1970s.

It is true of course that the area cultivated was reduced in the drought years from 1980 to 1983, but loss of agricultural work in that period was at least partially compensated by the availability of work in well deepening and by the Food for Work Program implemented by the state government. Cultivators in Randam reported a total expenditure of Rs 127,000 on well deepening during the drought, and employment equivalent to 50 days per annum for every agricultural labor household in the village in each of the three drought years.

Meanwhile, according to data on village labor markets, it appears that real wages have increased. This finding is confirmed in two of the other three villages for which I have comparable data (Table 4.1). The village that does not show clear evidence of real wage increases, Veerasambanur, is relatively remote and has poor irrigation facilities. Production there has stagnated, probably because of low groundwater potential. It may be noted that this is a village in which land values have apparently fallen (see Table 4.2).

What of the supply of agricultural labor? As discussed elsewhere (Chapter 6), the overall rate of population growth has been comparatively low in eastern North Arcot. My own censuses for Randam show an increase of as little as 8.7 percent from April 1973 to January 1984. This particularly low rate of increase may be partly accounted for by net emigration (33 households and 150 individuals having migrated out and 25 households and 98 individuals having come in), with a loss of agricultural-labor households in particular having occurred (13 households left and only 4 came in). However, some of this was purely local emigration, as people moved to new houses or new house sites just outside the bounds of the residential area of Randam village. The low rate of increase also reflects a reduced rate of population growth resulting from declining fertility. The use of family planning, usually though not exclusively through tubectomy, has increased considerably since 1973, and family sizes are smaller among the numerically predominant Agamudaiyan Mudaliars.

Among the other villages, the population of one (Duli) has grown much faster than the average (by 37 percent, according to census data).

TABLE 4.1
Agricultural Wages (Rs/day)

	Randam				Veerasambanur				Vinayagapuram				Duli			
		1984 Deflated				1984 Deflated				1984 Deflated				1984 Deflated		
Task	*1984 Actual*	*(a)*	*(b)*	*1973*	*1984 Actual*	*(a)*	*(b)*	*1973*	*1984 Actual*	*(a)*	*(b)*	*1973*	*1984 Actual*	*(a)*	*(b)*	*1973*
Ploughing (with animals)	10	4.57	5.26	2.5	5	2.28	2.63	0.75	5	2.28	2.63	2.0	7	3.30	3.68	2.0
Male coolie	5	2.28	2.63	2.0	3	1.37	1.58	2.0	4	1.83	2.10	1.7	5	2.28	2.10	1.3
Female transplanting	3	1.37	1.58	1.0	2	0.91	1.05	1.25	2	0.91	1.05	0.70	3	1.37	1.58	1.5

Notes: (a) Deflator based on general consumer price index for agricultural labor in Tamil Nadu.
(b) Deflator based on difference in paddy prices in Randam village between December 1973–February 1974 and 1983–84.

TABLE 4.2
Land Prices (Rs/acre, current prices)

Village	*Year*	*Wetland with Well & Pump Share*	*Wetland*	*Dryland*
Randam	1971–74	12,900	8,900	2,500
	1979–83	14,000	8,700	3,450
Veerasambanur	1971–74	—	7,000	1,300
	1978–80	—	6,700	1,000
Vinayagapuram	1971–74	16,600	—	3,300
	1979–83	23,000	6,000	3,300
Duli	1971–75	—	5,000	1,600
	1979–83	—	18,000	2,000
Dusi	1970–74	—	11,100	1,500
	1980–83	—	24,600	4,400

Source: Data from recorded land sales and purchases.

The village has attracted some immigrants taking advantage of a favorable employment situation because the village is near the fast-growing town of Cheyyar. The populations of Vinayagapuram and Veerasambanur have grown less than the average. There has been net emigration from both villages, people from both having moved, especially to Vellore (the district capital), to Madras, and to Bangalore for work. These details are necessary to understand the data on employment.

Analysis of principal occupation by household in Randam (see Table 4.3) shows that the number of households dependent primarily upon cultivation increased by 6 percent between 1973 and 1984; that the number depending primarily upon agricultural labor decreased by 10 percent; and that the number dependent upon other occupations increased by 35 percent. Analysis of the primary occupations (usual status) of individual men and women gives a slightly different impression (see Table 4.4). It appears that the number of men whose principal occupation is own cultivation actually decreased by nearly 20 percent from 1973 to 1984; that both the absolute number of men working principally as agricultural laborers and their share in the total labor force changed very little; and that the proportion of men working in activities other than cultivation and agricultural wage labor increased from 31 percent to 40 percent of the total. Meanwhile, the number of women working both in own cultivation and as agricultural laborers increased. Though I am doubtful as to the reliability and the comparability of these data on women's employment, I believe that there has

TABLE 4.3
Principal Occupations of Households, Randam (number of households)

Occupation	1973	1984
Cultivation	102 (37)[a]	108 (36)
Agricultural labor	93 (34)	84 (28)
Other	80 (29)	108 (36)
Trade	11	11
Livestock	6	9
Artisans/functionaries	12	18
Transport	2	2
Service[b]	36	45
Dependents	11	18
Money lending	2	2
Rents/interest	—	3

[a]Figures in parentheses are percentages of total.
[b]The category "service" is meant in the conventional Indian usage and refers to employment in government service or in private-sector jobs that offer at least roughly comparable terms and conditions of work. It is not used in the sense of "domestic service."

TABLE 4.4
Occupational Structure of the Labor Force, Randam (number of workers)

Primary Occupation	*Men*		*Women*	
	1973	*1984*	*1973*	*1984*
Owner cultivation	137 (38)	109 (29)	8	18
Agricultural labor	107 (30)	114 (30)	136	158
Other	112 (31)	151 (40)	14	25
Total	356	374		

Note: Figures in parentheses are percentages of total.

certainly been an increase in the size of the female agricultural labor force.

The clearest and firmest conclusion from these data is that activities other than cultivation and agricultural wage work have become relatively more important in Randam. "Other activities" that have expanded over the decade are paddy dealing, in which only two households were involved in a minor way in 1973, but which is now the principal occupation in four households and a subsidiary source of income in five others; (silk handloom) weaving, which was the principal activity in one household in 1973 and in nine in 1984; herding sheep, the principal occupation of six households in both 1973 and 1984, but the main activity of half as many men again in 1984 as in 1973; and a variety of service occupations, including local government jobs such as working in the Tamil Nadu government's Nutritious Noon Meals Program.

Another change of importance since 1973, but one that does not appear in these data, is the increased importance of dairying. The Arni Milk Cooperative set up a depot in the village after 1973, and this and the credit made available by the cooperative have made dairying a more important source of income. In spite of the drought, which led to a 21 percent decrease in the numbers of draft animals held by Randam cultivators, the number of cows owned by people in the village increased by 25 percent between April 1973 and January 1984, and the number of households owning milk cattle increased from 21 percent of the total to 34 percent. Both this change and, even more so, the increased importance of sheep in the village economy have resulted from the expansion in the availability of cheap formal-sector credit for these purposes in the past 10 years.

In addition to the increase in the importance of activities other than cultivation and agricultural wage work in the village, there has been some increase in the number of dependent households (from 11 to 18); in four cases, households are now dependent upon remittances from relatives employed in Vellore, Bangalore, or Madras. Whereas in 1973 one person from Randam worked in Bombay, this number has now increased to five.

The decline in the number of households depending primarily upon agricultural labor—which seems to have taken place, even if the number of individuals working as agricultural laborers has not changed much—is partly due to emigration, for whereas 21 former agricultural-labor households moved into other occupations (15) and tenant cultivation (6), 18 households moved from these activities and from petty cultivation into primary dependence upon agricultural labor. It is of some importance, therefore, to know why 13 agricultural-labor households left the village, and where they went. Seven have migrated purely locally and continue to be employed as agricultural laborers; two have moved to local towns for employment as casual labor; two have gone to work in textile mills in Bombay; and one has gone to Madras for casual work. The movement of the last is unknown. It is not the case that people have been moving out of agricultural labor into "desperation" activities outside the agricultural economy.

It may be deduced from these observations that there has been some shift in Randam away from primary dependence upon agriculture toward other activities, though cultivation has continued to absorb roughly the same absolute numbers of people (388 in 1973 and 399 in 1984). It seems that the diversification of occupations locally (paddy trading, weaving, service employment) and increased migration for

TABLE 4.5
Occupational Structure of the Labor Force, Veerasambanur, Vinayagapuram, Duli, and Dusi (number of workers)

Sample Estimates	*Veerasambanur* 1973	*Veerasambanur* 1984	*Vinayagapuram* 1973	*Vinayagapuram* 1984	*Duli* 1973	*Duli* 1984	*Dusi* 1973	*Dusi* 1984
Men								
Owner-cultivation	27 (48)	17 (38)	29 (60)	25 (49)	20 (42)	22 (34)	32 (46)	25 (30)
Agricultural labor	29 (52)	15 (33)	12 (25)	9 (18)	23 (48)	18 (28)	5 (7)	5 (6)
Cattleherd			1			4 (6)		
Weaving		7 (16)		9 (18)			17 (25)	35 (42)
Wage earning		2 (4)				20 (31)		4 (5)
Service			3 (6)	3 (6)	5 (10)		4 (6)	2 (2)
Petty business		1		2 (4)		1	8 (12)	7 (8)
Profession			3 (6)	2 (4)				1
Remittances		3 (7)						
Money lending				1				
Other							3 (4)	4 (5)
% of male population in labor force	59	54	63	59	55	58	66	64
Women								
Owner-cultivation	6 (18)	22 (42)	6 (25)	19 (51)	1	12 (35)	20 (59)	10 (21)
Agricultural labor	27 (82)	27 (51)	17 (71)	13 (35)	10 (91)	16 (47)	3 (9)	12 (25)
Petty trade		1				5 (15)	6 (18)	18 (38)
Service (noon meals scheme)						1		
Dhobi			1	3 (8)				
Domestic service		1		1				8 (16)
Weaving		1		1				
Tailor		1						
Other							5 (14)	
% of female population in labor force	34	51	29	47	18	43	27	37

Note: Figures in parentheses are percentages of totals.

work in larger, distant urban centers have tightened the agricultural labor market. It is probably significant in this connection that the number of *padials* (permanent, "attached" laborers) employed by Randam cultivators has increased also.

In my earlier analysis I argued that the effects of the expansion of groundwater irrigation and of HYV cultivation in these circumstances of rather intensive cultivation, far from leading to reduced employment of permanent laborers (as predicted in some of the green revolution literature), actually enhanced cultivators' interests in attaching labor to themselves (see Harriss 1982, Chapter 4). This seems to have been borne out by subsequent experience because the number of *padials* employed by Randam farmers has increased from 37 in 1973 to 46 in 1984.

Further qualitative evidence of a tightening of the local labor market is the observation that there has been some reduction in the length of the working day (commented upon widely by cultivators in the area), and an increase in the frequency with which early-morning "shift" work is carried on (whereby women work from about 6.30 A.M. until about 8:30, and may then work for the remainder of the day on a separate contract). (Note that in the calculations of wages in Table 4.1, I have used the wage for the standard working day, and this may be slightly shorter in 1984.)

Analysis of individual occupations in the sample households in the other four villages produces results that strongly confirm the tendency observed in Randam. In each of the villages there has been some decline in the number of men depending primarily upon own cultivation; a decline in the number dependent primarily upon agricultural labor; and a marked increase in the number primarily engaged in and dependent upon other occupations (notably, weaving both in the old weaving village of Dusi and in Veerasambanur and Vinayagapuram, where it was not previously carried on; and urban wage work in Duli; see Table 4.5).

The results for female employment are problematic, for I am much less certain of the comparability of data between the two observation points, particularly with regard to the number of those whose primary activity is owner cultivation. It seems possible, however, that overall female participation has increased, and unlikely that the number of those engaging in agricultural labor has declined.

There has been net emigration from two villages (Veerasambanur and Vinayagapuram) and only limited migration into a third (Duli). Indeed, in the cases of all three villages my estimates of the population size of the whole village in 1984, which are based on sample estimates, correspond closely with the 1981 census figures. I am confident, then, that for these three villages my samples have not led me to ignore immigration into them. The picture in Dusi is more complicated, and there I believe there has been immigration of outsiders into the village, though not mainly for work in agricultural labor (see Guhan and Bharathan 1984).

In short, the conclusion that there has been some decline locally in the size of the male agricultural labor force seems justified, and findings for all the villages are strikingly consistent in pointing to a decline in the relative share of primary dependence upon cultivation activities as more employment outside agriculture has become available both locally and in major urban centers such as Madras and Bangalore. There has been a corresponding improvement in agricultural wages in all except one village, where cultivation has generally failed to expand.

It seems, therefore, that proletarianization of labor has been taking place over the last decade, at least in the sense that there has been a marked increase in the number of people and of households depending in some way upon wage work (including handloom weaving, which can properly be seen as a form of disguised wage work). Thus, in Vinayagapuram 25 percent of households now have members in regular or short-term wage work in Madras or Vellore; in Duli 33 percent of households have members working in Cheyyar; and in Veerasambanur 28 percent of households have members with nonagricultural wage incomes. But does this kind of "proletarianization" mean that increasing numbers of people in the villages have been fully separated from ownership of means of production? Has there been that widely anticipated tendency toward greater concentration of landholdings with the development of capitalist agriculture following the introduction of HYVs? Has there been a tendency for smaller landholders to be dispossessed as they resort to distress sales of land? Is there evidence of the kind of social and economic marginalization within the rural economy referred to by some writers (such as Pearse 1980) and quite often assumed to be taking place generally in India?

Differentiation of Peasantry? Land Transactions and Household Mobility

In the case of Randam village, I have data on the landholdings inherited by all households and details of subsequent purchase, sale, and other transactions. (The procedures employed here follow Cain 1981.) These data have been closely checked against official ownership records, and data collected in 1984 have been checked against those collected in 1973. The same data were also obtained for sample households in the other four villages. In all cases the 1984 data were checked against those collected in 1973, but only for Veerasambanur and Dusi was it possible to check against the official records. I believe that the data are good for Randam and Veerasambanur, and least reliable for Vinayagapuram. Using these data I have analyzed the distribution of landownership holdings at the time of inheritance, in 1973, and in 1984, charted shifts in landownership and the mobility of households among landholding categories, and analyzed reasons for land sales and the sources of funds for land purchases. Note that data on landholding at inheritance are for the households still present in the villages in 1984, allowing for partitioning since 1973; and that the data for 1973 are for the households present in the village at that time (i.e., including those of people who have subsequently migrated out).

The results of a painstaking and time-consuming analysis may be rather quickly summarized as follows.

Changes in the Distribution of Land

Table 4.6 shows that in Veerasambanur there has been little change in the incidence of landlessness; in Dusi the incidence of landlessness has declined since inheritance and shows little change between 1973 and 1984; in Vinayagapuram landlessness has increased since inheritance, though from a low base; in Randam, though there has been no change in the incidence of landlessness between the time of inheritance and the present, there has been some increase since 1973 among the households living in the village in 1984. This is the result of partitioning of landless households and because of the downward mobility, in terms of landholding, of 17 households. These cases are mainly the result of women having been widowed and of indebtedness arising from drink. Finally, there is very clear evidence in Duli of increased landlessness from inheritance to 1984.

The distribution of landownership has become distinctly less unequal since inheritance in Dusi; it shows little change between inheritance and the present, and between 1973 and 1984 in Randam, Veerasambanur, and Vinayagapuram; and it has become markedly more unequal only in Duli (Table 4.6).

These observations are amplified by further data on changes in shares of land owned from inheritance (see Table 4.7). In Randam, Veerasambanur, and Vinayagapuram the members of the upper quintile of landholders at the time of inheritance have, in aggregate, lost land. Those in the lower quintiles have generally gained land in Randam and Veerasambanur, but the pattern is a little more complex in Vinayagapuram, with both loss and gain in the middle of the inheritance

TABLE 4.6
Changes in Distribution of Landownership

	Randam			*Veerasambanur*			*Vinayagapuram*			*Duli*			*Dusi*		
	At Inheritance	*1973*	*1984*	*At Inheritance*	*1973*	*1984*	*At Inheritance*	*1973*	*1984*	*At Inheritance*	*1973*	*1984*	*At Inheritance*	*1973*	*1984*
Landless households (% total households)	44.0	41.0	44.0	21.0	23.0	21.0	5.5	11.0	11.0	11.8	19.4	20.6	38.3	32.6	34.0
Percentage of total land area owned by:															
Top size decile[a]	53.4	55.2	51.7	28.7	32.3	30.7	50.0	54.0	49.0	28.6	43.3	40.1	47.2	45.9	39.0
Lower half of size distribution[a]	1.5	1.7	1.2	12.0	11.0	12.8	13.4	10.4	10.2	19.5	12.9	11.3	4.0	7.8	5.9

[a]The size distribution of households includes the landless.

TABLE 4.7
Changes in Area of Land Owned from Inheritance to 1984 by Size Group (acres)

Ownership Category at Inheritance (by quintile)	*Randam*	*Veerasambanur*	*Vinayagapuram*	*Duli*	*Dusi*
Poorest	0	+2.77	+0.87	+1.00	+4.75
2	+37.67	+4.54	+4.84	−0.77	+8.02
3	+57.05	+1.59	−3.85	−4.66	+10.01
4	+37.18	−1.37	+11.58	+29.84	−0.86
5	−24.72	−14.64	−8.88	+5.86	+7.26

Note: Figures are the changes in the total land area held by all farms in each size group. They are not expressed on a per farm basis.

distribution. In Dusi there have been relatively much greater gains of land in the middle and lower quintiles, loss in the fourth quintile, and a small gain in the uppermost quintile. Only in Duli have the members of both the upper quintiles gained land, and those in the lower quintiles remained the same or lost land.

It is remarkable that in all five villages the number of "gainers" of land since inheritance outweighs—though not always by much—the number of "losers" of land (Tables 4.8 and 4.9). Again, though, there is a difference between Duli and the other four villages. In Duli alone does the group of the largest landholders at inheritance include more gainers than losers, while the group of smallest landowners at inheritance includes more losers than gainers of land. It can reasonably be concluded, therefore, that except in the case of Duli there is no evidence for increased concentration of landholdings or loss of land by the smallest landholders, but rather the reverse. The reason for the tendency toward increased concentration observed in Duli is that people in that village have steadily been buying back land from Sengunda Mudaliar moneylenders and master weavers in the town of Cheyyar, who acquired control of large amounts of village land, probably during the depression in the 1930s. (This occurred in Vinayagapuram too. In the 1930s, all the land of that village reportedly came under the control of a single Chettiar banker in Polur.) The buying back of land in Duli has led to increased concentration of landholding because the larger village landholders have been doing most of the purchasing. Increased concentration does not appear to have been the result primarily of transfers of land from smaller to larger landholders.

This argument is supported by analysis of household mobility between landholding classes from inheritance to the present. The greatest amount of mobility occurred in Vinayagapuram, where 42 percent of

TABLE 4.8
Gains and Losses of Land from Inheritance to 1984, Randam (number of households)

	Ownership Category at Inheritance (by quartile)					
	Landless	*1*	*2*	*3*	*4*	*Total*
Gainers	18 (14)	13 (31)	13 (32)	11 (27)	8 (20)	63 (21)
No change	112 (86)	24 (57)	19 (46)	11 (27)	14 (34)	180 (61)
Losers	0	5 (12)	9 (22)	19 (46)	19 (46)	52 (18)
Total	130	42	41	41	41	295

Note: Figures in parentheses are percentages.

TABLE 4.9
Gains and Losses of Land from Inheritance to 1984, Veerasambanur, Vinayagapuram, Duli, and Dusi (number of households)

	Ownership Category at Inheritance (by tercile)				
	Landless	*1*	*2*	*3*	*Total*
Veerasambanur					
Gainers	3	4	3	2	12 (36)
No change	4	3	2	2	11 (33)
Losers	0	2	4	4	10 (31)
Total	7	9	9	8	33
Vinayagapuram					
Gainers	1	5	4	5	15 (42)
No change	1	5	2	3	11 (30)
Losers	0	2	5	3	10 (28)
Total	2	12	11	11	36
Duli					
Gainers	0	3	3	5	11 (32)
No change	4	4	4	2	14 (41)
Losers	0	3	3	3	9 (26)
Total	4	10	10	10	34
Dusi					
Gainers	4	5	2	5	16 (34)
No change	14	4	4	2	24 (51)
Losers	0	1	4	2	7 (15)
Total	18	10	10	9	47

Note: Figures in parentheses are percentages.

the households changed positions, but here and in Randam, Dusi, and Veerasambanur there was more upward than downward mobility. The least mobility and the only instance of more downward than upward mobility were found in Duli.

There thus appears to be quite strong evidence against the simpler versions of the classic differentiation thesis, which supports the findings of Attwood for a village in Maharashtra (Attwood 1979) and of Cain for several villages in the semiarid tropics of India (Cain 1981). These are the only studies known to me that offer dynamic analysis at the household level comparable to that presented in this chapter.[1] However, the evidence presented thus far of course does not permit one to conclude that concentration of agricultural capital has not been occurring, especially in circumstances like these where there is so much difference in productivity between irrigated and nonirrigated land. The loss of land by larger landholders in Randam, Veerasambanur, and Vinayagapuram could be accounted for as the result of land sales to finance investments. To some extent this probably is the case, particularly in Randam, where 40 percent of land sales by the largest landholders at inheritance were for investment in land. Yet analysis of the distribution of landownership by value in 1973 and 1984 in Randam—using average values of land of different types in the periods 1971–74 and 1979–83—shows virtually no change at all. Since the most substantial component of agricultural capital is made up of wells and pumps, and investments in these are reflected in land values, it seems fair to conclude that in Randam there has been no increase in the concentration of agricultural capital since 1973.

In sum, there is very little evidence here for the existence of a process of differentiation involving increased concentration of landownership and the ownership of agricultural capital more generally, and losses of land by smaller landholders.

Land Transactions

Analysis of land sales and purchases in the villages shows that the land market is generally more active than is commonly supposed to be the case in rural India, and indeed that it may be more active than in Western Europe, where about 1 percent of the total stock of land is bought or sold each year (information from Harrison 1985). In Randam in the 1970s the corresponding figure was 1.5 percent per annum, in Vinayagapuram 2.7 percent, and in Duli 3.5 percent.

In Randam and Duli more than one-third of the land area sold since inheritance has been for investment in other land or in groundwater irrigation; and in each case one-third of the total number of sales transactions has been for these purposes also. In Duli such sales have been almost entirely by the largest landowners, but in Randam smaller holders have also engaged in sales for these purposes. If we consider house

1. Since the time of writing, comparable analysis has been offered in Athreya, Djurfeldt, and Lindberg 1990 and in Walker and Ryan 1990.

construction and marriage payments to be investments too, as well as purchase of cattle and tractors, then we find that in Randam 68 percent of the area sold and 63 percent of transactions have been for investment; in Veerasambanur 40 percent of the area and 39 percent of transactions; in Vinayagapuram 76 percent of the area and perhaps 79 percent of transactions; and in Duli 48 percent of the area and 50 percent of transactions. In Dusi only 18 percent of the total land sold and 10 percent of transactions were for consumption or medical expenses (27 percent and 19 percent, respectively, if the category of land sold in order to repay outstanding cooperative debts is included). These sales were made by landholders in the medium and large categories. A more common reason for the sale of land was to finance investment, including purchase of land of better quality and land improvement (19 percent of transactions and 23 percent of the land area sold). In Dusi also, other important reasons for sales include marriage cost, house construction, and education, which together account for 37 percent of both the area sold and the total number of transactions.

It may be significant that the villages with the highest proportion of land sold and frequency of transactions for consumption purposes are the two villages with poor irrigation, Veerasambanur and Duli. In all the villages it is remarkable that sales for purposes of direct consumption—what might in principle be "distress sales"—have been made at least as much and usually more by the bigger landholders. (In Randam this was 15 percent of the area sold from the top quartile, 39 percent of that sold from the third quartile, and only 11 percent in each case from the first and second quartiles. Only among those originally landless does it go over 50 percent of the area sold.)

Thus, the available evidence shows that the incidence of distress land sales is rather low, certainly less than 20 percent of all land sales, further supporting the conclusion that concentration of landholdings as a result of the development of capitalist agriculture or of distress sales by poorer landholders is not taking place.

Class Mobility in Randam

The data for Randam allow more detailed examination of household mobility and of mobility between agrarian classes for the period of burgeoning green revolution from 1973 to 1984. The matrix shown in Table 4.10 records cases of mobility among agrarian classes as these were distinguished in my earlier work (see Harriss 1982, Chapters 4 and 5).

In the matrix "A" refers to capitalist farmers, defined as those who

TABLE 4.10
Class Mobility, Randam (number of households)

	Total 1973	1984 A	B	C	D	Agric. Labor	Other	Migrated Out	Extinct
A	9	7	5	—	—	—	—	—	—
B	22	3	25	10	—	—	4	1	—
C	32	—	2	22	4	—	5	2	1
D	39	—	—	—	21	12	12	5	—
Agric. labor	93	—	—	—	6	62	15	13	5
Other	80	—	—	1	4	6	50	12	8
Migrated in		—	—	3	6	4	12	—	—
Total 1984		10	32	36	41	84	98	33	14

Note: A = capitalist farmers, B = rich peasants, C = middle peasants, and D = poor peasants. See text for definitions of these terms.

own sufficient resources to be able to produce surplus equivalent to more than 12 months' household livelihood requirements, employing wage labor, and not themselves engaging directly in productive labor. "B" refers to rich peasants, defined as those who own sufficient resources to be able to produce surplus equivalent to 12 months' livelihood requirements or more, employing wage labor, and themselves engaging in productive work on their lands. "C" refers to middle peasants, defined as those who own sufficient resources to be able to produce some surplus above their own 12 months' household livelihood requirements, who employ labor, and who themselves work on their lands but do not hire themselves out to work for others. "D" refers to poor peasants, who own insufficient resources to be able to produce their own household livelihood requirements for 12 months, and who work for other people more than they employ others to work on their lands. The category "other" includes all those households in which an activity other than cultivation or agricultural wage work supplies the principal source of livelihood, though these households may be engaged in cultivation or in agricultural labor as subsidiary activities. (The matrix includes cases of partitioning, and so the horizontal rows do not add up to the number of households in each category present in 1973.)

In general what the matrix shows is a perhaps remarkable stability in the absolute numbers of households in each class category—except for the marked increase in "other"—in spite of a good deal of movement, rather more of it downward than upward among the classes of cultivators, though there are indications of cyclical mobility.

Among the reasons for mobility, what Shanin refers to as "substantive changes" (see Shanin 1972) figure importantly, especially the effects of partitioning. Few cases can be attributed in one way or another to the effects of the green revolution. In summary:

Mobility from A to B ("capitalist farmer" to "rich peasant"): Five cases of downward mobility, four due to partitioning, one to poor irrigation wells.

Mobility from B to A ("rich peasant" to "capitalist farmer"): Three cases of upward mobility. Demographic factors are involved, as in two cases there was only a single son, while in the third two brothers remain in a joint family. All are involved in money lending; one has a teaching income.

Mobility from B to C ("rich peasant" to "middle peasant"): Ten cases of downward mobility, seven of them due to partitioning and three to hazard (one because of a serious fire, one because of the failure of a well, and one because of the death of the former household head and with him a money-lending business).

Mobility from B to "other" (from "rich peasant" to "other"): Four cases, two being dependent old men and one a divorced and separated wife. Only one case can be considered one of downward mobility because of large cultivation debts brought about by poor management (this followed from psychological problems). The former rich peasant concerned now makes a living from a small cycle hire business.

Mobility from C to B (from "middle peasant" to "rich peasant"): Two cases of upward mobility, each because of the availability of supplementary income from paddy trading, in a joint family.

Mobility from C to D (from "middle peasant" to "poor peasant"): Four cases of downward mobility, because of hazard, failure of wells, and illness. One case is due to demographic factors, the effects of large family size.

Mobility from C to "other" (from "middle peasant" to "other"): Five cases altogether: two of Harijans downwardly mobile because of the hazards of failure of a well in one case and a family dispute in the other; one of a Harijan who is now dependent upon rental income because of old age; one case of a move into weaving following the partitioning of a household, where property has not yet been divided; and the last one a move into a service occupation following the failure of a well.

Mobility from D to agricultural labor (from "poor peasant" to "agricultural labor"): Twelve cases of downward mobility, six of them because of the cessation of sharecropping arrangements, three as a result of partitioning, and three because of the effects of drought and poor wells.

Mobility from agricultural labor to "other": Ten cases that can be considered "downward," seven of them a result of partitioning; and two cases that are upward, partly resulting from decisions to remain in joint families.

Mobility from agricultural labor to "poor peasant": Six cases, four of them a result of the acquisition of land for sharecropping, and two the result of land purchases made possible by earning additional income from sharecropping.

In summary, "substantive changes" relating to the demographic character of households and to partitioning appear to have been the single most important influence on downward mobility, involved in 25 out of 41 cases of downward mobility, excluding those involving cessation of sharecropping arrangements; and these factors have also been significant in influencing upward mobility, for among the rather few clear cases of upward mobility most have involved, among other factors, decisions to remain in a joint family. The "substantive changes" have mostly had the effect of leveling down. Among other factors that have affected mobility among the agrarian classes, the most important has been the quality of access to groundwater. These data from Randam also do not appear to support the thesis that the new technology accelerates and intensifies the differentiation of the peasantry.

Credit and the Reproduction of Households

My analysis of the agrarian economy of northern Tamil Nadu in the early 1970s emphasized the crucial role of traders' credit. I argued that product and credit markets are interlinked, that mercantile credit played a key function in the reproduction of small-scale production—advances from traders being crucial to the renewal of the productive cycle—and that the dependence of small producers on paddy traders in particular was instrumental in maintaining rates of profit in trade higher than those available in agricultural production itself.

This argument seemed to be confirmed by my first conversation with farmers during the fieldwork I carried out in 1983–84, in Veerasambanur, where I found farmers relating a tale closely comparable with my analysis. It was true, they said, that the new varieties and the advent of electric pumpsets had increased their production of paddy. But, they maintained, they derived no benefit from this increased output: "All the benefit goes to those two, Mudaliar X and Chettiar Y, for they buy all the paddy from these four villages [Veerasambanur and its neighbors] and we are all in debt to them. We can do nothing if they underweigh or deduct from our payments." However, the data from Veerasambanur and the other villages (see Tables 4.11 and 4.12) do not entirely support the thesis that I advanced for the early 1970s.

The interlinking of transactions in commodity and credit markets continues to be significant. *Mundy* loans (advances from paddy traders) remain important sources of credit in Randam, Veerasambanur, and Vinayagapuram, though not in Duli (where most paddy is sold in a regulated market in Cheyyar) or in Dusi (where advances from master weavers and credit obtained from the mortgaging of land are much

TABLE 4.11
Structure of Outstanding Credit by Purpose of Loan, 1984 (percent of total outstanding debt)

Village	*Consumption*	*Cultivation Costs*	*Cultivation & Consumption*	*Marriage & Ritual Expenses*	*Well Investment*	*Cattle or Sheep Purchase*	*Housing*	*Other*[a]
Randam	10	13	16	10	14	9	9	19
Veerasambanur	14 (46)[b]	15 (31)	9	14 (20)	42 (37)	4	1	1
Vinayagapuram	9	16	7	15	13	10	—	30
Duli	13 (44)	33 (44)	5	3	20 (25)	11	2	13
Dusi	6	8	11[c]	39	2	6	8	20

[a]Includes purchases of tractors and land.
[b]Figures in parentheses are the percentage of households with this category of credit.
[c]Includes cost of weaving as well as of cultivation.

more extensive). In Randam and Veerasambanur all but a handful of cultivators, and in Vinayagapuram still a majority of cultivators, have a more or less permanent relationship with a particular *mundy*, regularly obtaining credit from the *mundy* owner. The amount of credit that can be obtained varies systematically according to the class of peasant—up to about Rs 20,000 for capitalist farmers in Randam, Rs 2,000–3,000 at a time for rich peasants, Rs 500–2,000 for middle peasants, and Rs 200–1,000 for poor peasants. In terms of the regularity with which this source of credit is used and the numbers of cultivators availing themselves of it, it is especially important. It is the first link in a chain of relationships that are instrumental in channeling resources out of agriculture, and to a large extent out of the rural economy altogether.

It may be noted that there is no evidence to suggest that the uses of money in commerce are less attractive investments now than they were in 1973–74. It was argued (by B. Harriss 1981 and J. Harriss 1982) that higher rates of profit in commercial activities tended to constrain productive investment in agriculture or outside. Information on investment preferences among business people in Arni in our 1983 survey confirms this argument (Harriss and Harriss 1984).

What is otherwise most striking in these data on credit is the importance of formal credit in all the villages—though less in Vinayagapuram than elsewhere—and the amount of credit that is available from within each village. In Randam the amount outstanding to other villagers is reported as being over 3.5 *lakhs* of rupees (Rs 364,220) or the equivalent of Rs 1,200 per household. The total sum outstanding represents the equivalent of the net returns from cultivation of twice the amount of paddy land held by people in the village. Though a number of individuals have contributed disproportionately to the village credit in circulation, it is not dominated by one or two moneylenders, as it is in Vinayagapuram where two big men account for 70 percent of the village credit in circulation and for 22 percent of all the loans in circulation in the village. Their preeminence in the credit, land, and labor markets of the village may help to account for the smaller share of formal credit in the outstanding loans of Vinayagapuram.

The interest rates charged on private loans—larger ones generally on bonds—are modest, 24 percent being the rate most commonly charged within the village, though rates as low as 12 percent are not at all unusual. Higher annual rates of interest, up to 60 percent or very occasionally more, are charged only on small loans when vessels or jewelry are pledged to small-scale moneylenders in the village (mostly women), or when loans are obtained from pawnbrokers in Arni. However, these loans make up only a small share of the total amount of credit in circulation. Thus, although I believe that traders' credit con-

TABLE 4.12
Source of Outstanding Credit, 1984 (percent of total outstanding debt)

Village	*Private Person in Village*	*Private Person Outside*	*Private Party in Nearby Town*	*Pawnbroker*	*Nationalized Bank*	*Land Development Bank*	*Coop*	*Other Formal*	*Other Informal*	*Total Formal Credit*
Randam	22	14	9	3	24	7	14	1	6	46
Veerasambanur	19	21	12	2	13	28	3	—	2	44
Vinayagapuram	31	24	13	2	20	5	3	—	2	28
Duli	13	6	10	9	19	10	32	—	1	61
Dusi	17	—	29	5	17	—	4	—	27	21

tinues to play an important role in the reproduction of peasant households in eastern North Arcot, the role of *usurious* money lending is less extensive than has been supposed to be the case in rural India.

A most significant trend over the past decade is the expansion of formal-sector credit, which now accounts for over 60 percent of outstanding credit in Duli, and more than 40 percent in Randam and Veerasambanur. Credit supplied through the land development banks is long term and mostly for investment in wells and pumps; but credit obtained from the nationalized banks, representing about 20 percent of the total, is often for short-term consumption and cultivation costs, as is cooperative credit. Credit extended under Integrated Rural Development Programs intended for the relief of poverty among specific target groups is significant too, making up 15 percent of all loans outstanding in Vinayagapuram, 10 percent in Duli, and 6 percent in Randam. These are mostly loans for purchase of sheep, and some for the purchase of bullock carts, but both types of loans are sometimes used for other purposes, including land purchases, house construction, and wedding and funeral payments. The rate of repayment of these loans appears to be low, as is that of crop loans made available through the nationalized banks. It is widely believed by people in the villages that if they hold out long enough, debts incurred as a result of failure to repay these loans will eventually be canceled, as they have been in the past (as they were, for example, after the state legislative assembly elections in 1980).

The expansion in the supply of formal-sector credit has surely contributed to the weakening of usury in the strict sense within this economy. (This argument has recently been put forward and elaborated more than I have been able to do here by Athreya and his co-authors with reference to the region of Tiruchy, further south in Tamil Nadu: see Athreya et al. 1985). It is significant in another way, too. The so-called needs-based lending, which has been given so much emphasis in public policy over the past decade, has further intensified the direct relationships between a broad spectrum of rural people and the state apparatus. A many-stranded relationship has developed between rural people and the state: it involves electricity supplies and tariffs, interventions in paddy and groundnut markets, the supply of basic consumer goods at regulated prices through so-called cooperative shops, the Food for Work Program, and lately the Noon Meals Scheme for schoolchildren, as well as credit supplied through Integrated Rural Development Programs. These different interventions have been instrumental in creating overlapping alliances of rural people, in a sense "against" the state though in a context in which the state is regarded as, and partially conforms to the role of, a patron. It is not the case that rural people are mobilizing to overthrow the state.

The Politics of the "Awkward Class" in South India

Trends of Change in North Arcot, 1973–1974

Paddy production has expanded appreciably over the past 10–15 years as a result of the introduction of the new technology of the green revolution. This expansion of production has yielded benefits that have been widely distributed. HYV paddy production does yield higher returns for most cultivators, though there has probably been a squeeze on the profitability of HYV cultivation since 1973, at least at some times. Real wages have increased for many if not for all agricultural laborers, and there is a greater diversity and volume of employment within the local economy, though not enough to have discouraged migration for work in the metropolitan cities both by members of the rural elite and by poor peasants and the landless.

These trends may be considered positive, and to run counter to the gloomier prognoses concerning the likely impact of the green revolution. But the possibility that the new technology has also increased the riskiness of paddy cultivation must be noted. It has also increased cultivators' need for credit, a need partly satisfied by the expansion of formal-sector credit. However, this expansion in the supply of formal-sector credit—together with the sensitivity of the issue of electricity tariffs and supply, and the problem of the relative prices of other agricultural inputs and outputs—has created conditions for confrontation between diverse groups of rural people and the state. This confrontation is reflected in the support that has been extended to the farmers' movements across a wide spectrum of agrarian social groups, and in the "farmerist" appeals of many politicians (see the report of interviews with candidates; B. Harriss 1984, pp. 274–77).

Class Formation and Agrarian Politics

The more or less conventional radical wisdom about the effects of the new technology, which was that intrarural class antagonisms would be intensified (perhaps the classic source for India is Frankel 1971) has not been borne out by the experience of the past 10 years.

There are several elements in the argument here:

1. Though benefits have certainly not been distributed equally, there is evidence that most groups of rural people have derived some benefit.

The potential antagonism between rich and poor peasants has been dampened because of the participation of poor peasants in the green revolution, and the shared experience of problems with the supply of power to pumpsets, supply of credit, and product prices.

2. There is little evidence of "depeasantization" and of increased landlessness and concentration of landholdings. (There is no evidence here of that more subtle kind of depeasantization detected by Byres [1981], who draws especially on research in Northwest India. These studies show reversion of formerly tenanted land and an increase in the incidence of reverse tenancy, and thus the loss of land area operated by poor peasants. Tenancy has been of little importance in North Arcot for a long time. There is evidence of, if anything, a slight increase in the incidence of land rented to poor peasants, rather than the reverse.) The distribution of landholdings appears generally to have become more rather than less equal.
3. There is no strong evidence of the swelling of the male agricultural labor force, but rather indications for the movement of labor, on relatively favorable terms, into other activities (Table 4.3). The absolute numbers of those engaged in agriculture as cultivators or as laborers appear to have remained roughly constant.
4. The employment of laborers on a (semi-) permanent basis has not declined and in some areas has actually increased; the significance of this is that such laborers are found, generally, to be less militant than casual laborers.

It is difficult to detect the crystallization of classes in themselves, and the class positions of many remain blurred in practice because of the combinations of activities in the same households.

The more subtle analyses of the relationships between the introduction of the new technology and class formation and class action, like that of Byres (1981), express a good deal of skepticism about the argument that the green revolution would turn red. However, these analyses do emphasize the way in which the new technology has served to consolidate further the rich peasantry as a powerful, dominant class, particularly in certain areas like Northwest India; and the way in which it may—again in certain areas with much more likelihood than in others—contribute to a consolidation and heightened self-awareness of the subaltern class(es). North Arcot district obviously has a small and economically very powerful rich peasantry, but it does not seem to me to exercise dominance in the way the North Indian rich peasantry does, according to Byres and others. It has not been able to keep down the level of real wages paid to agricultural labor, nor has it been successful, apparently, in persuading the state to raise the prices of agricultural products in relation to costs, as the rich peasantry of North India is said to have succeeded in doing, according to Byres and others. With regard to class action by the subordinated class, there are a few indications in eastern North Arcot that agricultural labor has increased its bargaining power, but there is still little indication of militant political organization among them. Militancy is much more likely to be caste based than class based, as in Veerasambanur where there are two men among the Paraiyans who are involved in the Anna DMK party, and who have on occasion made use of their party connections to bring pressure to bear, on behalf of the Harijan community as a whole, on the Mudaliars in the main caste village. Generalization is of course dangerous, and it is true that radical political action, dubbed "Naxalite" by the authorities, has been undertaken not too far away in the southwestern part of North Arcot, in the Javadi hills. But it has been localized, and seems exceptional, though it indicates the potential that exists.

The government of Tamil Nadu has lately allocated resources to rural people in a way that has been highly visible politically. Whether its appropriations and allocations of resources overall have been urban biased or rural biased is probably less important for politics than the visibility of a scheme like the noon meals scheme. This was slated for implementation in 1981–82 with a provision in the estimates of Rs 1 billion, which is equivalent to slightly more than 10 percent of the total budgeted allocation for development purposes in the revenue account (data from the Tamil Nadu economic appraisal for 1981; published by the Evaluation and Research Department of the state government in August 1983). The noon meals scheme, even at its inception—and it has grown subsequently—is equivalent to a large share of the development expenditure of the Tamil Nadu government, and given the distribution of the population as a whole, it represents resources paid over principally to rural people.

It is not only through the noon meals scheme and the ration shops that the state in Tamil Nadu apparently subsidizes rural people. There is an element of subsidy in the Food for Work Program; the provision of cheap credit under Integrated Rural Development Programs and the supply of credit and electricity to the cultivating peasantry represent a considerable drain on state resources. This is because of the volume of overdue debts owed the cooperative banking system, and the subsidizing of rural electricity supplies (the general argument here is made strongly by Shetty 1978).

Whether amounting to rural bias or not, some of these transfers have contributed to the building up and maintenance of support for the Anna DMK regime—none more clearly so than the noon meals scheme—and to the defusing of antagonisms in the countryside. At the same time the political issues posed by problems over electricity supplies and the electricity tariff, and outstanding debts to public banking institutions, create alliances between groups of people who are potentially divided by class-based antagonisms. These groups mobilize to make demands on the state.

It can be argued that the resources allocated to the rural sector undercut the potential for accumulation in the industrial sector. It is widely recognized that the state has been falling behind in industrial development and that a particularly important reason for this has to do with the problems of power supply. Part of the opportunity cost of a program like the noon meals scheme is the potential investment in power generation forgone. Given the problems faced by industry in Tamil Nadu, it is not surprising that both the DMK when it was in power between 1967 and 1975 and the Anna DMK since 1977 have generally been repressive toward the organized working class. The local state in Tamil Nadu shows contradictions like those observed in developing states elsewhere: policies of patronage and subsidy are pursued for political reasons even though they may actually undercut development objectives, in turn giving rise to conflicts between interest groups in which the state intervenes (there are points of comparison in Bates's work on African states; 1981, 1983).

What is distinctive about the state of Tamil Nadu is that the policies pursued by the Dravidian political parties in power, as well as their success in political mobilization—involving nationalist ideology, socialist rhetoric, populist appeals, and the skillful deployment of popular media, especially the cinema—have effectively precluded the development of class politics. Competition between the DMK and the Anna DMK, indistinguishable though they are in terms of ideology and policy, is very strong at local-level villages, in the cities, and among the organized working class. This competition cuts right across classes in themselves and creates vertical alliances. In Randam, in Veerasambanur, and in Duli, party allegiances bring together rich and poor peasants and landless laborers. These alignments certainly help to account for the apparently increased bargaining power of agricultural wage workers, for agricultural laborers can and do call on the support of rich peasants like the former *panchayat* president of Randam, who, as I described in my earlier work (Harriss 1982, Chapter 7), acquired his position of power by commanding their support. But the existence of these alignments also helps to account for the general, if not invariable, lack of class-based political organization among agricultural laborers, and contributes to the creation of alliances between rich, middle, and poor peasants such as has been seen in the farmers' movement in Tamil Nadu (Guruswamy 1985). As Shanin (1972) argued in relation to the Russian peasantry in the earlier part of this century, the peasants of

Tamil Nadu, though they are certainly not homogeneous and undifferentiated, do sometimes act together politically. They are an awkward class politically, and awkward for conventional categories of analysis.

Conclusions

This account of agrarian social and economic change in North Arcot exposes a number of generalizations that have been made about the political economy of Indian agriculture. I have referred at length to the limitations of a good deal of radical analysis of the green revolution. Here the point is not simply that eastern North Arcot doesn't seem to fit the interpretations offered, but also that this longitudinal case study shows up processes that are likely to be of more general occurrence and that have been neglected. Most important is the point that the tendencies that exert a push toward polarization also give rise to increased income-earning activities, which have the effect of stabilizing smallholding property (see Bhaduri, Rahman, and Arn 1986 on this point, referring to a Bangladesh case study). There does appear to have been a decline in the incidence of owner cultivation in the labor force, but there has been a decline also in the incidence of agricultural labor. While wage working has increased, people remain peasants, so there has been a pattern of proletarianization without depeasantization. Political alignments have become, if anything, more affected by the contradictory class locations of individuals and by vertical arrangements.

At the same time it is doubtful whether the green revolution in this case has had quite the dynamic effects claimed by its proponents. It is true that my findings with regard to the role of merchant-usurers' capital and of oligopoly power in the villages are not clear cut; but mercantile credit clearly remains important in reproduction of small property. The extent of dependence on usurious money lending is less than it was, and financial power is more diffuse than is taken to be the case in general models of agrarian semifeudalism. Yet given the continuing entrenchment of merchant capital (which appears also in our study of economic activity in Arni; Harriss and Harriss 1984), it would be premature to dismiss the analytical claims of these models. The burden of these last remarks is that if we recognize the limitations of our models, we must be wary of allowing them to drive particular historical analysis. Yet in the case of the green revolution, both radicals and liberals seem to me to have done precisely this.

CHAPTER 5

The Impact of Technological Change in Rice Production on Food Consumption and Nutrition

Per Pinstrup-Andersen and Mauricio Jaramillo

TECHNOLOGICAL CHANGE, such as the replacement of traditional with modern crop varieties and introduction of irrigation, has been effective in increasing the yields and production of various crops—notably rice and wheat—as well as incomes of farmers in developing countries (Pinstrup-Andersen 1982; Pinstrup-Andersen and Hazell 1985; Lipton 1989). However, the impact on food consumption and nutrition is poorly documented.

Technological change may influence human nutrition through its impact on (1) incomes acquired by households with malnourished members; (2) the prices they have to pay for food commodities; (3) the nature of the production systems among semisubsistence farmers; (4) risk and fluctuations in food production, prices, and incomes; (5) the nutrient composition of the foods available to them; (6) household income composition; (7) intrahousehold income and budget control; (8) women's time allocation; and (9) labor demand and energy expenditures.

Among these factors, the most important ones are likely to be household incomes and food prices. Thus, if the impact on these factors can be estimated for North Arcot, it may be possible to provide a rough estimate of the nutrition impact of the green revolution.

The conceptual model used for the analysis is as follows. Technological change influences rice yields and acreage, which in turn results in changes in rice production. The production of other crops may also change as a result of acreage substitution and reallocation of labor. The change in rice production will be reflected in rice sales or home consumption. Changes in rice sales and prices will be reflected in incomes of rice farmers, which in turn will influence calorie and protein con-

The authors are grateful to Barbara Harriss, John Harriss, Peter Hazell, Michael Lipton, and C. Ramasamy for many useful comments and suggestions on an earlier draft.

sumption and thus nutritional status. In North Arcot it is unlikely that changes in rice production will significantly influence state or national rice prices. Changes in labor demand may influence incomes and thus food consumption by labor households. These changes may also influence the nutritional status through changes in energy requirements.

Description of Study Households

The study draws on the village household data collected as part of the Cambridge-Madras universities and IFPRI-TNAU surveys. It focuses on three paddy-farming groups: (1) small paddy farmers—farmers whose principal crop was rice and who operated 1 hectare or less; (2) large paddy farmers—those whose principal crop was rice and who operated more than 1 hectare of land; and (3) landless laborers. The term *large* should be interpreted in a relative rather than an absolute sense, since the average farm size in that group was less than 3 hectares.

Table 5.1 presents the number of households, mean household size, and mean operated farm size for each of the three household groups by village group and year. The average household sizes increased from 1973/74 to 1982/83. The average operated holding of large farmers also increased during the decade, while the farm size among small farmers appears to have remained constant.

As discussed in Chapter 2, rice production increased during the 1970s as a consequence of widespread adoption of modern varieties and an increase in the number of irrigation wells. A severe drought caused a significant reduction in production for 1982/83, making it very difficult to assess the effect of technological change on the basis of direct comparison. As argued in Chapter 3, comparison between 1973/74 and 1983/84 is a much better approximation of the effects of technological change, though this comparison is limited to the poorly irrigated resurvey villages for which 1983/84 data are available.

Household Incomes and Expenditures

Per capita incomes and consumption expenditures were much higher in 1983/84 than in 1973/74 for all three household groups (Table 5.2). There was also an improvement in equity; small farmers and landless laborers gained relatively more than large farmers.

Food expenditures account for about 70 to 80 percent of total expenditure (Table 5.3), with little difference among the years and household types. That the share did not decline more significantly as incomes

TABLE 5.1
Characteristics of Study Households

	Sample Size	*Per Household Family Composition*		*Operated Farm Size (ha)*
		Persons	*Adult Equivalents*[a]	
1973/74 (resurvey villages)				
Small paddy farmers[b]	15	4.7	4.0	0.62
Large paddy farmers[b]	5	5.6	4.8	1.48
Landless laborers	17	4.0	3.4	
1982/83 (resurvey villages)				
Small paddy farmers	23	5.7	4.9	0.57
Large paddy farmers	41	7.0	5.8	2.75
Landless laborers	44	4.8	4.0	
1983/84 (resurvey villages)				
Small paddy farmers	11	4.5	4.0	0.50
Large paddy farmers	22	6.5	5.5	2.87
Landless laborers	23	5.1	4.2	
1973/74 (all villages)				
Small paddy farmers	31	5.1	4.2	0.58
Large paddy farmers	22	6.2	5.2	2.42
Landless laborers	48	3.6	3.0	
1982/83 (all villages)				
Small paddy farmers	72	5.6	4.7	0.59
Large paddy farmers	89	7.2	6.0	2.76
Landless laborers	114	4.4	3.7	

[a]1 adult equivalent = 1 man older than 14 years old = 2.94 babies < 1 year old = 1.69 children 1–5 years old = 1.27 women > 5 years old = 1.09 men 6–14 years old.

[b]A small paddy farmer is defined as one who operates 1 hectare or less. Large farmers operate more than 1 hectare.

increased is surprising and suggests that food intake also increased. However, the extent to which food intake did increase also depends on changes in food prices and the composition of the diet.

The cost of the diet—measured as the cost per 1,000 calories—increased faster than the general consumer price index (Table 5.4). The average real costs of the diet for all households increased by about 50 percent during the 10-year period. This increase reflects both increasing real food prices and, as we shall see, diet diversification toward foods providing more expensive calories. Real rice prices to the consumer declined slightly between 1973/74 and 1982/83 but then increased by about 20 percent from the drought year to the next. This was largely due to a reduction in explicit subsidies that kept consumer prices below producer prices in 1982/83. Although low rice prices are partly responsible, the low costs per 1,000 calories during the drought year relative to the following year illustrate how households coped with reduced

TABLE 5.2
Total Annual Consumption Expenditures and Incomes (1974 Rs/capita)

	Resurvey Villages			*All Villages*	
	73/74	*82/83*	*83/84*	*73/74*	*82/83*
Expenditures					
Small paddy farmers	250	318	743	293	350
Large paddy farmers	395	513	828	435	541
Landless laborers	254	295	580	304	316
Average paddy farmers[a]	311	412	784	352	442
Incomes					
Small paddy farmers	264	237	535	386	320
Large paddy farmers	525	431	657	770	578
Landless laborers	261	214	443	311	206
Average paddy farmers[a]	374	330	594	547	444

Notes: The expenditures and incomes figures above are not directly comparable. Incomes were calculated with farm-gate prices, while the value of the own-production share of expenditures was calculated with consumer prices. This explains why expenditures are greater than incomes in some cases.

Deflated using the CPI for Kunnathur village in Chingleput district.

[a]Weighted average using the weights given in chapter 3.

TABLE 5.3
Food Expenditures (percent of total expenditures)

	Resurvey Villages			*All Villages*	
	73/74	*82/83*	*83/84*	*73/74*	*82/83*
Small paddy farmers	81.4	77.4	77.7	79.8	79.3
Large paddy farmers	72.5	72.4	78.8	71.4	72.7
Landless laborers	84.1	79.7	77.7	81.9	83.1

incomes by emphasizing low-cost foods, and explain why the budget share going to food did not increase during the drought.

Household Energy and Protein Consumption

Dramatic increases occurred in household energy and protein consumption during the study period (Figure 5.1). The average calorie consumption per person increased by about two-thirds and protein consumption doubled between 1973/74 and 1983/84 in the resurvey villages (Table 5.5). The negative effect of the drought in 1982/83 was offset by positive effects brought about by other factors, including technological change between 1973/74 and 1982/83, leaving the 1982/83 consumption level slightly above the 1973/74 level. The negative effect of the drought cannot be isolated from other effects, such as increased

TABLE 5.4
Rice Prices and the Calorie Cost of the Total Diet

	Resurvey Villages			*All Villages*	
	73/74	*82/83*	*83/84*	*73/74*	*82/83*
Small paddy farmers (current Rs)					
Consumer rice price per kg	1.32	2.18	2.96	1.31	2.24
Cost per 1,000 calories	0.45	0.87	1.51	0.45	0.92
Small paddy farmers (1974 Rs)					
Consumer rice price per kg	1.32	1.19	1.47	1.31	1.21
Cost per 1,000 calories	0.45	0.47	0.75	0.45	0.49
Large paddy farmers (current Rs)					
Consumer rice price per kg	1.36	2.10	2.88	1.30	2.14
Cost per 1,000 calories	0.50	0.90	1.37	0.50	0.94
Large paddy farmers (1974 Rs)					
Consumer rice price per kg	1.36	1.14	1.43	1.30	1.16
Cost per 1,000 calories	0.50	0.49	0.68	0.50	0.51
Landless laborers (current Rs)					
Consumer rice price per kg	1.27	2.11	2.76	1.28	2.14
Cost per 1,000 calories	0.46	0.87	1.35	0.48	0.88
Landless laborers (1974 Rs)					
Consumer rice price per kg	1.27	1.14	1.37	1.28	1.16
Cost per 1,000 calories	0.46	0.47	0.67	0.48	0.48

availability of wheat and rice from public distribution outlets, on the basis of available data.

As expected, both per capita calorie and protein consumption were higher among large-scale farmers than among small-scale farmers and landless laborers. However, during the 10-year period small farmers increased consumption more than large ones, thus narrowing the gap between the two groups. An explanation is that large farmers have now reached calorie consumption levels that suffice for most households, and further increases in incomes are spent largely on more expensive calories and nonfoods rather than more calories. The increase in calorie and protein consumption among the landless was also substantial but less than the increase among farmers. Thus, from consuming at about the same level as small farmers in 1973/74, in 1983/84 the landless consumed about 450 calories per capita less or 20 percent less than the small farmers. This is a reflection of the smaller per capita income gains among the landless (Table 5.2).

The average daily energy consumption reported in Table 5.5 for 1973/74—about 1,900 calories/adult equivalent for the 11 villages and 1,700 for the resurvey villages—corresponds closely to estimates from other studies in the region. Rao et al. (1961) estimated daily energy consumption per adult equivalent unit to be 1,724 calories in 1958 and

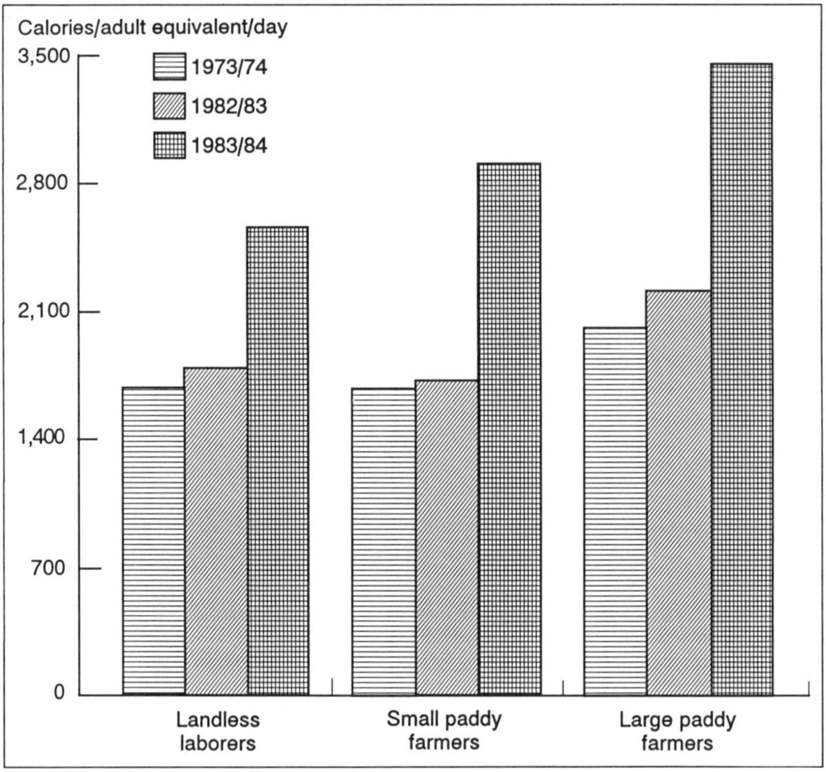

Fig. 5.1. Mean energy consumption in resurveyed villages.

1,716 in 1961, while Sundaraaraj and Pereira's (1971) estimate for 1971 was 1,732, and Harriss' (1982) estimates ranged from 1,298 to 2,214. These other estimates also indicate that no improvement in calorie consumption took place during the period 1958–74—that is, prior to the green revolution. Unfortunately, no reliable regional estimates from other sources have been found for the 1980s. Average daily calorie consumption per capita for rural India in 1973/74 was estimated to be 1,262 for the poorest 20 percent and 1,772 for the next-to-the-poorest quintile (Murty 1983). Thus, our per capita estimates of about 1,600 also fall in the range corresponding to that of the poorest 40 percent of the rural population of India.

As mentioned earlier, changes in the average price of the calories making up the diet reflect changes both in the commodity composition of the diet and in the prices of individual commodities. During the study period a remarkable change occurred in diet composition. The absolute amount of rice consumed per person changed little, but its share of

TABLE 5.5
Daily Energy and Protein Consumption

	Resurvey Villages			*All Villages*	
	73/74	*82/83*	*83/84*	*73/74*	*82/83*
Calories/person					
Small paddy farmers	1,386	1,494	2,606	1,592	1,602
Large paddy farmers	1,724	1,848	2,884	1,759	1,924
Landless laborers	1,426	1,495	2,154	1,604	1,642
Average paddy farmers[a]	1,528	1,664	2,739	1,662	1,756
Grams of protein/person					
Small paddy farmers	29	32	64	34	34
Large paddy farmers	37	40	69	37	42
Landless laborers	28	34	57	33	36
Average paddy farmers[a]	32	36	66	35	37
Calories/adult equivalent					
Small paddy farmers	1,630	1,729	2,953	1,893	1,882
Large paddy farmers	2,053	2,218	3,456	2,085	2,270
Landless laborers	1,673	1,783	2,572	1,919	1,962
Average paddy farmers[a]	1,807	2,407	3,194	1,973	2,068
Grams of protein/adult equivalent					
Small paddy farmers	34	37	73	40	40
Large paddy farmers	44	48	82	44	49
Landless laborers	33	40	67	39	43
Average paddy farmers[a]	38	42	77	42	44

[a]Weighted average using the weights given in chapter 3.

total calories declined sharply during the period (Table 5.6). This decline is due to substitution toward a more diversified diet, a phenomenon that usually occurs with increasing incomes. What is remarkable is not that it occurred, but the magnitude of substitution within a period of 10 years. The share of rice in total calories dropped by between 25 and 50 percent. The share of total calories coming from edible oils, fruits, vegetables, and grams each increased from virtually nothing in 1973/74 to up to almost 9 percent in 1983/84 in the resurvey villages (Table 5.7). Large percentage increases were also found for dairy products and meat, while the contribution of *ragi* (millet)—an inexpensive calorie source—increased to 1973/74 levels during the drought year but dropped to below 1973/74 levels in 1983/84.

Increased availability of subsidized wheat during the latter stages of the drought, together with lower rice production, played a role in diet diversification during the drought year as well as the beginning of 1983/84.

A large share of the food consumed by the farmers—particularly larger farmers—is home produced (Table 5.8). Large farmers obtained 60 to 70 percent of their total calories and 80 to 90 percent of their rice

TABLE 5.6
Daily Energy Obtained from Rice Consumption

	Resurvey Villages			*All Villages*	
	73/74	*82/83*	*83/84*	*73/74*	*82/83*
Calories/person					
Small paddy farmers	1,060	986	1,110	1,135	1,019
Large paddy farmers	1,246	1,143	1,456	1,295	1,139
Landless laborers	1,064	925	820	1,030	1,036
Percent of total calories					
Small paddy farmers	76.5	66.0	42.6	70.6	64.8
Large paddy farmers	72.3	61.9	50.5	73.7	61.7
Landless laborers	74.6	62.1	38.1	66.2	63.5
Calories/adult equivalent					
Small paddy farmers	1,245	1,147	1,248	1,354	1,214
Large paddy farmers	1,454	1,379	1,720	1,535	1,366
Landless laborers	1,252	1,110	996	1,237	1,238

calories from own production. A decrease in the degree of self-sufficiency was observed during the drought year for small farmers and landless laborers, and this lower rate continued into 1983/84. However, analysis of seasonal data shows that by mid–1984, rice consumption from own production for these groups had reverted to 1973/74 levels (Pinstrup-Andersen and Jaramillo 1989).

During 1973/74 landless laborers received a considerable proportion of the calories they consumed from in-kind wages. However, it appears that in-kind wages were reduced greatly both during the drought and subsequently. This was partly because of a shift toward cash payments (see Chapter 4), but also because of a sharp reduction in agricultural employment during the 1982/83 drought (see Chapter 3).

Apparent Energy Deficiencies and Nutritional Effect

Although changes in average calorie consumption for each group reported in Table 5.6 provide indications of the degree of household-level calorie sufficiency rates, group averages do not show the distribution of these rates among households. Thus, to complement earlier indicators, Table 5.9 shows the proportion of households with calorie consumption below both 100 and 80 percent of energy requirements. During 1973/74, about 90 percent of all households in the resurveyed villages consumed less than full requirements and about 70 percent consumed less than 80 percent of requirements. By 1983/84 these figures were lowered to about 30 and 20 percent, respectively. The worst sit-

TABLE 5.7
Mean Daily Energy Consumption, Resurvey Villages (percent of total calories)

Commodity	*1973/74* Small Paddy Farmers	*1973/74* Large Paddy Farmers	*1973/74* Landless Laborers	*1982/83* Small Paddy Farmers	*1982/83* Large Paddy Farmers	*1982/83* Landless Laborers	*1983/84* Small Paddy Farmers	*1983/84* Large Paddy Farmers	*1983/84* Landless Laborers
Rice	76.5	72.3	74.6	66.0	61.9	62.1	42.6	50.5	38.1
Ragi	20.6	19.5	22.0	17.4	18.7	22.2	12.7	11.6	17.2
Wheat	—	—	—	—	0.2	0.1	3.6	2.3	4.5
Other cereals	0.2	—	—	2.6	2.0	3.4	3.3	2.5	3.8
Grams	1.3	2.6	0.8	2.5	3.1	2.0	6.0	5.4	4.7
Dairy products & eggs	0.1	2.0	1.1	0.5	1.5	0.1	4.4	5.6	5.2
Meats	0.3	0.2	0.4	0.4	0.3	0.9	1.4	1.1	1.9
Vegetables	—	—	—	3.3	2.8	3.1	7.0	4.0	6.4
Fruits	—	—	—	0.2	0.5	0.1	2.0	1.6	2.0
Oils	0.6	1.8	0.9	5.0	5.9	4.9	8.6	7.1	6.8
Other foods	0.4	1.4	0.1	2.0	3.2	1.0	8.5	8.1	9.3
Total calories per capita	1,386	1,724	1,426	1,494	1,848	1,495	2,606	2,884	2,154

TABLE 5.8
Total Food Expenditure, Calorie Consumption, and Rice Consumption Obtained from Own Production or In-kind Earnings (percent of total)

	Resurvey Villages			*All Villages*	
	73/74	*82/83*	*83/84*	*73/74*	*82/83*
Small paddy farmers					
Total food expenditure	42.4	34.2	25.8	47.4	35.0
Calorie consumption	59.5	43.6	38.3	63.3	47.2
Rice consumption	71.4	53.2	55.2	77.9	61.2
Large paddy farmers					
Total food expenditure	41.8	45.2	47.6	53.4	45.7
Calorie consumption	62.7	62.1	69.7	71.7	62.6
Rice consumption	84.4	82.7	91.8	84.4	84.6
Landless laborers					
Total food expenditure	24.0	5.3	5.5	30.7	7.3
Calorie consumption	35.8	7.3	10.1	40.8	9.2
Rice consumption	43.2	9.0	10.1	57.2	11.0

TABLE 5.9
Households Consuming Below Recommended Daily Allowance for Energy (percent)

	Resurvey Villages			*All Villages*	
	73/74	*82/83*	*83/84*	*73/74*	*82/83*
Below 100 percent					
Small paddy farmers	93.9	81.7	34.3	81.8	78.2
Large paddy farmers	86.4	63.5	11.2	77.0	60.5
Landless laborers	91.5	80.8	51.6	81.6	75.2
Below 80 percent					
Small paddy farmers	82.2	64.6	22.9	68.3	56.8
Large paddy farmers	39.0	43.1	4.3	43.9	40.3
Landless laborers	73.4	67.2	28.3	56.5	57.5

Source: WHO 1985.
Note: The recommended daily allowance (RDA) for energy is 2,400 calories per adult equivalent, the daily requirements of a 55-kg adult man.

uation was found among landless laborers, where 28 percent of the households still consumed less than 80 percent of requirements in 1983/84.

The initial situation (1973/74) was much better in the nonresurveyed villages but the improvements by 1982/83 were less, thus reducing the difference between the two groups of villages. The lower degree of calorie deficiency in the nonresurveyed villages in 1973/74 reflects their higher income level. It is surprising, however, that the resurveyed villages, which were more severely affected by drought during 1982/83 than the nonresurveyed ones, nevertheless show a larger reduction in the proportion of households with severe calorie deficiencies.

There was a sharp increase in the proportion of both small- and large-scale paddy farmers consuming less than 80 percent of energy requirements during 1982/83 and an even sharper decrease after the 1982/83 drought (Figures 5.2, 5.3, and 5.4). The rate of deterioration during 1982/83 was less for landless laborers, primarily because the level was high prior to that year. However, the improvements after the drought were impressive for that group.

Since, as illustrated in Figures 5.2, 5.3, and 5.4, the proportion of households with severe calorie deficiencies kept falling during 1983/84, primarily because of recuperation from the previous year's drought, the average annual figures shown in Table 5.9 for 1983/84 are not representative of a "normal" situation. In fact figures from the latter months of 1983/84 would be more representative. As shown in Figures 5.2 and 5.3, the proportion of farming households consuming less than

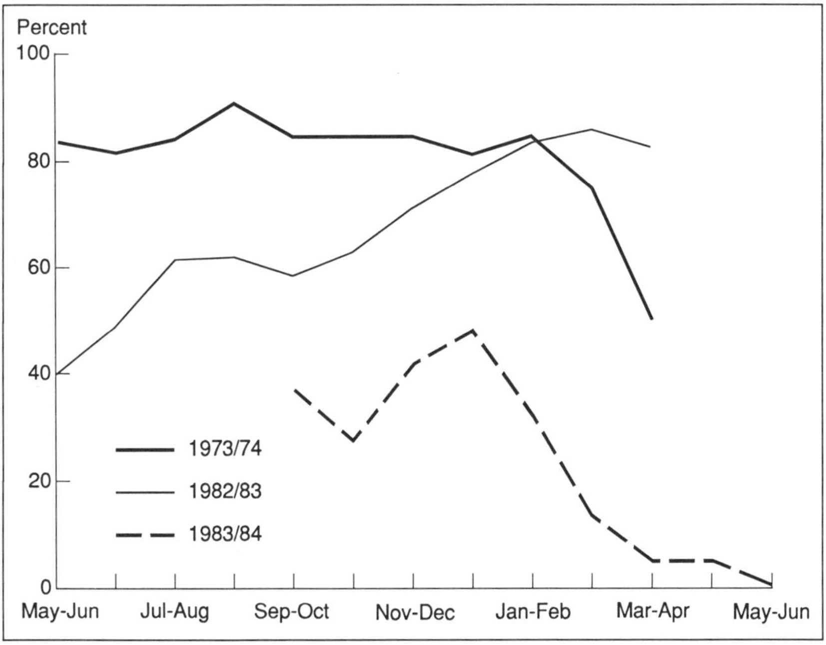

Fig. 5.2. Percent of small-paddy-farmer households consuming less than 80 percent of energy RDA, two-month moving averages, resurvey villages.
Note: Energy RDA (recommended daily allowance) equals 2,400 calories per adult equivalent per day.

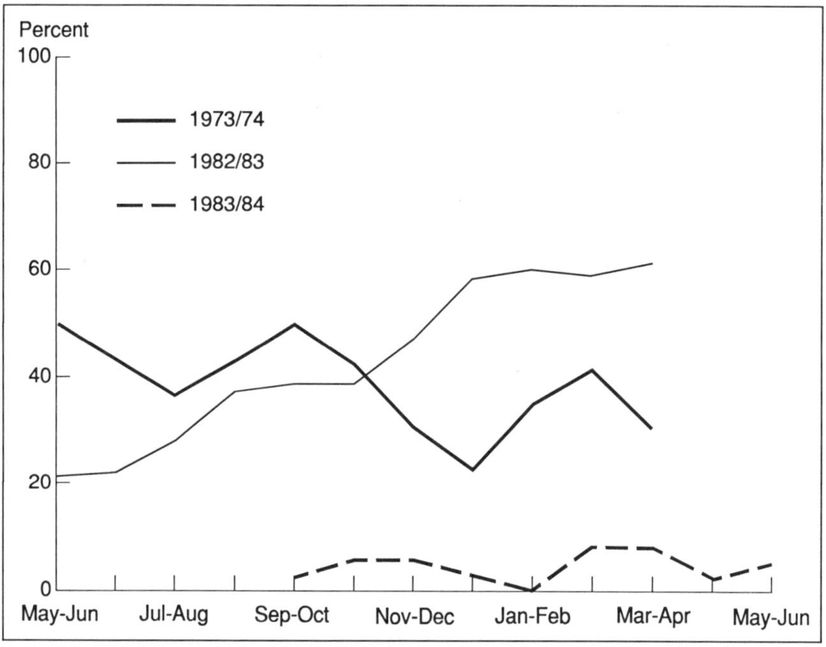

Fig. 5.3. Percent of large-paddy-farmer households consuming less than 80 percent of energy RDA, two-month moving averages, resurvey villages.
Note: Energy RDA (recommended daily allowance) equals 2,400 calories per adult equivalent per day.

80 percent of calorie requirements during the last couple of months of the 1983/84 survey was negligible, while it was about 15 percent for landless laborers (Figure 5.4).

Thus, except for the drought effect, it appears that by 1984 severe calorie deficiency remained a problem only among landless-labor households, with 10–15 percent being affected. This is an enormous improvement over the situation 10 years before.

Since no data were collected on the nutritional status of members of survey households, the impact of the reduced calorie and protein deficiencies on child growth and other nutritional indicators cannot be estimated. Data from the K. V. Kuppam development block in North Arcot district show a rather high prevalence of malnutrition among preschoolers in 1983 (Steinhoff et al. 1986). Almost 10 percent of the preschoolers studied suffered from both chronic and acute malnutrition. No regional data have been found to estimate the change in these indicators over time.

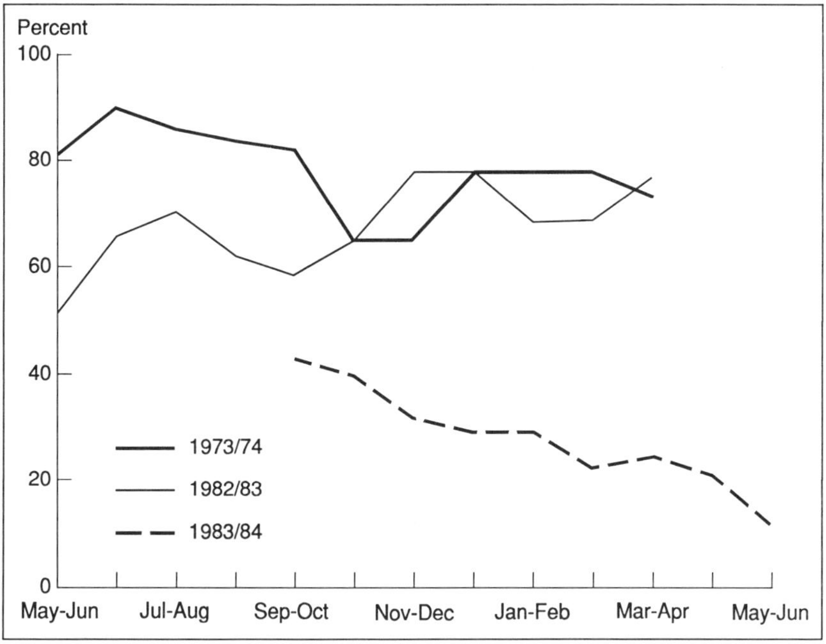

Fig. 5.4. Percent of landless-laborer households consuming less than 80 percent of energy RDA, two-month moving averages, resurvey villages.
Note: Energy RDA (recommended daily allowance) equals 2,400 calories per adult equivalent per day.

Impact of Changes in Incomes, Prices, and Other Factors on Food Consumption

In order to estimate the food consumption impact of changes in selected variables hypothesized to be influenced by technological change and in turn affecting food consumption, a multivariate regression analysis was undertaken. The analysis was done on monthly data for (1) each year (pooled monthly, cross-sectional data), and (2) all three years together.

The model specification included the following variables:

Dependent variables
- Total daily calorie consumption per person (calories/person/day)
- Rice consumption (calories/person/day)

Independent variables
- Total annual expenditure (log of Rs/person/year)
- Price of rice (Rs/kg)
- Price of *ragi* (Rs/kg)

TABLE 5.10
Income and Price Parameters and Other Coefficients Estimated from Consumption Functions, Paddy-Farm Households

Dependent Variable	*Year*	*Income Elasticity*	*MPC*[a]	*APC*[b]	*Price Elasticity of:* Rice	Ragi	*Dairy*	*Meat*	*Season's % of Annual Paddy Production*	*Paddy Production (kg/person /year)*	*Household Size*	*Intercept Dummies* 1982/83	*1983/84*	R^2
Calorie consumption (cal/person/day)	73/74	0.55	1,066	1,933	−0.16	[c]	−0.27	[c]	1.13	0.18	−41.3			0.53
	82/83	0.44	402	903	−0.46	−0.15	[c]	0.11	[c]	[c]	−34.9			0.42
	83/84	0.72	512	713	[c]	[c]	[c]	[c]	[c]	0.39	[c]			0.38
	Pooled	0.47	808	1,714	−0.30	[c]	−0.11	0.08	[c]	0.10	−35.3	−61.0	456.6	0.49
Rice consumption (cal/person/day)	73/74	0.45	629	1,397	−0.30	0.15	[c]	[c]	1.76	0.37	−57.0			0.42
	82/83	0.25	135	551	−0.49	−0.12	0.11	[c]	[c]	0.18	−28.6			0.23
	83/84	0.90	321	356	[c]	[c]	1.03	0.77	[c]	0.28	64.0			0.35
	Pooled	0.32	337	1,053	−0.28	[c]	0.23	[c]	[c]	0.24	−30.1	−158.1	−107.1	0.24

[a]Marginal propensity to consume: increase in calorie consumption for an increase in income of Rs 1 (current rupees for yearly functions, 1974 rupees for pooled three-year functions).

[b]Average propensity to consume: average calorie consumption per rupee spent (current rupees for yearly functions, 1974 rupees for pooled three-year functions).

[c]Indicates that the corresponding regression coefficient was found not significantly different from zero at the 90 percent level.

Price of milk (Rs/kg)
Price of meat (Rs/kg)[1]
Off-farm income for the month as a percentage of total income (cash flow) (landless labor only)
Percentage of annual paddy production harvested in the season to which month belongs (farmers only)
Paddy production (kg/person/year) (farmers only)
Household size (number of persons)
Intercept dummies for years (only in functions for three-year pooled data).

The principal results from the analyses are shown in Table 5.10 for rice farmers and Table 5.11 for landless households.

Income elasticities for total calorie consumption were around 0.5 and, as expected, are generally above the income elasticities for rice. A comparison between the income elasticities for total calorie consumption and the income elasticities for total food expenditures indicates the extent to which diet diversification occurred (Table 5.12). The difference between the two represents the income elasticity for total calorie cost, that is, the percentage change in the calorie cost of the diet associated with a 1 percent change in income.

On the basis of the estimates in Table 5.12, it appears that the desire to diversify the diet toward more expensive calories with increasing incomes was stronger in 1973/74 than in 1983/84. While the relative and absolute magnitudes of the three parameters for 1973/74 are in line with findings from several other studies of low-income households (Alderman 1986; Garcia and Pinstrup-Andersen 1987), it is surprising that the calorie income elasticity is higher and the calorie cost elasticity lower for 1983/84 than for 1973/74, in view of the much higher incomes in 1983/84. The difference between the food expenditure and the calorie income elasticity usually becomes larger with increasing incomes. The most plausible explanation is that efforts to regain the losses in calorie consumption due to the drought resulted in high calorie income elasticities during at least part of 1983/84. If this is the correct explanation, the estimates for both 1982/83 and 1983/84 reflect the economic hardships caused by the drought. Households emphasized calories over diet diversification initially to cope with the drought and subsequently to regain calorie losses. This implies that once the desired calorie levels were obtained, a larger proportion of income would be spent on improving the diet, and the calorie income elasticity would fall to a level below the 1973/74 level. Thus, for the purpose of estimating the effect of technological change on calorie consumption without the drought

1. A (consumption-) weighted average of beef and mutton prices.

TABLE 5.11
Income and Price Parameters and Other Coefficients Estimated from Consumption Functions, Landless Households

Dependent Variable	*Year*	*Income Elasticity*	*MPC*[a]	*APC*[b]	*Price Elasticity of:* *Rice*	Ragi	*Dairy*	*Meat*	*Cash Flow (%)*	*Household Size*	*Intercept Dummies* *1982/83*	*1983/84*	R^2
Calorie consumption (cal/person/day)	73/74	0.51	1,063	2,084	−0.28	0.20	−0.13	[c]	268.2	[c]			0.32
	82/83	0.57	639	1,115	−0.22	−0.47	−0.15	[c]	382.2	−57.4			0.49
	83/84	0.78	583	751	−0.51	[c]	[c]	−0.13	[c]	[c]			0.58
	Pooled	0.55	1,108	2,003	−0.24	−0.20	−0.14	[c]	355.6	−47.3	[c]	142.5	0.47
Rice consumption (cal/person/day)	73/74	0.32	430	1,328	−0.32	0.69	[c]	[c]	[c]	[c]			0.14
	82/83	0.41	289	703	−0.24	−0.61	[c]	[c]	[c]	−70.8			0.36
	83/84	0.87	248	286	−0.48	0.56	[c]	[c]	[c]	[c]			0.35
	Pooled	0.39	463	1,197	−0.17	−0.13	[c]	[c]	113.1	−54.6	[c]	−335.4	0.28

[a]Marginal propensity to consume: increase in calorie consumption for an increase in income of Rs 1 (current rupees for yearly functions, 1974 rupees for pooled three-year functions).

[b]Average propensity to consume: average calorie consumption per rupee spent (current rupees for yearly functions, 1974 rupees for pooled three-year functions).

[c]Indicates that the corresponding regression coefficient was found not significantly different from zero at the 90 percent level.

effect, it is probably more correct to use a calorie income elasticity of 0.4.

As expected, the marginal and average propensities to acquire calories and rice were found to be highest during 1973/74 and lowest during 1983/84 (Tables 5.10 and 5.11). This indicates the relative income levels. Only about one-half of the increase in calorie consumption would come from rice, implying a strong desire for diet diversification. This is supported by higher income elasticities for protein than for calories—that is, the desired diet diversification is in the direction of higher-protein foods.

It is clear from these parameters that income increases, whether generated by technological change or by other agents, have caused very significant increases in both calorie and protein consumption. As shown in Table 5.2, between 1973/74 and 1983/84 total annual real expenditures for paddy farmers in the resurvey villages increased by 473 rupees/capita, or 1.3 rupees/capita/day, while total annual real incomes increased by 220 rupees/capita or 0.6 rupees/capita/day. If, because of likely measurement errors, we take total expenditures to be a more correct estimate of household incomes than the data collected directly on incomes, this implies that increases in rice production, which account for about 40 percent of the increases in family incomes,[2] are associated with an increase in calorie consumption of about 373 calories/person/day.[3]

As shown in Table 5.13, other factors influenced calorie consumption. The price elasticity for rice with respect to total calorie consumption was estimated to be −0.30 for rice farmers and −0.24 for landless laborers. Therefore, the increase in real rice prices shown in Table 5.4 is expected to have reduced calorie consumption by 39 and 27 calories/person/day for farmers and landless laborers, respectively. Further downward pressure on per capita calorie consumption was caused by increasing household size (Table 5.1) and a negative association between household size and per capita calorie consumption (Tables 5.10 and 5.11).

2. The paddy income share, which was derived from information in Tables 3.3, 3.8, and 3.9, required making plausible assumptions about the crop allocation of farm costs. As in Chapter 3, we calculated a weighted average share for small and large farms.

3. The calculation is as follows. In 1973/74, the average per capita expenditure for paddy farmers was Rs 311 (Table 5.2). This increased by Rs 473 between 1973/74 and 1983/84, of which 40 percent, or Rs 189, was due to increased paddy production. The paddy income component is equivalent to an increase of 61 percent (189/311 × 100) in per capita expenditures. Given an expenditure elasticity for total calorie consumption of 0.4 and an initial 1973/74 consumption of 1,528 calories/capita/day (Table 5.5), then the 61 percent increase in income due to paddy production induced an increase of 373 calories/person/day (1,528 × 0.4 × 0.61).

TABLE 5.12
Relationship Among Income Elasticities

	Paddy Farmers			*Landless Labor*		
Year	*Food Expenditure Elasticity*	*Calorie Income Elasticity*	*Calorie Cost Elasticity*	*Food Expenditure Elasticity*	*Calorie Income Elasticity*	*Calorie Cost Elasticity*
1973/74	0.87	0.55	0.32	0.90	0.51	0.39
1982/83	0.80	0.44	0.36	0.85	0.57	0.28
1983/84	1.03	0.72	0.31	1.08	0.78	0.30

Note: All elasticities are calculated with respect to a change in income.

TABLE 5.13
Sources of Change in Calorie Consumption, 1973/74 to 1983/84, Resurvey Villages

Source	*Estimated Effect on Daily per Capita Calorie Consumption* — *Paddy Farmers*	*Landless*
Increases in:		
Income from rice production	373	0
Income from other sources	557	948
Rice prices	−39	−27
Ragi prices	0	−17
Milk prices	−28	−34
Meat prices	38	0
Household size	−14	−53
Cash flow changes (landless)	—	3
Other sources	324	−92
Actual change (Table 5.5)	1,211	728

Finally, negative price elasticities for *ragi* and milk with respect to total calorie consumption, combined with increasing real prices of these commodities, are estimated to have resulted in a decrease in calorie consumption, while a positive elasticity for meat caused an increase. Real prices for *ragi*, milk, and meat increased by 6, 17, and 31 percent, respectively.

Conclusions

In this chapter we have attempted to estimate the effect of technological change in rice production on calorie and protein consumption and household-level calorie deficiencies. A number of intervening factors, including a major drought during one of the three years for which data were collected, as well as large changes in incomes from activities other than rice production, made the attempt difficult. Thus, while the estimated changes in calorie and protein consumption and the effects of changes in incomes, prices, and other variables are believed to be reliable, the decomposition of the total effect between technological change and other sources—such as drought, increasing incomes from groundnuts, and off-farm employment—are less certain. Therefore, the estimated impact of technological change per se should be interpreted as orders of magnitudes rather than exact estimates.

Total energy and protein consumption increased dramatically during the study period. By the end of the last study year, virtually all rice-farming households in the resurvey villages were consuming more than 80 percent of recommended calorie levels, as opposed to only about

20 percent of small rice farmers and 60 percent of large rice farmers 10 years earlier. The average paddy-farm household increased its daily calorie consumption per adult equivalent by about 77 percent. The increase was smaller for the landless (54 percent), but only 10–15 percent of this group were still consuming less than 80 percent of calorie requirements during the last months of the study.

Large increases in incomes during the period are responsible for more than half of the improvements in calorie and protein consumption. Total expenditures on food and other consumption goods—usually a reliable proxy for incomes—more than doubled in real terms, after accounting for inflation. With an income elasticity for calorie consumption of 0.4, the resulting increase in calorie consumption for paddy farmers is estimated to be 930 calories/person/day, or 61 percent of the 1973/74 consumption level. It is estimated that about 40 percent of the income increase was due to increasing rice production. Thus, an increase of about 373 calories/person/day, or 31 percent of the total calorie increase, is attributable to increased rice production.

CHAPTER 6

Population, Employment, and Wages: A Comparative Study of North Arcot Villages, 1973–1983

John Harriss

ONE ASPECT OF the research undertaken in North Arcot in 1973/74 by the Cambridge project was a comparative study of the sample villages. Chambers and Harriss wrote of their study of intervillage variations:

> Comparative analysis involves an exercise in classification. Yet as many typologies of villages are possible as there are dimensions or scales against which villages can be assessed. The challenge in searching for a typology is to choose scales or dimensions which are both powerful in making sense of other factors and useful in seeing what might be done to improve rural livelihoods; so that the important result should be not so much the categories that are produced as the principles of classification . . . What is important is not that we should be able to say "This is A, that is B" but rather that we should understand the principal reasons for variations between villages, because it is probable that those reasons will tell us much about the critical variables in rural development. (1977, p. 303)

Starting from an analysis of long-term trends in village populations and examining possible reasons for the marked differences among villages in the extent to which they had apparently been able to absorb increasing numbers of people, Chambers and Harriss considered location, resources in relation to population, and the nature of the production process as "the mainly causal factors," and demographic trends, farming practices, aspects of labor relations, and wages as "mainly derivative factors." They argued finally that a major cause of variations was the differing extent of continuity in the processes of production in different villages. Villages with better-quality irrigation had more continuous production and had, on the whole, supported higher levels of increase in their populations, higher demand for labor, and contrary to some expectations had higher wage rates. The analysis highlighted the importance of seasonality (which Chambers went on to study in depth; see Chambers, Longhurst, and Pacey 1981), and the paper on intervillage variations concluded with the broad statement that "a North Arcot District with a quasi-industrial agriculture, with a continuous demand for labor throughout most of the year, is a target worth bringing into clearer focus" (Chambers and Harriss 1977, p. 322).

Systematic differences among villages were summarized as follows:

QUASI-INDUSTRIAL VILLAGES

Kalpattu, Randam: Indications of labor shortages, high wage rates; both sides have an interest in semipermanent labor contracts

Vegamangalam: This pattern disturbed by political strength of scheduled castes (no attached labor)

Vinayagapuram: The same level of demand for labor not evident; more equal distribution of landholdings associated with modest demand for labor

SEASONAL "EXPANSION" VILLAGES

Duli, Meppathurai: Modest wage rates, no *padials*, no continuous labor shortages

SEASONAL-PRODUCTION-PROCESS VILLAGES

Sirungathur, Veerasambanur, Vengodu: Indications of labor surplus strong; low wage rates; few meals (perquisites) given to laborers; little opportunity for semipermanent labor contracts

Vayalur: This pattern complicated by the fact that scheduled castes have some "independence" and by the availability of higher-paid employment outside

Amudhur: Indications of labor surplus and low wage rates, but pattern distinctive because of particular caste relations

In the absence of firm data on labor demand and supply and on variations in them through the year (for villages other than Randam), the argument depended on the observation of a positive correlation between the apparent quality of irrigation and both wage rates and incidence of labor attachment, and the presumptions—tautological, given that they were supported only by limited qualitative evidence—that production was more continuous and that labor shortages generally existed in these "good-irrigation/high-wage" villages.

This chapter takes the analysis of intervillage variation in 1973/74 as its starting point, but subjects the relationships postulated in that analysis to more rigorous scrutiny, using the Cambridge-Madras universities and IFPRI-TNAU survey data on household labor use and seasonal wages. It finds, essentially, that the earlier analysis probably overestimated the direct connections among quality of irrigation infrastructure, continuity of demand for labor, and levels of wages and the incidence of semipermanent labor contracts. It argues that the class and caste (status) structures of villages also exercise an important influence upon employment patterns and wages; and whereas the earlier analysis pointed to the significance of seasonality as a determinant of rural livelihoods, this chapter draws attention to the importance also of factors that contribute to the segmentation of rural labor markets.

The same general caveats that entered in the presentation of the 1973/74 study apply here. There are major difficulties over the definition of some villages. The sampling frame for the North Arcot surveys was the census list of villages. The villages in this list include different types of social units (see Chambers and Harriss 1977, p. 302); they are not always the same as the villages defined for revenue (administrative) purposes, and units may have been aggregated or disaggregated in different ways at different census points, so that it is sometimes difficult to trace a village from one census to another; it may also be uncertain as to whether the village surveyed by a research team is exactly the same as the unit listed by the census. A further set of difficulties arises from the fact that villages are not clearly bounded entities, and there is interpenetration by ownership of land, wells, and pumpsets, and by movements of labor. Finally, as was said of the 1973/74 analysis, "much of the argument which follows is based upon impressions and upon evidence of rather low reliability . . . But . . . a set of interpretations appears to hang together, and . . . raises policy issues" (Chambers and Harriss 1977 p. 303).

Population Trends

Comparison of the census results for the villages at different points is far from straightforward for the reasons just mentioned, and it is possible that the 1971/81 trends shown in Table 6.1 have been affected, in some cases, by boundary changes. It appears that the population in all 11 villages increased by only 14.8 percent over the decade—compared with 17.2 percent for the population of Tamil Nadu as a whole—though with considerable variation between the −2.5 percent recorded for Meppathurai and +37.1 percent for Duli. We believe that both of these extreme results partially reflect boundary changes. Taking the figures at their face value, it would appear that the higher rates of growth have generally been experienced in what were considered to be seasonal-production-process villages in 1973/74. This may not be altogether surprising, given the facts that there has been some intensification of agricultural production in these villages over the decade, and that some of the continuous-process villages (like Randam) were thought already to have become saturated with population even by 1973/74.

TABLE 6.1
Village Populations

Village	*1971 Census*	*1973 Survey*	*1981 Census*	*1983 Survey*	*Percent Change 1971–81*	*Percent Change 1973–83*
Amudhur	934	942	1,121	986	20.0	4.7
Duli	450	456	617	538	37.1	18.0
Kalpattu	1,942	1,537	2,228	1,393	14.7	−9.4
Meppathurai	804	551	784	747	−2.5	35.6
Randam[a]	1,446	1,388	1,614	1,487	11.6	7.1
Sirungathur	980	948	1,172	1,049	19.6	10.7
Vayalur	634	639	739	692	16.6	8.5
Veerasambanur	540	565	560	620	3.7	9.7
Vegamangalam	1,028	1,023	1,214	1,062	18.1	3.8
Vengodu	1,061	1,046	1,274	1,165	20.1	11.4
Vinayagapuram	784	750	846	814	7.9	8.5
Total	10,603	9,845	12,169	10,553	14.8	7.2
Total excluding Kalpattu & Meppathurai[b]	7,857	7,757	9,157	8,413	16.5	8.5

[a]Randam is a pseudonym for Nesal (see Chapter 4).
[b]For Kalpattu and Meppathurai, there are particularly acute uncertainties as to the comparability of survey and census units, *and* the comparability of 1973 and 1983 survey units.

There is also the possibility, discussed below, that there has been some decline in fertility, and this more in advanced, continuous-process villages than in the poorer, seasonal-process ones. The overall increase of 14.8 percent is appreciably higher, however, than the 10.1 percent increase recorded for these villages for the decade 1961–71, which might be taken to suggest the greater capacity of the local production system to support increases in population (even though there are still indications of net emigration from some villages, such as from Randam, Veerasambanur, and Vinayagapuram; see Chapter 4).

In each case (comparison of the Cambridge-Madras survey results for 1973 with the 1971 census, and of the 1983 IFPRI-TNAU results with the 1981 census), it appears that the survey listings have tended to produce lower estimates of population than the preceding censuses, though more so in the case of the 1983 survey (8.1 percent difference compared with 1.3 percent difference between 1971 and 1973—for villages excluding Kalpattu and Meppathurai, in which cases comparability is very doubtful). This higher difference in 1983 compared with 1973 may reflect the fact that the survey was conducted in the midst of a series of three agroclimatically very poor years, during which there was a lot of short-term migration from the villages to local towns and to the cities of Madras and Bangalore. But even allowing for this factor and excluding the difficult cases of Kalpattu and Meppathurai, it seems either that the census operation actually tends to inflate population numbers or that household surveys systematically underestimate them.

In 1983/84, already aware of the discrepancies between census and survey figures, stringent efforts were made by the IFPRI-TNAU survey team to check the accuracy of data on village populations. Even after correction of initial household listing figures—which are expected to be on the low side because of investigators' lack of familiarity with the villages—the disparity shown in Table 6.1 remained. The accuracy of the survey figures is broadly confirmed by the independent measurement of the population of the main village of Randam by anthropological investigation. This showed an increase of 8.65 percent between April/May 1973 and January/February 1984, corresponding quite closely with the 7.1 percent increase shown in the comparison of the survey results from 1973 and 1983. There does seem to be a possibility that the census results for 1981 overestimate the village populations, and that the overall rate of population growth over the decade has not been as high as the 15 percent that appears.

In view of the general importance of labor absorption and support for natural population increase within the rural economy (this was also the organizing theme of the work by Chambers and Harriss on intervillage variation), it is striking that the sample villages in eastern North Arcot should have supported so small an increase in population (even 15 percent could be considered relatively low and possibly indicative of emigration), especially over a decade of rather rapid growth of agricultural production. In the absence, at the time of writing, of full census records for North Arcot for 1981, the analysis cannot be pursued much further. The extent of local migration is indicated by the fact that the urban population of North Arcot district as a whole grew by 29.6 percent according to census data, and one of the market towns in the study region, Arni, saw population grow by 27 percent over the decade. The possibility that there has been migration from villages to towns in North Arcot, as well as to the more distant cities of Madras and Bangalore, is borne out by evidence of such movements of people from Randam, Veerasambanur, Vinayagapuram, and Duli (for which more detailed information is available; see Chapter 4).

Account must also be taken of the possibility that there has been some decline in fertility. The situation in some villages in eastern North Arcot seems in general to resemble that in an area in Karnataka state, to the west of the city of Bangalore, studied by Caldwell, Reddy, and Caldwell (1985). The population in their study area has hardly changed in the recent past because net emigration, mostly to Bangalore, is more or less equal to the natural increase. There is also strong evidence in this very detailed microdemographic study of fertility decline, brought about by a range of interlocking factors, but including especially the desire of parents to keep their sons and even their daughters at school, which has increased the costs of having children. Parents want to educate their sons in order to increase their chances of obtaining urban jobs or local off-farm employment, and thereby of gaining access to potential for extra earning; and they wish to educate their daughters in order to improve their chances of marrying them to men in such jobs. The expansion in urban jobs and off-farm employment has made these expectations reasonable. Much the same aspirations and intentions were expressed to the author in Randam (though not uniformly across classes; more among wealthier high-caste landholders than among landless laborers), and the possibility of fertility decline there was suggested by evidence of the increased use of family planning.

The predictions of the 1973/74 study of intervillage variation—that population growth would be supported differentially according to the character of the production process in different villages—are difficult to test, therefore, in view of the data problems, but they are also questionable because of the likelihood of changes in the demographic process. In relation to our main concern with employment and wages, what seems most important are the indications of local migration from the villages to towns. The extent to which this may be the result of growth linkages from agriculture is the focus of other chapters in this book.

Trends in Occupational Structure

Following from the foregoing consideration of population trends, the question is raised about the nature of changes in the occupational structure of the region. Data on occupational structure in the sample villages come from the initial household listing surveys in 1973 and 1982, made when the investigators were unfamiliar with the villages. Given this fact and the difficulty of assigning individuals to discrete occupational categories when they may work at several occupations, the data unfortunately cannot be considered very reliable.

Changes in the numbers of those reporting their main occupation as agricultural labor are shown in Table 6.2. It seems that there has been an absolute increase overall of 364 agricultural laborers in the 11 villages, and that the rate of increase in their numbers (16.9 percent) has been rather higher than that of the population as a whole. The picture differs a good deal among villages, however, and the general

TABLE 6.2
Number of Agricultural Laborers by Village

Village	*1973* *Persons*	*1973* *Percent of Total Population*	*1983* *Persons*	*1983* *Percent of Total Population*	*Independent Estimates*[a] *1973*	*Independent Estimates*[a] *1983*
Amudhur	275	29.2	357	36.0		
Duli	90	19.8	137	25.5	100	103
Kalpattu	298	19.4	233	16.7		
Meppathurai	89	16.2	128	17.1		
Randam	355	25.6	376	25.3	243	272
Sirungathur	179	18.9	310	29.6		
Vayalur	166	26.0	110	15.9		
Veerasambanur	158	28.0	131	21.1	162	150
Vegamangalam	216	21.1	246	23.2		
Vengodu	213	20.4	235	20.2		
Vinayagapuram	114	15.2	254	31.2	145	110
All villages	2,153	21.9	2,517	23.9		

[a]See J. Harriss 1986.

increase is substantially made up by the large increases recorded for Vinayagapuram (140), Sirungathur (131), and Amudhur (82).

An independent estimate for Vinayagapuram, based on a one-fifth stratified random sample (reported in Chapter 4), leads to an entirely contrary conclusion for this village of a decline in the numbers of agricultural laborers, from 145 in 1973 to 110 in 1983. It seems possible in this case that there was underestimation of their numbers in the 1973 survey (total 114) and overestimation in 1983 (total 254). For Veerasambanur, surveys and independent investigation alike suggest a decline in the numbers of agricultural laborers; both sources suggest a small increase in Randam (19 and 29); and the survey results for Duli show a sizable increase (47), while the independent sample estimates indicate little change in absolute numbers (from 100 to 103). In view of the difficulties inherent in the collection of labor force data in circumstances like those of North Arcot villages, no firm conclusions can be drawn. It seems possible that the numbers of those employed mainly as agricultural laborers have declined or remained constant in some villages, and it is unlikely that there has been a disproportionate increase in their numbers overall. The independent studies referred to indicate a slight absolute decrease; and we can say that there is no very clear or very strong evidence from these villages of the process of "depeasantization" and expansion of the agricultural labor force, which has often been supposed to be the prevailing tendency.

Irrigation and Agriculture

In 1973/74, Chambers and Harriss considered the irrigation facilities of the villages to be as follows:

QUASI-INDUSTRIAL
(i.e., fairly continuous irrigation and labor demand throughout the year)
Kalpattu—very reliable wells
Vegamangalam—perennial spring irrigation
Vinayagapuram—two crops a year from tank and river channel
Randam—86 percent of wells have pumpsets

SEASONAL-CUM-INDUSTRIAL
Amudhur, Vengodu, Veerasambanur, Vayalur, Meppathurai, and Sirungathur—combinations of small tanks, wells, and some pumpsets, with water supplies of varying reliability and depth

SEASONAL
Duli—wells negligible, reliance on one crop a year from small tank

It seemed possibly to be significant that the three villages that had experienced the lowest intercensal rates of population increase between 1961 and 1971 were those that had received electricity connections most recently and had, correspondingly, only just begun to see much development of groundwater irrigation by 1973 (Vinayagapuram, Vengodu, and Veerasambanur). In view of this late start, it is not surprising that of these three, Vinayagapuram and Vengodu should have seen the greatest expansion in mechanized groundwater pumping since 1973 (see Table 6.3). By the same token, it is striking that the number of pumps in Veerasambanur has hardly increased at all—indicative of the general

TABLE 6.3
Expansion of Groundwater Irrigation, 1973–83

Village	*Increase in Number of Pumpsets (percent)*
Amudhur	5.4
Duli	266.0
Kalpattu	4.3
Meppathurai	21.0
Sirungathur	47.0
Vayalur	9.0
Veerasambanur	8.0
Vegamangalam	57.9
Vengodu	92.0
Vinayagapuram	281.0

Note: No data are available for Randam.

failure of agricultural development there, which has been associated with emigration and probably falling real wages (in contrast to the situation in other villages; see Chapter 4). Other villages in which there has been expansion in mechanized pumping over the decade are Vegamangalam (remarkably, perhaps, for a village that received an electricity connection at a very early stage), Sirungathur, and Duli (from a very low base). These developments cannot be associated very clearly with population trends for reasons that have been explained. Also, they do not appear to have very much affected the distinctions between villages that were made earlier, for they are borne out quite consistently by the 1982/83 cropping indices for the villages (computed from the IFPRI-TNAU farm survey data and shown in Table 6.4; note these low indices for a year of acute drought, a pattern also evident in Table 3.2).

The question is then raised as to the seasonality of labor demand: How strong are differences among villages, and do they fit with the statements made about variations in quality of irrigation? Then, to what extent have seasonal variations changed between 1973/74 and 1983/84? The data are problematic, however. As we go on to explain in the next section, the survey data on household labor use are an imperfect guide to the level of and variation in labor demand in different villages because of variations among villages in the extent to which the household samples include "seigneurial" landowners who seek to avoid involvement in labor on the land. Further, directly comparable data were not recorded in 1973/74 on a month-by-month basis for use of household labor on own farm.

Comparisons for the resurvey villages between 1982/83 and 1983/84, and between resurvey and continuous-process villages for 1982/83, show that there was generally higher variance in the nondrought year,

TABLE 6.4
Cropping Indices, 1982/83

Village	*Cropping Index*
Amudhur	1.16
Duli	0.62
Kalpattu	1.32
Meppathurai	1.10
Randam	1.83
Sirungathur	0.77
Vayalur	1.20
Veerasambanur	0.83
Vegamangalam	1.56
Vengodu	1.02
Vinayagapuram	1.33

though the lows were less pronounced than in the drought year (unsurprisingly). In 1982/83 there were not significant differences between continuous-process villages and others—though this finding cannot be considered significant, given that the continuous-process villages especially include those with seigneurial landowners. It is worth pointing out that whereas Pinstrup-Andersen and Jaramillo (1989) report very little indication of seasonal variations in labor use when they aggregate data from different villages, marked seasonal variations still appear when the data are examined for each village separately. Because peaks and troughs come close together and are not recorded as occurring in precisely the same months in every village, putting data for different villages together may produce a quite misleading effect of uniformity through the year.

Employment and Wages

We begin by reporting some basic facts insofar as we have been able to establish them from the survey data. The ranking of the villages in 1982/83 in terms of the average number of person-days of labor performed per household per month in all activities (employment in agriculture, in nonagriculture, in family nonfarm business, and in work on own farm) was as follows (see Table 6.5):

Meppathurai
Veerasambanur, Kalpattu
Vinayagapuram
Sirungathur, Vegamangalam
Vayalur, Randam, Vengodu
Duli
Amudhur

There is no obvious correspondence between this ranking and the variations among villages in terms of the quality of irrigation and intensity of cropping. Comparison of the results for the five villages that were resurveyed in 1983/84 with those for 1982/83 suggests that Amudhur was especially hard hit in the drought year, but the ranking of the other four villages is the same. Overall, it seems fair to suppose that the effects of the drought have not exercised a distorting influence on the relative positions of different villages.

Table 6.6 reports wage rates—where possible, those actually paid according to farm survey data, rather than those said usually to be paid in the village—for the main (*samba*) season, for the principal operations performed by men and by women. Table 6.7 reports data on in-kind

TABLE 6.5
Household Labor Use (average person-days/month/household)

Village	*1982/83* *Male*	*Female*	*Total*	*1983/84* *Total*
Amudhur	11.5	5.9	17.4	50.3
Duli	18.4	1.4	19.8	34.8
Kalpattu	18.6	17.2	35.8	n.a.
Meppathurai	30.3	12.3	42.6	59.9
Randam	18.7	7.7	26.4	n.a.
Sirungathur	23.7	4.5	28.2	n.a.
Vayalur	21.8	4.3	26.1	44.1
Veerasambanur	25.0	11.9	36.9	51.1
Vegamangalam	19.2	9.0	28.2	n.a.
Vengodu	19.6	6.7	26.3	n.a.
Vinayagapuram	19.4	11.5	30.9	n.a.

wages for harvesting and threshing. In view of the importance of these payments for agricultural laborers' income, it is very unfortunate that with the data available it is impossible to be confident of knowing whether or not there have been changes in them, or even about differences between villages. There are two reasons for this. One is that the payments were made traditionally in terms of bundles of paddy on the stalk, or of local volumetric measures of grain. Different measures, though sometimes with the same name, were used in different parts of even a small region like the study area. Attempts have lately been made to standardize these measures in terms of liters or kilograms. The result has been that cultivators and laborers may say they have paid or have received a certain number of traditional measures, when the payment has been made out of a standard liter measure—or perhaps the other way round. People still refer to harvesting and threshing payments in terms of a particular number of measures. There is no clear evidence that these ideas of standard payments have changed, except perhaps in Vinayagapuram and Amudhur, where they may have increased. The picture is made even more complicated by a second consideration: over the decade there has been a shift away from the standard daily payments that were still the norm in 1973/74 to much more employment of labor on the basis of various specific contracts. These contracts mean that it is possible for the individual laborer to earn more than, or less than, the traditional rate for the day.

In these circumstances it seems most sensible to rely on comparison of payments for the principal operations paid for in cash, in the main paddy season. Neither in 1973/74 nor in 1982/83 is it easy to rank villages, because of differences between relative payments to men and

TABLE 6.6
***Samba* Season Wages (Rs/day)**

Village	Plowing (men) 1973/74	Plowing (men) 1973/74 (Inflated to 1982/83)	Plowing (men) 1982/83	Plowing (men) 1983/84	Plucking (men) 1973/74	Plucking (men) 1973/74 (Inflated to 1982/83)	Plucking (men) 1982/83	Plucking (men) 1983/84	Transplanting (women) 1973/74	Transplanting (women) 1973/74 (Inflated to 1982/83)	Transplanting (women) 1982/83	Transplanting (women) 1983/84
Amudhur	2.00[a]	3.67	2.75	5.50	1.80[a]	3.30	n.a.	6.00	1.30	2.40	2.00	2.37
Duli	2.00[a]	3.67	3.00	7.20	1.00	1.84	n.a.	5.00	1.50	2.75	2.50	3.00
Kalpattu[b]	3.50	6.44	5.00	n.a.	1.00	1.84	n.a.	n.a.	1.00	1.84	2.00	n.a.
Meppathurai[b]	2.80[a]	5.14	5.00	3.22	2.00	3.67	3.00	4.30	1.50	2.75	2.10	3.18
Randam	2.50	4.60	4.62	n.a.	2.50	4.60	5.50	5.00	1.50	2.75	2.70	3.00
Sirungathur	2.50[a]	4.60	5.00	n.a.	2.00[a]	3.67	n.a.	n.a.	1.00	1.84	2.25	n.a.
Vayalur	2.00	3.67	6.33	5.60	2.00[a]	3.67	7.50	8.00	1.00	1.84	2.66	4.00
Veerasambanur[b]	2.33	4.28	3.00	2.83	2.00[a]	3.67	2.83	3.00	1.20	2.20	2.00	2.00
Vegamangalam	3.00[a]	5.50	5.00	n.a.	3.00	5.50	5.37	n.a.	1.00	1.84	3.16	n.a.
Vengodu	2.00	3.67	4.10	n.a.	1.00	1.84	3.00	n.a.	1.57	2.87	2.13	n.a.
Vinayagapuram	2.00[a]	3.67	3.00	4.37	1.70[a]	3.12	3.00	4.00	0.70[a]	1.29	2.00	2.00

Source: Plot data from the Cambridge-Madras universities and IFPRI-TNAU surveys.

[a]Average wage for village, not plot means.

[b]The wages for Kalpattu, Meppathurai, and Veerasambanur are for the *navarai* season.

TABLE 6.7
Harvesting and Threshing In-kind Wages (mm/day)

Village	*Harvesting (women)*		*Threshing (men)*	
	73/74	*83/84*	*73/74*	*83/84*
Amudhur	2.5	6.0	3.5	8.0
Duli	3.5	2.5	1.0	6.0
Kalpattu	3.5	3.5	3.5	3.5
Meppathurai	3.0	3.0–4.0	4.5	4.5–6.0
Randam	3.0	3.0	6.0	6.0
Sirungathur	4.0	4.0	4.0	4.0
Vayalur	2.5	3 kg	5.0	6 kg
Veerasambanur	3.0	3.0	6.0	6.0
Vegamangalam	4.0	n.a.	4.0	n.a.
Vengodu	3.5	5 liters	3.0	6 liters
Vinayagapuram	2.1	4 kg	2.3	6 kg

Note: mm = one *padi,* or measure of paddy.

to women in different places. In 1973/74, looking across the cash wages and harvesting payments, and noting that the data for these operations were reduced to a standard measure, it appears that Randam and Vegamangalam had fairly high wages, though Meppathurai also had quite high cash wages while Vinayagapuram especially and Vayalur had lower wages than elsewhere. Cash wages were low in Veerasambanur also. Given that paddy is relatively unimportant in Kalpattu and that payments to labor in the cultivation of bananas and turmeric are comparatively high, it is thought that wage rates should be considered to have been high there. In 1982/83 wage rates seem still to have been generally high in Vegamangalam and less clearly so in Randam, but high also now in Vayalur and perhaps in Sirungathur. Cash wages were clearly lower than elsewhere in Vinayagapuram, Veerasambanur, and Amudhur.

Evidence on changes in real wages is mixed. Only in one village, Vayalur, is there a clear indication of an increase in the real wage paid for plowing. For the other operations, real wages seem to have remained roughly constant or to have increased in Vayalur, Vinayagapuram, Randam, Sirungathur, and Vegamangalam. They appear to have declined in Meppathurai, Veerasambanur, and perhaps in Amudhur, though the picture for all these villages, and for Duli, appears rather more favorable when we consider the wages paid after the drought year in 1983/84. It is certainly interesting that the evidence on wages for the drought year, however, offers an indication of an increase in real wages over 1973/74 in continuous-process villages (Randam, Vegamangalam, Vinayagapuram) and in a seasonal-process village that has seen a good deal of expansion of groundwater irrigation (Sirungathur), while it shows decline in other seasonal-process villages.

The principal hypothesis put forward concerning intervillage variations by Chambers and Harriss was that better irrigation endowment, leading to more intensive cultivation, generates higher and more continuous labor demand through the year, and probably higher wage rates too. The hypothesis was qualified by the recognition that proximity to a town or the existence of a diversified village economy might also, because of opening up alternative income-earning opportunities, increase overall labor demand in a village. In this respect the villages appeared to be differentiated according to 1982/83 household labor use data as follows:

NONAGRICULTURE AND NONFARM BUSINESS EMPLOYMENT IMPORTANT:

Randam	(37 percent of total male employment; 25 percent female)
Sirungathur	(26 percent male and 12 percent female)
Kalpattu	(29 percent male and 6 percent female)
Vayalur	(16 percent male and 19 percent female)
Vegamangalam	(16 percent male and 15 percent female)

NONAGRICULTURE AND NONFARM BUSINESS EMPLOYMENT LOW:

Veerasambanur	(11 percent male and 0 female)
Vengodu	(10 percent male and 0 female)
Meppathurai	
Duli	
Amudhur	
Vinayagapuram	

Nonagriculture and nonfarm business employment is more important in villages nearer to towns or small service centers (Randam, Sirungathur, Vayalur, Vegamangalam) or with an especially diversified economy (Kalpattu). Nonagricultural employment is more important in the periurban village of Duli than the survey data show, according to an independent sample (see Chapter 4). Laboring and carting in Cheyyar are important sources of income.

In relation to the principal hypothesis proposed, the relatively low levels of household labor use in Randam and Vegamangalam, with their good irrigation, intensive cultivation, and nonagricultural employment opportunities, appear at first to be hard to explain, as do the levels of labor use in Veerasambanur and Meppathurai, with their less good irrigation and lower cropping intensities. Relatively low household labor use but relatively high wages in Randam, Vegamangalam, and Vayalur (close to a service center where alternative employment is available) are probably explained by the fact that these are villages with a fairly numerous and high-ranking dominant caste from which come a number of larger and richer cultivators who do not themselves participate very much in cultivation work. If this argument holds, we should expect to observe (1) relatively low participation in cultivation by paddy farmers and (2) relatively high employment of hired labor and semipermanent labor. Data shown in Table 6.8 confirm that Randam, Vegamangalam, and Vayalur are in the lower half of the range for "adult family males working on farm" among paddy farmers, and that Randam and Vegamangalam are low in the range for "adult family females working on farm." Semipermanent labor is employed in all three villages, and Vegamangalam and Randam are among the highest employers of agricultural labor. The explanation cannot be rejected, therefore.

Other villages in which semipermanent labor is employed and which are high employers of agricultural labor are Duli, Amudhur, and Vinayagapuram. They are also—especially Duli and Amudhur—low with regard to "adult family males working on farm" among paddy farmers. These are also villages in which there are households with the kind of seigneurial lifestyle of the richer households of Randam, Vegamangalam, and Vayalur. In terms of number of days of work per household in agricultural wage labor among landless households, however (Table 6.9), Duli and Amudhur are rather low, while Vinayagapuram is relatively high. The small amount of employment for landless-labor households in Duli and Amudhur may reflect the poor irrigation and low intensity of cultivation in these villages. Kalpattu has relatively high household labor use because of its diversified agricultural economy and high employment opportunities outside agriculture, in the context of

TABLE 6.8
Total Paddy-Farm Labor Use, 1982/83 (person-days/month/household)

Village	*Family Male Labor*	*Family Female Labor*	*Hired Labor*
Amudhur	14.6	7.6	9.0
Duli	16.6	0.8	11.0
Kalpattu	21.7	14.5	8.8
Meppathurai	30.0	10.3	9.3
Randam	24.8	5.6	10.0
Sirungathur	30.6	7.2	3.5
Vayalur	23.3	7.0	5.8
Veerasambanur	23.9	9.2	2.7
Vegamangalam	22.9	5.4	12.0
Vengodu	25.9	5.2	5.9
Vinayagapuram	27.9	4.1	15.2

TABLE 6.9
Farm Employment, Landless Households, 1982/83 (person-days/month)

Village	*Days of Employment*
Amudhur	15.4
Duli	23.7
Kalpattu	31.8
Meppathurai	55.2
Randam	27.6
Sirungathur	17.7
Vayalur	28.2
Veerasambanur	44.8
Vegamangalam	40.0
Vengodu	29.8
Vinayagapuram	39.7

fairly good irrigation, and because it is a Vanniya-dominated village. The Vanniyas are a numerous but historically quite low-ranking caste community not much given to the seigneurial style of the Agamudaiyans of Randam, the Mudaliars of Vegamangalam, or the self-styled Kshatriyas of Vayalur. They engage a good deal in cultivation.

Pursuing the logic of these arguments—which is that the effects of the irrigation and cultivation systems and of access to nonagricultural employment are moderated by the nature of the class and status structures of different villages, as well as by labor supply factors—it is possible to suggest the typology of villages in terms of labor use and wages, which is shown in Figure 6.1. The explanation for this is as follows:

RANDAM, VEGAMANGALAM

Randam —agricultural labor, 25 percent
scheduled caste, 50 percent

Vegamangalam—agricultural labor, 23 percent
scheduled caste, 33 percent

Middle to low overall household labor use but high wages; high use of hired labor; employment of semipermanent labor and relatively low on-farm work by paddy-farming households; high nonagricultural and nonfarm employment.

Interpretation: These are villages with seigneurial high caste and quite big landowners, seeking to employ others and not working much on the land themselves. High wages because of high demand for hired labor and, in each case, proximity to town.

KALPATTU

agricultural labor, 17 percent
scheduled caste, 11 percent

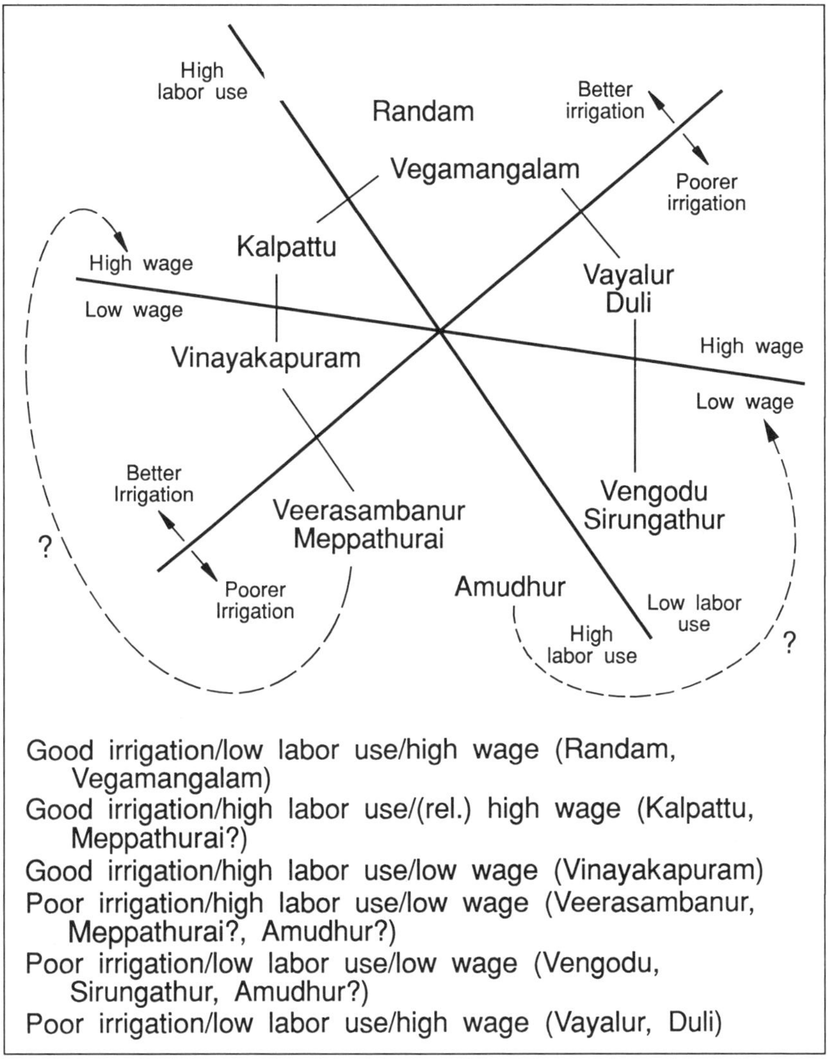

Fig. 6.1. Schematic classification of North Arcot villages, 1980s.

High overall household labor use, fairly high wages, fairly high use of hired labor (especially female), some employment of labor on semi-permanent basis, relatively high on-farm work by paddy-farming households.

Interpretation: High demand agriculture and high nonagricultural and nonfarm business employment. More of a working-peasant type of larger landholder from Vanniya caste. Relatively low supply of labor in the village.

VINAYAGAPURAM

agricultural labor, 31 percent
scheduled caste, 24 percent

Fairly high overall household labor use, with wages apparently still rather low though having seen real increases over the decade; high hired labor use and employment of labor on semipermanent basis; average to high on-farm work by paddy-farming households.

Interpretation: Relatively high demand agriculture, in a context with a few seigneurial-type (Brahmin) larger landholders, but predominantly working-peasant Vanniyas. Lower wages here because of high local supply of labor and lack of access for landless to alternative employment opportunities.

VEERASAMBANUR, MEPPATHURAI, AMUDHUR

Veerasambanur—agricultural labor, 21 percent
scheduled caste, 47 percent
Meppathurai —agricultural labor, 17 percent
scheduled caste, 28 percent
Amudhur —agricultural labor, 36 percent
scheduled caste, 33 percent

Patterns not wholly consistent with each other but alike in showing high overall household labor use (taking evidence for Amudhur in 1983/84) and low wages (less clearly so in Meppathurai, but it was like the other two villages in showing decline in real wages from 1973/74 to 1982/83) in a context of indifferent irrigation and lower cultivation intensity. Some employment of semipermanent labor in all three villages, average to high hired labor use in Meppathurai and Amudhur but low in Veerasambanur. High on-farm labor in paddy-farming households in Meppathurai, fairly low in Veerasambanur and Amudhur.

Interpretation: Meppathurai, where irrigation is probably rather better than in the other two villages, has a pattern similar to that of Kalpattu. In the other two villages, the combination of high overall labor use, low wages, but quite low participation in on-farm work in paddy-farming households may be explained by the presence in these villages of large numbers of scheduled caste and of agricultural-labor households, together with poor but would-be seigneurial landholders (Agamudaiyans in Veerasambanur and Brahmins and Reddiars in Amudhur). The context is one in which opportunities for nonagricultural and nonfarm business employment are limited.

VENGODU, SIRUNGATHUR

Vengodu —agricultural labor, 20 percent
scheduled caste, 15 percent
Sirungathur—agricultural labor, 30 percent
scheduled caste, 67 percent

Low to average overall household labor use and middling wages; low use of hired labor and high on-farm work by paddy-farming households; few semipermanent laborers.

Interpretation: These villages show similarities with Veerasambanur, Meppathurai, and Amudhur, but they appear to be distinguished by the absence of would-be seigneurial landholders and lower levels of labor use among their landless households. It is not clear why this last fact should obtain.

VAYALUR, DULI

Vayalur—agricultural labor, 16 percent
scheduled caste, 21 percent

Duli —agricultural labor, 21 percent
scheduled caste, 18 percent

Low overall household labor use but high wages (especially Vayalur); high hired labor use in Duli and increased employment of labor on semipermanent basis; low on-farm work by paddy-farming households (see 1983/84 data); fairly high employment in nonagriculture and in nonfarm business (even in Duli; see data in Chapter 4).

Interpretation: In these villages it seems that wages are relatively high because of the combination of seigneurial landholders and the availability of alternative employment outside agricultural wage work, and in a context with quite low intravillage labor supply.

Conclusions

When we turn the microscope as low as the level of individual villages and compare "specimens," it is not surprising that it is possible to discern—or at least to suggest the existence of—complex, subtle, and highly specific combinations of factors that must seem confusing to those who have not peered so intently through the same lens. If we turn the objective of the microscope back up a little and take into the field of view all 11 villages again—and the reader might care to simulate this by looking at Figure 6.1—then it may be suggested that the pattern discerned by Chambers and Harriss, defined by the irrigation-cultivation intensity and continuity dynamic, still seems to obtain. But it is clearly modified or blurred by access to nonagricultural employment opportunities, and by the effects of class and status structures in different villages (particularly the extent to which villages are dominated by working-peasant or by at least would-be seigneurial landholders). The net result might appear to be a palimpsest. But it is probably more accurately described as a labor market that is still quite highly segmented and influenced by institutional factors. The circumstances are different, but the basic finding is similar to that of Rudra and Bardhan in their studies in West Bengal (see Rudra 1984; Bardhan and Rudra 1986).

This conclusion is broad and may be unsatisfactory, but it is a salutary reminder of the existence of forces that almost certainly mean that in securing access to such new employment opportunities as have been created by the growth linkages from agriculture in eastern North Arcot, certain social groups have been discriminated against. It was found, for example, in the comparison of the structure of business activity and employment in the market town of Arni in 1973 and 1983 that for all the increased employment in the town, members of the scheduled castes are still discriminated against in a wide range of activities (Harriss and Harriss 1984). That this is a more general tendency may be indicated by the fact that the proportion of scheduled caste people in the village populations has increased in five of the sample villages and appears to have decreased in only two of them. Part of the explanation for this may be that scheduled caste people have been less successful in gaining access to work outside agriculture and outside the villages.

Part II

The Indirect Effects

CHAPTER 7

A Social Accounting Matrix of the Regional Economy, 1982/83

Peter B. R. Hazell, C. Ramasamy, V. Rajagopalan, and Neal Bliven

THIS CHAPTER USES an estimated social accounting matrix (SAM) to provide a detailed quantitative description of the North Arcot study region in 1982/83. The SAM framework provides a consistent, comprehensive, and detailed picture of the transactions in an economy. Production activities, commodities, factors, government, households, and other institutions can all be accommodated, and the pattern in which incomes are distributed takes its place alongside the sources of income generation. The SAM also provides the basis for the construction of a model of the regional economy, as discussed in Chapter 8.

An Overview of the SAM

A SAM combines the principles of national income accounts in matrix form and the Leontief input-output model of production (see, for example, Pyatt and Round 1985). A SAM is always square, for under every account there are both receipts and expenditures. By convention, the entries in the matrix represent receipts when read across rows and expenditures when read down columns. Since the principles of double-entry bookkeeping apply, each row total is identical to its corresponding column total.

Table 7.1 illustrates in schematic form the SAM estimated for the North Arcot study region. Some interpretive comments follow.

ROW 1. Households receive income from transfers among each other (column 1), from government transfers (column 2), from self-employment in production activities (column 3), from leasing out factors, including labor (column 5), and as remittances from outside the region, for example, pensions and transfers from relatives (column 7). The ways in which this income is spent are summarized in *column 1.*

TABLE 7.1
Schematic Social Accounting Matrix for North Arcot

	Households (1)	*Government Current Account (2)*	*Private Production Sectors (3)*	*Commodities (4)*	*Factors (5)*	*Capital (6)*	*Rest of World (7)*	*Row Sums (8)*
Households (1)	Income transfers between households	Subsidies and other income transfers	Payment of profits to households		Factor payments to households		Remittances from outside region	Household total incomes
Government current account (2)	Personal taxes	Taxes paid by government-operated businesses	Business and commodity sales tax	Commodity supplied by government	Interest payments to nationalized banks		Transfers from district and state government	Government total fiscal receipts
Private production sectors (3)				Commodity supplied by private firms	Interest payments to private financial institutions			Gross outputs
Commodities (4)	Household consumption expenditures	Government procurements from within region	Production intermediates purchased within region			Investment demands for locally procured commodities	Exports	Total commodity demands
Factors (5)	Interest payments on consumer loans	Government salaries, rents, etc.				Factor payments for investment activities	Factor earnings outside region	Total factor earnings
Capital (6)	Household savings	Government savings	Earnings retained by incorporated firms				Net capital inflow (outflow if negative)	Total capital receipts
Rest of world (7)		Government procurement of direct imports	Private firm procurement of direct imports	Indirect imports		Investment demands for direct imports		Total payments to outside region
Column sums (8)	Household expenditures	Total government expenditures	Total costs of production	Total supplies of locally traded commodities	Total factor payments	Total investment	Total receipts from outside region	Total regional transactions

It goes to interhousehold transfers (row 1), to direct tax payments (row 2), to consumption expenditures (row 4), to factor payments (mostly interest payments on consumer loans) (row 5), and to household savings (row 6). Total household expenditure (row 8, column 1) must be equal to total household income (row 1, column 8).

ROW 2. In its current account, the government receives tax payments from households (column 1), tax collections from government-operated businesses, for example, civil supply shops (column 2), and business and sales taxes from private businesses (column 3). In addition, government earns income from the sales of commodities, for example, foods and kerosene (column 4), and from interest earnings by nationalized banks (column 5), and receives fiscal transfers from the district and state governments (column 7). Outlays (*column 2*) consists of transfers to households (row 1), tax payments by government-operated businesses (row 2), factor payments, especially salaries (row 5), and the procurement of goods and services, both from local suppliers (row 4) and from suppliers based outside the region (row 7). In addition, government saves any surplus fiscal funds, which are then available to fund its investment activities (row 6).

ROW 3. Production sectors produce goods and services whose value is the private-sector gross output of the regional economy. This amount includes total commodity sales (column 4) and interest payments received by private financial institutions (column 5). In order to produce these goods and services, various inputs are required as summarized in *column 3*. These inputs consist of intermediate commodities purchased from within the region (row 4) or from outside the region (row 7), and the employment of factors of production (row 5). Part of the remaining income is paid as business and sales taxes to government (row 2), part is retained by incorporated firms for reinvestment, especially private banks (row 6), and any remaining income is allocated to the households owning or operating the businesses as payment for their own factor use (row 1).

ROW 4. The demands for locally transacted commodities in the region consist of household expenditures (column 1), government procurements on current account (column 2), production intermediates (column 3), government and private demands for investment (column 6), and export demands from outside the region (column 7). The supplies of locally traded commodities are portrayed in *column 4*. They arise from government-operated businesses (row 2), from private businesses (row 3), and from regional imports (row 7).

ROW 5. Payments received by factors that are traded or leased within the region include labor, land, bullocks, buildings, and capital. Households pay interest on consumer loans (column 1), government hires workers and rents buildings and land on its current account (column 2), private businesses hire workers, bullocks, land, and buildings and pay interest on borrowed credit (column 3), and factors are also hired for government and private investment activities (column 6). Finally, some factors earn income from outside the region; these are mostly earnings by white-collar workers who commute to Vellore (column 7). *Column 5* shows who receives the factor earnings. Most factor earnings go directly to the households who own the factors (row 1), but interest payments collected by nationalized banks go to government (row 2), and interest payments collected by private financial institutions go to production (row 3).

ROW 6. The capital account is a combined account for all government and private investment. The sources of capital are household savings (column 1), government savings (column 2), retained earnings by incorporated firms (column 3), and net capital inflows from outside the region (column 7). *Column 5* shows how the capital funds are spent. They are used to buy capital goods from within the region (row 4) or from outside it (row 7), and to hire factors, especially labor, to undertake investment activities (row 5).

ROW 7. The region's imports consist of imports purchased directly from outside the region by the government on its current account (column 2), by private businesses for production or local trade (column 3), and by government and private businesses for investment purposes (column 6). In addition, imports are purchased for local trading (column 4). The region's earnings from outside are summarized in *column 7*. They consist of commodity exports (row 4), factor earnings (row 5), remittances to households (row 1), and transfers to government from district or state sources. In addition, there may be a net capital inflow or outflow for the region (a capital outflow if the entry in row 6 is negative).

Estimation of the SAM

Most of the SAM was estimated using data from the IFPRI-TNAU surveys undertaken in 1982/83 and described in Chapter 2. The surveys provide detailed information on the incomes and expenditures of representative samples of rural and urban households, and of the different types of farm and nonfarm businesses in the region.

The availability of these data had two important implications for the estimation of the SAM. First, the accounts for households, production sectors, and commodities could be defined at a highly disaggregate level. Some aggregation was desirable to keep things manageable, but this aggregation was rarely required to overcome any deficiencies in the data. Second, since all transactions were recorded in the surveys in the prices households and businesses actually paid or received for each commodity, it turned out to be easiest to define many of the commodity accounts by price level (i.e., producer, wholesale, or retail) as well as by type of commodity. Trade and distribution margins are captured in the SAM through explicit representation of the transactions of different types of wholesale and retail establishments. For example, paddy wholesalers buy paddy at producer prices in the SAM and sell it to mills at wholesale prices. The difference in the value of these two transactions is the sum of all the trade and distribution costs (including profits) charged by the wholesalers. The composition of the margin is given explicitly by the cost structure of the paddy wholesaler sector in the SAM.

The commodities are defined in Table 7.2; there are 134 in all, though, as discussed above, many are the same commodity defined at more than one price level. Only commodities traded within the region are included in the commodity accounts. Commodities purchased outside the region and not traded locally are treated as direct imports and enter the "rest-of-world" account under the account of the purchasing institution. Many items procured by government fall into this category, being delivered by suppliers based outside the study region at prices that are not available locally. Commodities involving only small amounts of money were aggregated with other like commodities.

The production sectors are defined in Table 7.3. There are 59 sectors, including 4 types of agricultural activity and 55 types of nonfarm business. The latter were aggregated from the 120 types of firms identified in the IFPRI-TNAU nonfarm business survey (see Chapter 2). Sectors are defined largely on the basis of the major commodity they produce or trade. However, since all transactions are recorded by commodity, the account definitions do not lead to any loss of information in the case of multiproduct firms. Further, since commodities are defined by price level as well as by type of commodity, it was necessary to keep separate accounts for firms producing or trading at different stages of the marketing channel. For example, by having separate accounts for farmers, agricultural wholesale merchants, rice mills, and

TABLE 7.2
Structure of Commodity Transactions, 1982/83 SAM

Account Number	Commodity Name	Total Transactions (thous Rs)	Percent Total Commodity Transactions	Percent Imported	Percent Commodity Sold to:				
					Households	Government	Production	Investment	Exports
87	Paddy (farm gate)	502,560	7.90	8.66	35.7	—	64.3	—	
88	Paddy (wholesale)	228,077	3.59	—	—	8.6	57.0	—	34.5
89	Rice & rice products (mill gate)	300,786	4.73	—	—	—	100.0	—	—
90	Rice & rice products (wholesale)	324,136	5.10	—	—	7.3	67.8	2.2	22.6
91	Rice & rice products (retail)	285,016	4.48	—	99.6	0.1	0.3	—	—
92	Wheat & wheat flour (retail)	14,378	0.23	—	92.5	—	7.5	—	—
93	Other grains (farm gate)	103,264	1.62	31.47	16.7	—	83.3	—	—
94	Other grains & flour (wholesale)	115,288	1.81	—	—	0.2	99.8	—	—
95	Other grains & flour (retail)	127,623	2.01	—	100.0	—	—	—	—
96	Pulses (farm gate)	39,856	0.63	87.95	9.3	—	90.7	—	—
97	Pulses (wholesale)	68,760	1.08	—	—	7.4	92.6	—	—
98	Pulses (retail)	73,575	1.16	—	98.8	0.1	1.1	—	—
99	Groundnuts & gingelly (farm gate)	458,557	7.21	—	5.0	9.7	85.3	—	—
100	Groundnuts & gingelly (wholesale)	446,727	7.02	—	—	—	84.6	—	15.4
101	Edible oils (mill gate)	421,870	6.63	—	—	1.3	19.0	—	79.7
102	Edible oils (retail)	139,258	2.19	—	99.8	—	0.2	—	—
103	Spices (wholesale)	116,272	1.83	97.68	—	2.1	97.9	—	—
104	Spices (retail)	128,325	2.02	—	99.7	—	0.3	—	—
105	Jaggery & sugarcane (farm gate)	3,468	0.05	98.79	1.3	0.4	98.3	—	—
106	Jaggery & sugarcane (wholesale)	3,751	0.06	—	—	—	100.0	—	—

107	Jaggery & sugarcane (retail)	4,167	0.07	—	97.6	—	2.4	—	—
108	Vegetables & fruit (farm gate)	94,602	1.49	51.07	11.4	2.3	86.3	—	—
109	Vegetables & fruit (retail)	108,957	1.71	—	95.5	2.9	1.6	—	—
110	Livestock feed (mill gate)	32,394	0.51	—	—	—	66.0	—	34.0
111	Livestock feed (retail)	26,113	0.41	—	—	—	100.0	—	—
112	Sugar, sugar products, & honey (retail)	28,866	0.45	—	95.0	—	5.0	—	—
113	Milk (farm gate)	45,848	0.72	—	29.3	51.7	19.0	—	—
114	Milk & fresh milk products (retail)	43,637	0.69	—	65.8	3.4	1.9	—	29.0
115	Alcoholic beverages (retail)	21,284	0.33	—	95.9	—	4.1	—	—
116	Meats, fish, & poultry (retail)	54,195	0.85	5.61	99.1	—	0.9	—	—
117	Eggs (farm gate)	4,680	0.07	—	29.1	—	61.5	—	9.4
118	Eggs (retail)	3,298	0.05	—	98.2	—	1.8	—	—
119	Wholesale import services	24,470	0.38	—	—	—	100.0	—	—
120	Baby foods & processed milk products (retail)	3,434	0.05	—	100.0	—	—	—	—
121	Ice cream (factory gate)	1,554	0.02	—	—	—	100.0	—	—
122	Ice cream (retail)	204	—	—	100.0	—	—	—	—
123	Snack foods (retail)	13,185	0.21	—	95.7	—	4.3	—	—
124	Bakery products (factory gate)	423	0.01	—	—	—	100.0	—	—
125	Bakery products (retail)	5,376	0.08	62.44	91.4	—	8.6	—	—
126	Tea & coffee powder (retail)	7,728	0.12	—	84.8	1.5	13.7	—	—
127	Meals & drinks out (retail)	17,066	0.27	—	99.4	0.6	—	—	—
128	Soft drinks (factory gate)	2,548	0.04	61.16	—	—	100.0	—	—
129	Soft drinks (retail)	2,931	0.05	—	100.0	—	—	—	—
130	Fertilizers (retail)	90,094	1.42	—	—	—	100.0	—	—
131	Flowers (farm gate)	876	0.01	—	—	—	100.0	—	—
132	Flowers (retail)	1,388	0.02	—	100.0	—	—	—	—

TABLE 7.2
Continued

Account Number	Commodity Name	Total Transactions (thous Rs)	Percent Total Commodity Transactions	Percent Imported	Percent Commodity Sold to: Households	Government	Production	Investment	Exports
133	Live animals (farm gate)	119,447	1.88	14.25	1.8	—	84.0	14.2	—
134	Live animals (wholesale)	48,072	0.76	—	—	—	17.7	17.7	64.6
135	Manures (retail)	10,059	0.16	30.41	—	—	100.0	—	—
136	Farm tools & implements (retail)	11,566	0.18	—	—	—	17.2	82.8	—
138	Seeds & seedlings (farm gate)	2,772	0.04	—	—	—	100.0	—	—
139	Seeds & seedlings (retail)	14,593	0.23	—	—	0.7	95.7	—	3.6
140	Agrochemicals (retail)	11,122	0.17	—	—	—	55.1	44.9	—
141	Silt (retail)	499	0.01	—	—	—	—	100.0	—
142	Fodder (retail)	20,179	0.32	—	—	—	100.0	—	—
143	Rice & flour milling services (retail)	8,236	0.12	—	100.0	—	—	—	—
144	Decortication & oil extraction service	470	0.01	—	100.0	—	—	—	—
145	Personal services	7,046	0.11	—	100.0	—	—	—	—
146	Tailoring	5,840	0.09	—	100.0	—	—	—	—
147	Cycle repair & rental	789	0.01	—	100.0	—	—	—	—
148	Repair of motor vehicles (private)	4,048	0.06	—	83.6	12.8	3.7	—	—
149	Repair of motor vehicles (government)	1,317	0.02	100.00	—	100.0	—	—	—
150	Professional services	2,922	0.05	—	84.5	15.5	—	—	—
151	Medicine & private medical & veterinary services	27,269	0.43	—	99.2	—	0.8	—	—
152	Education services	6,252	0.10	30.07	100.0	—	—	—	—
153	Taxi, bus, & rickshaw rides	39,894	0.63	—	98.8	1.2	—	—	—

154	Rail transport (passengers & freight)	3,432	0.05	—	66.3	26.9	—	—	6.8
155	Truck transport	43,523	0.68	—	—	11.2	12.3	—	76.5
156	Machinery hire	16,925	0.27	36.60	—	1.3	54.4	44.2	—
157	Machinery service & repair (incl. blacksmithing)	27,724	0.44	1.45	—	5.3	43.0	51.7	—
158	Post & telecommunication	13,216	0.21	—	56.5	41.3	2.3	—	—
159	Printing	4,172	0.07	—	—	48.3	13.7	—	38.0
160	Entertainment	14,480	0.23	—	100.0	—	—	—	—
161	Storage services	755	0.01	—	—	100.0	—	—	—
162	Hardware (wholesale)	21,448	0.34	86.01	—	—	86.7	13.3	—
163	Hardware (retail)	37,534	0.59	—	—	12.9	68.5	18.6	—
164	Optical & photographic services	729	0.01	—	100.0	—	—	—	—
165	Laundry & drycleaning	4,623	0.07	—	100.0	—	—	—	—
166	Boarding services	1,098	0.02	—	—	—	—	—	100.0
167	Insurance	1,908	0.03	100.00	100.0	—	—	—	—
168	Tobacco, beedies, & betel (producer)	32,664	0.51	94.14	—	—	100.0	—	—
169	Tobacco, beedies, & betel (retail)	36,608	0.58	—	100.0	—	—	—	—
170	Electricity	69,393	1.09	—	15.7	3.0	81.3	—	—
171	Lumber, timber, & sawmilling (producer)	31,527	0.50	23.98	—	10.3	89.7	—	—
172	Firewood & charcoal (retail)	15,586	0.24	—	90.0	—	10.0	—	—
173	Cow dung (retail)	6	—	—	—	—	100.0	—	—
174	Kerosene	20,554	0.32	—	100.0	—	—	—	—
175	Fuel & oils	67,995	1.07	—	8.9	22.4	68.7	—	—
176	Toiletries	8,041	0.13	—	96.4	3.6	—	—	—
177	Soft furnishings (producer)	2,507	0.04	—	—	9.3	—	—	90.7
178	Soft furnishings (retail)	2,877	0.05	—	81.7	11.5	6.8	—	—
179	Electrical appliances	17,765	0.28	—	57.6	6.0	32.2	4.2	—
180	Metal vessels & pottery (producer)	1,701	0.03	—	—	—	100.0	—	—
181	Metal vessels & pottery (retail)	9,085	0.14	—	100.0	—	—	—	—
182	Kitchenware (producer)	884	0.01	—	—	—	100.0	—	—

TABLE 7.2
Continued

Account Number	Commodity Name	Total Transactions (thous Rs)	Percent Total Commodity Transactions	Percent Imported	Percent Commodity Sold to: Households	Government	Production	Investment	Exports
183	Kitchenware (retail)	2,141	0.03	—	60.4	—	—	—	39.6
184	Cycles (retail)	2,120	0.03	—	100.0	—	—	—	—
185	Wood furniture	2,769	0.04	—	22.4	—	—	77.6	—
186	Metal furniture	1,555	0.02	—	36.1	—	—	—	63.9
187	Cotton & artificial cloth, ready-made clothes (producer)	50,531	0.79	35.88	—	—	100.0	—	—
188	Cotton & artificial cloth, ready-made clothes (retail)	86,054	1.35	—	99.8	—	0.2	—	—
189	Silk cloth (producer)	224,167	3.52	—	—	—	3.2	—	96.8
190	Silk cloth (retail)	10,701	0.16	—	99.5	—	0.5	—	—
191	Cotton yarn (wholesale)	12,957	0.20	100.00	—	—	100.0	—	—
192	Silk yarn (wholesale)	145,905	2.29	99.45	—	—	100.0	—	—
193	Leather (producer)	27	—	100.00	—	100.0	—	—	—
194	Footwear & leather products (retail)	24,040	0.38	—	1.4	—	—	—	98.6
195	Skins & hides (producer)	28,698	0.45	—	—	—	100.0	—	—
196	Matches & paper products (producer)	12,464	0.20	—	—	0.1	63.1	—	36.8
197	Matches & paper products (retail)	6,824	0.11	—	70.9	4.9	24.2	—	—
198	Soap & candles (producer)	20,416	0.32	61.29	—	—	100.0	—	—
199	Soap & candles (retail)	24,536	0.39	—	94.4	—	5.6	—	—
200	Motor vehicles	1,894	0.03	—	21.9	—	33.6	—	44.5
201	Jewelry (retail)	18,818	0.30	21.91	92.0	—	8.0	—	—
202	Lottery tickets	5,772	0.09	—	100.0	—	—	—	—
203	Irrigation water	2,256	0.04	—	—	—	100.0	—	—
204	Industrial water	585	0.01	100.00	—	18.0	82.0	—	—
205	Chemical products (producer)	7,671	0.12	13.65	—	8.9	91.1	—	—

206	Chemical products (retail)	5,037	0.08	—	—	12.8	37.7	49.5	—
207	Plastic products (producer)	1,240	0.02	63.48	—	—	100.0	—	—
208	Plastic products (retail)	809	0.01	—	—	1.1	98.9	—	—
209	Tile, bricks, & stone (retail)	24,660	0.39	—	—	7.0	69.8	23.1	—
210	Cement (retail)	27,123	0.43	—	—	—	98.9	1.1	—
211	Metal products & materials	16,036	0.25	51.65	—	8.0	92.0	—	—
212	Raw & scrap metal	4,107	0.06	—	—	—	100.0	—	—
213	Educational aids	8,236	0.13	—	93.5	6.5	—	—	—
214	Fiber, coir, & jute materials (producer)	3,117	0.05	70.82	—	—	100.0	—	—
215	Fiber, coir, & jute materials (retail)	1,443	0.02	—	—	—	100.0	—	—
216	Twine & thread	1,702	0.03	—	—	—	100.0	—	—
217	Glass products	1,311	0.02	—	—	—	100.0	—	—
219	Fancy goods	1,827	0.03	—	—	—	100.0	—	—
220	Construction & carpentry services	180,127	2.83	—	25.5	—	1.6	72.9	—
	Total	6,361,693	100.00	9.10	27.7	2.9	51.8	3.5	14.1

Note: All prices are final demand prices unless otherwise indicated.

TABLE 7.3
Structure of Private-Sector Production, 1982/83 SAM

Account Number	Sector Name	Gross Output[a] (thous Rs)	Value Added (thous Rs)	Value Added/ Gross Output Ratio (%)	Share of Sector in Regional: Gross Output (%)	Share of Sector in Regional: Value Added (%)
28	Small farms (rural)	335,166	259,938	77.56	5.53	11.71
29	Large farms (rural)	806,317	634,853	78.74	13.29	28.61
30	Other agriculture (rural)	52,642	38,344	72.84	0.87	1.73
31	Agriculture (urban)	50,438	34,906	69.20	0.83	1.57
32	Agricultural inputs & machinery service centers	100,160	49,436	49.36	1.65	2.23
33	Rice mills	302,346	52,774	17.45	4.98	2.38
34	Other grain mills	17,311	7,407	42.79	0.29	0.33
35	Oil extraction mills	451,871	71,901	15.91	7.45	3.24
36	Agricultural wholesale merchants	1,162,305	131,106	11.28	19.16	5.91
37	Livestock traders	48,061	3,581	7.45	0.79	0.16
38	Chemical products manufacturing	17,528	8,128	46.37	0.29	0.37
39	Printing	4,171	1,965	47.10	0.07	0.09
40	Leather products manufacturing & sales	52,707	18,179	34.49	0.87	0.82
41	Tobacco manufacturing	1,914	1,317	68.83	0.03	0.06
42	Matches & paper products manufacturing	12,464	6,241	50.07	0.21	0.28
43	Plastic & rubber products manufacturing (including tire retreading)	742	383	51.66	0.01	0.02
44	Metal products manufacturing	10,627	4,795	45.12	0.18	0.22
45	Handicrafts & *khadi*	8,492	5,059	59.57	0.14	0.23
46	Pottery	3,772	2,174	57.64	0.07	0.11
47	Furniture manufacturing & sales	4,345	2,491	57.34	0.07	0.11

48	Engineering works	27,429	13,849	50.49	0.45	0.62
49	Motor vehicle repairs, service, & sales	4,811	2,382	49.51	0.08	0.11
50	Blacksmiths	3,083	2,407	78.08	0.05	0.11
51	Sawmills, carpentry & timber shops	19,899	12,859	64.62	0.33	0.58
52	Electrical goods servicing	1,680	1,092	65.02	0.03	0.05
53	Soda & ice cream manufacturing	2,544	1,297	51.00	0.04	0.06
54	Jewelry & goldsmith services	14,695	9,343	63.58	0.24	0.42
55	Silk textiles	224,967	78,603	34.94	3.70	3.54
56	Cotton textiles	25,031	10,310	41.19	0.41	0.46
57	Vessel & metal goods sales	8,399	4,137	49.26	0.14	0.19
58	Hardware & electrical goods sales	60,422	25,317	41.90	1.00	1.14
59	Firewood & charcoal manufacturing & sales	15,023	8,473	56.40	0.25	0.38
60	Cycle shops	2,209	1,105	50.03	0.04	0.05
61	Photo & optical shops	729	486	66.64	0.00	0.02
62	Truck transport services	43,523	25,034	57.52	0.72	1.13
63	Bus & taxi services	18,768	11,569	61.64	0.31	0.52
64	Pawnbrokers & local financial services	31,128	30,868	99.17	0.51	1.39
65	Lottery agents	5,574	1,994	35.77	0.09	0.09
66	Cinemas	14,480	8,168	56.41	0.24	0.37
67	Restaurants & hotels	17,382	8,458	48.66	0.29	0.38
68	Personal services	13,104	12,263	93.58	0.22	0.55
69	Textile shops	98,375	41,770	42.46	1.62	1.88
70	Handlooms	4,199	2,663	63.42	0.07	0.12
71	Gasoline, diesel, & kerosene sales	75,651	26,622	35.19	1.25	1.20
72	Medicine shops & private medical services	27,269	15,380	56.40	0.45	0.69
73	Liquor sales	21,284	10,106	47.48	0.35	0.46
74	Commercial godowns & gunny sales	1,514	792	52.31	0.02	0.04

TABLE 7.3
Continued

Account Number	Sector Name	Gross Output[a] (thous Rs)	Value Added (thous Rs)	Value Added/ Gross Output Ratio (%)	Share of Sector in Regional: Gross Output (%)	Share of Sector in Regional: Value Added (%)
75	Petty shops	38,474	10,815	28.10	0.63	0.49
76	Tea & snack food shops (incl. bakeries)	11,961	6,643	55.54	0.20	0.30
77	General provisions & grocery shops	788,245	112,182	14.23	12.99	5.06
78	Vegetable, fruit, & flower shops	100,216	17,528	17.49	1.65	0.79
79	Dairy, fish, & meat shops	68,427	16,796	24.55	1.13	0.76
80	Installment plan shops	2,732	1,208	44.23	0.05	0.05
81	Masonry materials manufacturing & sales	45,549	24,820	54.49	0.75	1.12
82	Wholesale importers	24,470	3,626	14.82	0.40	0.16
83	Commercial banks	4,737	4,015	84.76	0.08	0.18
84	Professional services	2,922	1,919	65.68	0.05	0.09
85	Construction contractors	179,673	97,706	54.38	2.96	4.40
86	Laundry & drycleaning	4,623	2,680	57.97	0.08	0.12
	Total private sector	5,498,580	2,002,263	36.26	90.64	90.22

[a]Gross output is defined here as total sales, and we have not netted out the cost of commodities that are simply bought and sold by trading establishments. The gross outputs for trading establishments are therefore higher than would normally be the case and their ratios of value added to gross output are correspondingly lower.

general provision shops, the various transactions involved in moving paddy from the farm to the mill and rice from the mill to the consumer are all explicitly traced in the SAM.

This method of accounting also led us to define the gross output for each sector as total sales. By convention, the gross output of trading establishments is usually defined net of the cost of commodities that are simply purchased and resold without any intermediate processing or production activity. Our definition, therefore, leads to much higher gross outputs for trading establishments, and to lower ratios of value added to gross output for these sectors.

The four agricultural sectors are small farms (1 hectare or less) and large farms (greater than 1 hectare) in the rural villages; other rural agriculture, predominantly livestock production by landless workers; and urban agriculture, the farming activities of landed households and landless workers residing in urban villages and towns. The agricultural sectors were not disaggregated by commodity because of difficulties in allocating many overhead costs. However, since all transactions are recorded by commodity in the SAM, the purchase of farm inputs and the disposition of output are recorded by commodity.

The government accounts are defined in Table 7.4. These are the major types of accounts used by the government itself. Detailed information on revenue and costs were obtained at the district and *taluk* levels for most types of account. Where only district-level data were available, these were scaled down to the study region using some appropriate factor, such as the share of the district's schools, rail line, or population located within the study region.

The household groups were defined following the sampling strata used in the IFPRI-TNAU surveys (Table 7.5). The definition of the factor accounts is also shown in Table 7.5. Only actual transactions of factors are recorded in the SAM. Payments to own factors by self-employed persons are treated as profits rather than factor payments. Land rents and sales are recorded in separate accounts, but the renting and sale of buildings were combined because of the small value of transactions involved.

In estimating SAM entries from survey data, sample means for households or firms had to be multiplied by relevant population estimates. In the case of households, we had access to the 1981 population census. We first extrapolated the rural and urban population counts to 1982/83 using the average annual growth rates between the 1971 and 1981 population censuses. Then, assuming the same family sizes and distribution of household types as observed in the 1982/83 IFPRI-TNAU rural and urban surveys, we were able to estimate the number of households and people in each of our household categories in 1982/

TABLE 7.4
Structure of Government Sector Production, 1982/83 SAM

Account Number	*Sector Name*	*Gross Output (thous Rs)*	*Value Added (thous Rs)*	*Value Added/ Gross Output Ratio (%)*	*Share of Sector in Regional:*	
					Gross Output (%)	*Value Added (%)*
13	Agriculture & marketing	14,966	8,396	56.10	0.25	0.38
14	Animal husbandry, forestry, & fishing	5,723	3,193	55.80	0.09	0.14
15	Irrigation & drainage	3,367	1,837	54.57	0.06	0.08
16	Health & education	120,127	82,083	68.33	1.98	3.70
17	Highways & buildings	16,413	2,407	14.67	0.27	0.11
18	Railways	9,761	3,754	38.46	0.16	0.17
19	Post & telecommunications	8,871	6,749	76.08	0.15	0.30
20	Cooperatives	164,336	62,300	37.91	2.71	2.81
21	Banking (nationalized)	16,145	12,286	76.10	0.27	0.55
22	Electricity	69,393	10,020	14.44	1.14	0.45
23	Road transport	21,812	3,695	16.94	0.36	0.17
24	Civil supplies	82,191	2,466	3.00	1.35	0.11
25	Other	12,634	8,951	70.85	0.21	0.40
26	Local government	21,841	8,815	40.36	0.36	0.40
	Total government	567,580	216,952	38.22	9.36	9.78

83 (Table 7.5). In the case of nonfarm businesses, an estimate of the population size of each type of business was available from the sampling frame used in the IFPRI-TNAU survey (see Chapter 2).

Two simplifications were introduced in estimating the SAM. First, we did not attempt to estimate the full matrix of interhousehold income transfers, but only the total of all transfers paid and received by each household type. Second, apart from agriculture, the profits from all production sectors were accumulated into a single account before allocating to households. This greatly simplified the number of allocations to be made and was also consistent with the nature of the available survey data.

Since most of the income and expenditure entries in the SAM were estimated from survey data, it was not surprising to find imbalances between the row and column sums for most accounts. Part of the discrepancies can be attributed to sampling errors, but part is undoubtedly due to incorrect answers from respondents and to errors in entering and processing the data. In general, we gave greater credence to expenditure rather than income data and adjusted the latter where necessary. We found particularly large discrepancies between the commodity transactions reported by rice millers and agricultural wholesale merchants, and independent data provided from official sources on the amounts of agricultural commodities produced and traded in the study region. We used the latter to correct the transactions data but used the survey data to estimate unit costs.

The least satisfactory data were for savings and capital flows. We simplified the estimation by defining a single combined capital account for the region, but even then most of the entries in the row account had to be derived as residuals to balance the SAM.

Finally, it needs to be noted that there are no accounts in the SAM to record changes in stocks. Such data are simply not available at a regional level. Accordingly, estimated commodity transactions in the region incorporate the value of any stock changes as well as the value of production during the accounting year. This is particularly troublesome for livestock, since more animals than usual were sold in 1982/83 as a result of the severe drought.

An Aggregate SAM for 1982/83

The full SAM is discussed in the next section. Here we highlight a few key features of the region's economy in 1982/83 with the aid of the aggregated SAM in Table 7.6.

TABLE 7.5
Sources of Household Income, 1982/83 SAM (thous Rs)

	Rural Villages				Urban Villages			Towns			
Income Source	*Small Farmers*	*Large Farmers*	*Landless*	*Other*	*Agric. Dependent*	*Self-Employed Nonagric.*	*Employed Nonagric.*	*Agric. Dependent*	*Self-Employed Nonagric.*	*Employed Nonagric.*	*Total*
Transfers from:											
Government	—	—	—	—	—	—	—	—	—	29	29
Other households	3,890	8,957	1,857	3,444	1,168	221	310	372	413	829	21,459
Rest of world	14,474	24,221	11,815	9,619	5,194	1,925	1,953	1,861	4,437	16,994	92,494
Factor earnings											
Interest & dividends	—	50	1,800	—	182	62	74	2,614	6,758	1,054	12,594
Bullock hire	7,782	5,643	3,274	—	270	—	—	532	—	—	17,500
Land rents	5,439	9,942	623	—	1,298	—	—	78	—	—	17,380
Land sales	34,429	74,902	—	—	—	—	—	—	—	—	109,331
Building rents & sales	—	53	37	—	752	447	379	892	7,735	2,402	12,697
White-collar employment	14,651	51,513	325	35,233	3,275	30,853	19,013	400	2,781	76,932	234,977
Agric. labor	55,870	17,368	104,926	8,621	12,869	1,116	970	8,661	222	3,286	213,909
Nonagric. labor	52,046	11,186	35,430	21,035	6,035	2,473	8,280	3,994	9,325	68,289	218,095
Business earnings											
Farm	207,637	455,473	32,408	—	17,023	—	—	9,864	—	—	722,405
Nonfarm	142,350	64,162	7,321	42,324	1,538	19,870	1,784	7,075	286,730	42,016	615,169
Total	538,568	723,470	199,816	120,276	49,604	56,967	32,763	36,343	318,401	211,831	2,288,039
Rs/capita	717	1,543	384	628	1,005	2,698	1,285	1,139	4,165	1,349	998
No. of households	154,771	96,652	107,161	39,489	9,587	4,100	4,950	5,595	13,411	27,543	463,259
Population	750,639	468,762	519,731	191,522	49,373	21,115	25,493	31,892	76,443	156,995	2,291,965

HOUSEHOLDS. Total household income was Rs 2,288 million. Given an estimated population of 2.3 million, this implies a per capita income of Rs 998 (about US$100). Gross national product (GNP) was US$260 per capita in 1983 (World Bank 1986), so our estimate is not unreasonable for this predominantly rural economy, especially in a drought year. Household savings were 21.5 percent of total income, despite the drought year.

GOVERNMENT. In its current account, the government received Rs 127 million in local taxes and a net transfer of Rs 44 million from district and state governments. Its productive earnings included Rs 320 million from the sale of commodities and Rs 76 million from factor earnings (actually interest payments collected by state banks). Thus, 70 percent of total government expenditure was paid from earnings and only 30 percent from taxes and transfers. Local government is therefore predominantly a productive rather than an extractive institution, and we shall treat it as such in reporting the region's income. On this basis, the government produced Rs 568 million of gross output and Rs 217 million of value added. The ratio of value added to gross output is 38.2 percent.

PRODUCTION. Gross output in the private sector was Rs 5,499 million, and value added (profits + factor payments + taxes + retained earnings) was Rs 2,002 million. The average ratio of value added to gross output in the private sector was therefore 36.4 percent, which is very similar to the government-sector ratio.

Adding the government and private sectors together, total regional income is as follows:

	Gross Output (million Rs)	*Value Added (million Rs)*
Government	568	217
Private sector	5,499	2,002
Total	6,067	2,219

Considering that the net domestic product for the entire district was Rs 3,285 million in 1980/81 (see Chapter 2), our estimate of regional value added seems reasonable.

COMMODITIES. The total value of all commodity transactions in the region was Rs 6,362 million. (This does not include the value of noncompetitive imports purchased directly from outside the region.) Of this amount, Rs 578 million was imported by local traders and the rest

TABLE 7.6
Summary of 1982/83 SAM (thous Rs)

	Households	*Government*	*Taxes*	*Production*	*Commodities*	*Factors*	*Capital*	*Rest of World*	*Row Sums*
Households	21,460	29		1,337,575		836,482		92,494	2,288,039
Government			126,764		320,350	75,940		44,524	567,578
Taxes	5,068	3,635		118,062					126,764
Production					5,462,718	35,864			5,498,580
Commodities	1,762,927	186,731		3,291,150			222,219	898,665	6,361,692
Factors	5,800	210,399		546,008			134,680	51,399	948,286
Capital	492,784	2,900		504				−88,233	407,955
Rest of world		163,884		205,285	578,623		51,055		998,847
Column sums	2,288,039	567,578	126,764	5,498,580	6,361,691	948,286	407,954	998,849	17,197,741

Note: Discrepancies in totals are due to rounding.

was supplied from local production. Commodity exports were valued at Rs 898 million.

CAPITAL. Total gross investment in the region was Rs 408 million, which was entirely funded with local savings. There was also a net capital outflow from the region of Rs 88 million, despite the fact that 1982/83 was a drought year.

BALANCE OF PAYMENTS. The region imported commodities worth Rs 998 million and exported only Rs 898 million worth. There were remittances to households and governments of Rs 92 million and Rs 44 million, respectively, and factor earnings brought in another Rs 51 million. This leaves a net surplus of Rs 88 million, which enters the SAM as a net capital outflow from the region.

A Full SAM for 1982/83

The full SAM is too large to include in this volume, but copies are available from the International Food Policy Research Institute upon request. Some salient features of the economy are highlighted here.

COMMODITIES. The value of each commodity transaction, their relative importance, and end user identities are given in Table 7.2.

The commodity transactions can be summarized as follows:

Commodity Group	*Percent Total Transactions*
Agricultural commodities	
Farm gate	21.6
Mill gate	11.9
Wholesale	21.2
Foods (retail)	17.0
Durables	0.6
Services	2.6
Transport	1.4
Fuels and energy	2.7
Farm inputs	2.9
Public utilities	0.2
Other goods	
Factory	7.3
Wholesale	2.8
Retail	7.6

Taken together, agricultural commodities and foods account for 72 percent of the region's commodity transactions, clearly demonstrating the agrarian nature of the local economy.

The importance of agriculture is also shown in the structure of the region's exports:

	Value of Exports (thous Rs)	*Percent Total Exports*
Paddy (wholesale)	78,586	8.8
Rice and rice products (wholesale)	73,386	8.2
Groundnuts and gingelly (wholesale)	68,687	7.6
Edible oils (mill gate)	335,836	37.4
Other agricultural commodities	55,659	6.2
Truck transport	33,284	3.7
Silk cloth (producer)	217,055	24.2
Other nonagricultural commodities	36,171	4.0
Total	898,664	100.0

Agriculture accounts for 68 percent of the region's exports and, because of the drought, groundnuts and edible oils were much more important than paddy and rice in 1982/83. Silk cloth is the most important nonagricultural export, even though its production is limited to the vicinity of a single town—Arni (see Chapter 9).

PRODUCTION. The production transactions for the private sector are summarized in Table 7.3. Agriculture (sectors 28–31) accounts for 20.5 percent of gross output and 43.6 percent of value added in the region's economy. Other important sectors are rice milling (2.4 percent of regional value added), oil extraction mills (3.2 percent), agricultural wholesalers (5.9 percent), general provision and grocery shops (5.1 percent), silk textiles (3.5 percent), and construction services (4.4 percent).

GOVERNMENT. The government's current account is disaggregated into 14 heads of account. Investment activities, including drought relief employment schemes, are included in the capital account. The transactions are summarized in Table 7.4.

FACTORS. The factor accounts record all transactions involving the hiring (or renting) and sale of factors. They do not include any payments to own factors from business activities (these payments are distributed as profits from production sectors to households in the SAM). The value of the factor transactions are as follows: capital—interest payments on loans, Rs 122 million; white-collar workers, Rs 235 million; agricultural labor, Rs 214 million; nonagricultural labor, Rs 218 million;

land rents, Rs 17 million; land sales, Rs 109 million; building rents and sales, Rs 13 million; and bullock rental, Rs 18 million.

HOUSEHOLDS. Table 7.5 summarizes the sources of income for each household group and their per capita incomes. In calculating income, all home-produced foods consumed by the household were valued at farm-gate prices.

The per capita incomes range from Rs 384 for the rural landless laborers to Rs 4,165 for self-employed persons in the urban towns. The average income is Rs 998 per capita, or Rs 4,939 per household.

Within the rural villages, agriculture accounts for the lion's share of the income of the farmers and landless laborers. Taken together, farm income and agricultural factor earnings account for 58 percent of the income of small farmers, 78 percent for large farmers, and 71 percent for landless laborers. In contrast, the nonagricultural households in the villages, which account for 10 percent of the total number of rural households, obtain 93 percent of their income from nonagricultural sources. It is instructive to calculate the number of rupees earned per capita from nonagriculture, either from wage earnings or self-employment. These earnings amount to Rs 259 for small farmers, Rs 161 for large farmers, Rs 82 for landless laborers, and Rs 331 for other nonagricultural households. Thus, although the share of nonagricultural earnings in total income tends to be low for the agriculturally dependent households, sizable earnings are nevertheless obtained from nonagricultural sources. This is encouraging in that it suggests that growth in the nonfarm economy, perhaps as a result of agricultural growth, may have the potential to benefit a broad range of rural households.

Table 7.7 summarizes the ways in which the different household types spend their income. On average, 21.5 percent of household income is saved in the region, but savings range from negative for the poorer rural groups—a reflection, perhaps, of the drought—to 65 percent for the self-employed households in the urban towns. Tax payments are generally low, and most of the income that is not saved is allocated directly to consumption. The average household allocates 74 percent of its total commodity expenditure to foods.

Finally, as a check on our SAM income estimates, we can compare the rural household incomes in the SAM with the direct sample estimates provided by the IFPRI-TNAU household survey in Chapter 3. After converting the latter to 1982/83 prices, the relevant comparisons are to be found in Table 7.8.

There is reasonable agreement between the SAM and survey estimates of total household incomes. Greater discrepancies arise in esti-

TABLE 7.7
Sources of Household Outlays, 1982/83 SAM (thous Rs)

	Rural Villages				*Urban Villages*			*Towns*			
Income Outlay	*Small Farmers*	*Large Farmers*	*Landless*	*Other*	*Agric. Dependent*	*Self-Employed Nonagric.*	*Employed Nonagric.*	*Agric. Dependent*	*Self-Employed Nonagric.*	*Employed Nonagric.*	*Total*
Transfers to other households	4,207	9,521	797	1,428	380	94	2,536	51	2,327	119	21,460
Taxes	1,955	321	78	27	6	2	249	114	1,963	353	5,068
Interest payments	611	1,976	174	269	71	200	584	23	267	1,627	5,802
Commodities											
Foods (retail)	277,370	227,311	181,936	84,041	20,723	12,189	15,572	22,001	77,222	136,695	1,055,060
Foods (farm gate)	87,459	140,559	10,502	3,515	3,651	108	1,113	2,699	726	942	251,274
Transport	10,642	16,926	2,835	3,467	904	542	1,106	574	1,841	2,865	41,703
Durables	2,360	7,646	2,186	5,257	263	323	1,378	306	1,960	2,639	24,319
Services	22,080	26,928	6,451	6,516	2,020	1,151	2,517	1,627	6,064	13,690	89,044
Household fuels	8,093	8,378	3,528	1,747	1,154	760	1,139	1,653	6,109	12,922	45,483
Vehicle fuel & oils	2,990	558	1,297	557	—	7	177	—	438	39	6,063
Public utilities[a]	2,092	1,306	1,448	534	130	79	637	86	400	751	7,463
Other goods (retail)	47,851	113,207	19,444	16,459	5,334	1,654	4,282	2,563	12,288	19,436	242,518
Savings	70,855	168,828	−30,860	−3,540	14,968	39,859	1,475	4,646	206,798	19,755	492,784
Total	538,568	723,467	199,816	120,276	49,604	56,968	32,765	36,343	318,403	211,833	2,288,040

Note: Discrepancies in totals are due to rounding.
[a]Electricity, post, and telecommunications.

TABLE 7.8
Rural Household Incomes, 1982/83 IFPRI/TNAU Survey and 1982/83 SAM (1982/83 prices)

Income Source	*Small Farms* 1982/83 Survey[a]	*Small Farms* SAM	*Large Farms* 1982/83 Survey[a]	*Large Farms* SAM	*Landless* 1982/83 Survey[a]	*Landless* SAM	*Other Rural* 1982/83 Survey[a]	*Other Rural* SAM
Farm income	2,271	1,392	5,388	4,772	26	334	63	—
Agricultural wage earnings	378	361	146	181	946	979	260	218
White-collar earnings	77	94	463	533	4	4	846	892
Other wage earnings	227	335	129	116	315	330	699	533
Nonfarm business income	293	920	394	664	41	68	544	1,071
Other income	194	153	444	448	157	151	317	330
Total income	3,440	3,255	6,964	6,713	1,488	1,865	2,728	3,045

Note: Discrepancies in totals are due to rounding.
[a]Does not include nonpaddy farms.

mating the composition of total income for both small and large farms. This is partly because the survey estimates in Table 7.8 pertain only to paddy farms, whereas the SAM estimates include the less profitable nonpaddy farms. It is also because the survey gave a higher estimate of regional groundnut production than is consistent with the regional data used in the SAM. The SAM also gives higher values of nonfarm business income for all household groups. Since the SAM is based on a more exhaustive and consistent set of nonfarm business data for the region, we conclude that there may have been some underreporting of nonfarm income in the survey during the 1982/83 drought.

Conclusions

A number of salient features of the regional economy emerge from the SAM. First, agriculture is clearly the mainstay of the regional economy. In 1982/83, agriculture accounted for 44 percent of the region's income and agro-industry accounted for another 14 percent. Agricultural commodities also accounted for 68 percent of the region's exports and for 72 percent of the total commodity transactions within the region.

Second, the region's 2.3 million people had an average per capita income of Rs 998 (approximately US$100) in 1982/83, which was about 40 percent of the national per capita income. Per capita incomes ranged from Rs 384 for the landless to Rs 4,165 for self-employed persons living in local towns. Remittances from outside the region were not generally important, accounting for only 4 percent of average household income.

Third, government activity accounted for about 10 percent of regional value added in 1982/83. The government also generated 70 percent of its own revenue from commodity sales and factor earnings, so that overall it was a productive rather than an extractive institution. Local tax revenues from households, businesses, and commodities amounted to Rs 127 million, or about Rs 55 per capita.

Fourth, in 1982/83 there was a net capital outflow from the region of Rs 88 million—an amount equal to 18 percent of total private savings. Part of the reason for this outflow must lie with more attractive investment opportunities available elsewhere in India, but it also represents a significant loss of investable resources that might have been used to foster the region's further development.

CHAPTER 8

An Analysis of the Indirect Effects of Agricultural Growth on the Regional Economy

Peter B. R. Hazell, C. Ramasamy, and V. Rajagopalan

THIS CHAPTER DEVELOPS an extended input-output model to provide a quantitative analysis of the direct and indirect impacts of increased agricultural production on the regional economy. The model is calibrated for 1982/83 using the 1982/83 social accounting matrix (SAM) (see Chapter 7).

Increases in paddy and groundnut output have been the predominant sources of growth in the regional economy in the past decade, and these have inevitably generated downstream growth in many other sectors of the economy. However, there have been other sources of growth that are not related to the production of these crops. These include substantial government expenditures on health, education, water, bus services, and rural electrification, and autonomous private investments in industries such as silk weaving, chemical manufacturing, and tanneries. Milk production has also increased in response to Operation Flood. There have also been significant changes in the relative prices of many commodities since the early 1970s. The real price of paddy, for example, has declined by about 10 percent, while the price of groundnuts has increased by 50 percent.

In order to unravel the impact of increases in paddy and groundnut production from all these other autonomous sources of growth in the economy, it is necessary to construct a picture of the regional economy as it would have been in the early 1980s had agricultural growth not been achieved. A key element in our analysis is to use the model to construct an estimate of this hypothetical situation for the economy, and then to make comparisons against the situation with agricultural growth.

A Model of the Regional Economy

The SAM and Its Accounting Identities

Since the SAM is a double-entry accounting system, we can use either the row or column accounts to write it out in mathematical form. The rows provide the statement of receipts for each account, whereas the columns provide the statement of expenditure. For example, the row for the *h*th household type in Table 8.1 reads:

$$Y_h = \Sigma_{h^*} H_{hh^*} + \Sigma_g H_{hg} + \Sigma_j V_{hj}$$

$$[\text{Income}] = \begin{bmatrix}\text{Transfers}\\ \text{from other}\\ \text{households}\end{bmatrix} + \begin{bmatrix}\text{Transfers from}\\ \text{government}\end{bmatrix} + \begin{bmatrix}\text{Profits received}\\ \text{from production}\\ \text{activities}\end{bmatrix}$$

$$+ \Sigma_f F_{hf} + R_h$$

$$+ \begin{bmatrix}\text{Factor}\\ \text{payments}\\ \text{received}\end{bmatrix} + \begin{bmatrix}\text{Income from}\\ \text{outside region}\end{bmatrix}$$

whereas the corresponding column is:

$$Y_h = \Sigma_{h^*} H_{h^*h} + T_h + \Sigma_i C_{ih}$$

$$\begin{bmatrix}\text{Total}\\ \text{outlays}\end{bmatrix} = \begin{bmatrix}\text{Transfers to}\\ \text{other households}\end{bmatrix} + [\text{Taxes}] + \begin{bmatrix}\text{Consumption}\\ \text{expenditures}\end{bmatrix}$$

$$+ S_h + \Sigma_f F_{fh}$$

$$+ [\text{Savings}] + \begin{bmatrix}\text{Factor}\\ \text{payments}\end{bmatrix}$$

By definition, total outlays must equal total receipts for each and every account, so that the row and column sums are identical in each and every case. Since we shall be building a model to predict the variables X, Y, Z, G, and F, it will be more useful to work with the row accounts. These are stated below for the regional SAM in Table 8.1 (figures in parentheses against the account name are the number of equations).

HOUSEHOLD ACCOUNTS (h)

$$Y_h = \Sigma_{h^*} H_{hh^*} + \sum_g H_{hg} + \sum_j V_{hj}$$

$$[\text{Income}] = \begin{bmatrix}\text{Transfers}\\ \text{from other}\\ \text{households}\end{bmatrix} + \begin{bmatrix}\text{Transfers from}\\ \text{government}\end{bmatrix} + \begin{bmatrix}\text{Profits}\\ \text{received from}\\ \text{production}\end{bmatrix}$$

$$+ \quad \Sigma_f F_{hf} \quad + \quad R_h$$

$$+ \begin{bmatrix}\text{Factor}\\ \text{payments}\\ \text{received}\end{bmatrix} + \begin{bmatrix}\text{Income from}\\ \text{outside region}\end{bmatrix}$$

GOVERNMENT DEPARTMENT ACCOUNTS (g)

$$G_g = R_g + \Sigma_i D_{gi}$$

$$[\text{Revenue}] = \begin{bmatrix}\text{Revenue allocation}\\ \text{from total tax}\\ \text{receipts}\end{bmatrix} + \begin{bmatrix}\text{Sale of}\\ \text{commodities}\\ \text{and services}\end{bmatrix}$$

$$+ \quad \Sigma_f F_{gf}$$

$$+ \begin{bmatrix}\text{Interest}\\ \text{and rents}\\ \text{collected}\end{bmatrix}$$

TAX ACCOUNT (1)

$$T = \sum_h T_h + \sum_g T_g + \sum_j T_j$$

$$[\text{Taxes}] = \begin{bmatrix}\text{Personal}\\ \text{taxes}\end{bmatrix} + \begin{bmatrix}\text{Taxes paid by}\\ \text{government}\\ \text{departments}\end{bmatrix} + \begin{bmatrix}\text{Business}\\ \text{taxes}\end{bmatrix}$$

$$+ \quad R$$

$$+ \begin{bmatrix}\text{Net transfers}\\ \text{from state}\\ \text{and district}\\ \text{government on}\\ \text{current account}\end{bmatrix}$$

PRIVATE-SECTOR PRODUCTION ACCOUNTS (j)

$$X_j = \Sigma_i D_{ji} + \sum_f F_{jf}$$

$$\begin{bmatrix}\text{Gross}\\ \text{sales}\end{bmatrix} = \begin{bmatrix}\text{Sale of}\\ \text{commodities}\\ \text{and services}\end{bmatrix} + \begin{bmatrix}\text{Earnings on}\\ \text{rented factors}\end{bmatrix}$$

COMMODITY ACCOUNTS (i)

$$Z_i = \Sigma_h C_{ih} + \sum_g C_{ig} + \Sigma_j C_{ij}$$

$$\begin{bmatrix}\text{Total}\\ \text{sales}\end{bmatrix} = \begin{bmatrix}\text{Household}\\ \text{consumption}\\ \text{demands}\end{bmatrix} + \begin{bmatrix}\text{Government}\\ \text{current account}\\ \text{demands}\end{bmatrix} + \begin{bmatrix}\text{Intermediate}\\ \text{demands}\end{bmatrix}$$

TABLE 8.1
Schematic Version of the SAM for North Arcot

	Households *(h^*)*	*Government Departments* *(g)*	*Taxes*	*Production* *(j)*	*Commodities* *(i)*	*Factors* *(f)*	*Combined Capital*	*Rest of World*	*Row Sums*
Households (h)	Inter-household transfers H_{hh^*}	Government transfers H_{hg}		Profits V_{hj}		Factor earnings F_{hf}		Remittances from outside region R_h	Y_h
Government departments (g)			Revenue allocation to departments R_g		Commodities supplied by government D_{gi}	Factor earnings F_{gf}			G_g
Taxes	Personal taxes T_h	Taxes paid by government businesses T_g		Business taxes T_j				Net transfers from state and district government on current account R	T

Production (j)					Commodities supplied by private firms D_{ji}	Factor earnings F_{jf}			X_j
Commodities (i)	Consumption expenditure C_{ih}	Current account expenditure C_{ig}		Intermediate inputs C_{ij}			Investment expenditure I_i	Exports E_i	Z_i
Factors (f)	Factor payments F_{fh}	Factor payments F_{fg}		Factor payments F_{fj}			Factor payments I_f	Factor earnings outside region R_f	F_f
Combined capital	Household savings S_h	Public savings S_g		Retained profits S_j				Net capital inflow B	I
Rest of world		Direct imports M_g		Direct imports M_j	Indirect imports through local firms M_i		Direct import of investment goods I_m		M
Column sums	Y_h	G_g	T	X_j	Z_i	F_f	I	M	

$$+ \quad I_i \quad + \quad E_i$$

$$+ \begin{bmatrix}\text{Investment}\\ \text{demands}\end{bmatrix} + [\text{Exports}]$$

FACTOR ACCOUNTS (f)

$$F_f = \sum_h F_{fh} + \Sigma_g F_{fg} + \Sigma_j F_{fj}$$

$$\begin{bmatrix}\text{Factor}\\ \text{income}\end{bmatrix} = \begin{bmatrix}\text{Payments by}\\ \text{households}\end{bmatrix} + \begin{bmatrix}\text{Payments by}\\ \text{government}\end{bmatrix} + \begin{bmatrix}\text{Payments}\\ \text{by firms}\end{bmatrix}$$

$$+ \quad I_f \quad + \quad R_f$$

$$+ \begin{bmatrix}\text{Payments for}\\ \text{investment}\\ \text{activities}\end{bmatrix} + \begin{bmatrix}\text{Factor earnings}\\ \text{outside region}\end{bmatrix}$$

COMBINED CAPITAL ACCOUNT (1)

$$I = \sum_h S_h + \Sigma_g S_g$$

$$\begin{bmatrix}\text{Total}\\ \text{investment}\end{bmatrix} = \begin{bmatrix}\text{Household}\\ \text{savings}\end{bmatrix} + \begin{bmatrix}\text{Government}\\ \text{savings}\end{bmatrix}$$

$$+ \quad \sum_j S_j \quad + \quad B$$

$$+ \begin{bmatrix}\text{Retained}\\ \text{profits}\\ \text{by firms}\end{bmatrix} + \begin{bmatrix}\text{Net capital}\\ \text{inflow to}\\ \text{region}\end{bmatrix}$$

REST-OF-WORLD ACCOUNT (1)

$$M = \Sigma_g M_g + \Sigma_j M_j + \Sigma_i M_i$$

$$\begin{bmatrix}\text{Total}\\ \text{imports}\end{bmatrix} = \begin{bmatrix}\text{Direct}\\ \text{imports by}\\ \text{government}\end{bmatrix} + \begin{bmatrix}\text{Direct}\\ \text{imports by}\\ \text{production}\\ \text{sectors}\end{bmatrix} + \begin{bmatrix}\text{Indirect}\\ \text{imports}\end{bmatrix}$$

$$+ \quad I_m$$

$$+ \begin{bmatrix}\text{Direct}\\ \text{imports for}\\ \text{investment}\end{bmatrix}$$

In all, there are $h + g + j + i + f + 3$ identities and $h^2 + 4h + hj + 2hf + 5g + gh + 2gi + 2gf + 4j + 4i + 2ij + 2fj + ih + 3f + 6$ variables. If all but $h + g + j + i + f + 3$ variables are given preassigned values, then the remaining variables can be uniquely determined from the system. However, because the number of variables that need to be predetermined is large in relation to the number of equations, the SAM identities have limited value as a device for estimating variables for years, or situations, other than the one on which the SAM is based. To provide a more versatile model for our purposes, it is necessary to introduce some assumptions about how certain variables are determined in the regional economy. Such assumptions convert the SAM from a set of accounting identities into an economic model that purports to characterize the workings of the economy.

Assumptions for the Regional Model

As in a Leontief system, we assume that all the structural relations (both behavioral and technological) are linear, or at least that they can be usefully approximated by linear functions. Our specific assumptions are stated below.

PRODUCTION. The first set of assumptions impose proportional relationships between all inputs and outputs in all production sectors:

$$C_{ij} = a_{ij}\, X_j, \text{ all } i, j \tag{8.1}$$

$$M_j = a_{mj} X_j, \text{ all } j \tag{8.2}$$

where a_{ij} and a_{mj} are, respectively, the values of domestic and directly imported intermediates required for the production of one unit of gross output in sector j.

Value added from production in sector j is:

$$VA_j = X_j - \Sigma_i C_{ij} - M_j$$

$$= (1 - a_{ij} - a_{mj})\, X_j$$

and this is also assumed to be allocated in fixed proportions of gross output. Part is used to pay for hired factors, part is retained for reinvestment, and the remaining value added is allocated to households contributing unpaid factors as owners (profits). More specifically:

$$F_{fj} = \lambda_{fj} X_j, \text{ all } f, j \tag{8.3}$$

$$V_{hj} = \omega_{hj} X_j, \text{ all } h, j \tag{8.4}$$

$$S_j = s_j X_j, \text{ all } j \tag{8.5}$$

where λ_{fj}, and ω_{hj} are, respectively, the shares of gross output paid to hired factors and to households and s_j is the marginal savings rate for sector j.

Production sectors also pay various business and commodity taxes to government. These payments are assumed to be proportional to output, so that:

$$T_j = t_j X_j, \text{ all } j \tag{8.6}$$

where t_j is the tax share.

COMMODITIES. Commodities are supplied locally from private-sector production, by importers, and by government. Government is particularly important in supplying foods and general provisions through civil supply shops, and in providing transport through public bus companies. Most other government services are provided free or do not compete with the private sector.

Government departments are divided into two groups—those that sell goods and services according to consumer demand, and those that provide services (usually free) at a predetermined level of output or capacity. The first group is assumed to maintain constant shares in the region's total supply of the relevant commodities, whereas the second group has exogenously fixed output levels. Mathematically these assumptions can be expressed as:

$$D_{gi} = \begin{cases} d_{gi} Z_i & \text{if } g \epsilon P \\ \overline{D}_{gi} & \text{otherwise} \end{cases} \tag{8.7}$$

where $g \epsilon P$ denotes the set (P) of government departments whose output is endogenous to the model, d_{gi} is the relevant market share for those departments, and $\overline{D}_{gi}$ denotes the exogenously fixed value of sales for government departments not belonging to P.

We assume that local firms and importers maintain constant shares in the total supply of each commodity after any government sales. That is:

$$D_{ji} = d_{ji} \, (Z_i - \sum_g D_{gi}), \text{ all } i, j \tag{8.8}$$

$$M_i = d_{mi} \, (Z_i - \sum_g D_{gi}), \text{ all } i \tag{8.9}$$

where d_{ji} and d_{mi} are, respectively, the shares of local production and imports.

HOUSEHOLDS. Tax collections from households are assumed to be a linear function of income:

$$T_h = \overline{T}_h + t_h Y_h, \text{ all } h \tag{8.10}$$

where t_h is the marginal tax rate levied on income for households of type h, and $\overline{T}_h$ is a constant that includes house taxes and water charges.

Households are assumed to save a fixed proportion of aftertax income:

$$S_h = s_h (Y_h - T_h), \text{ all } h \tag{8.11}$$

where s_h is the marginal propensity to save for households of type h.

We assume that factor payments, interhousehold income transfers, and remittances from abroad are exogenously given, so that:

$$F_{fh} = \overline{F}_{fh}, \text{ all } f, h \tag{8.12}$$

$$H_{hh^*} = \overline{H}_{hh^*}, \text{ all } h, h^* \tag{8.13}$$

$$R_h = \overline{R}_h, \text{ all } h \tag{8.14}$$

Further, we assume that household preferences for goods may be expressed by the linear expenditure system, so that:

$$C_{ih} = \gamma_{ih} + \beta_{ih} (Y_h - T_h - S_h - \sum_f \overline{F}_{fh} - \sum_{h^*} \overline{H}_{h^*h}), \text{ all } i,h \tag{8.15}$$

such that $\Sigma\gamma_{ih} = 0$ and $\Sigma_i\beta_{ih} = 1$. Here β_{ih} is the marginal budget share of the hth household for the ith commodity, and γ_{ih} is an intercept coefficient. Note that factor (interest) payments and transfers to other households must be deducted from the disposable income available for consumption.

GOVERNMENT. Turning to the governments' current account, we assume that for those departments whose sales are endogenously determined by the region's demand, their costs are proportional to output. However, for those government departments whose output is fixed, the cost structure is also exogenously given. These assumptions can be written as:

$$C_{ig} = \begin{cases} e_{ig}G_g \text{ if } g \epsilon P \\ \overline{C}_{ig} \text{ otherwise} \end{cases} \tag{8.16}$$

$$M_g = \begin{cases} e_{mg}G_g \text{ if } g \epsilon P \\ \overline{M}_g \text{ otherwise} \end{cases} \tag{8.17}$$

$$F_{fg} = \begin{cases} \lambda_{fg}G_g \text{ if } g \epsilon P \\ \overline{F}_{fg} \text{ otherwise} \end{cases} \tag{8.18}$$

$$T_g = \begin{cases} t_g G_g \text{ if } g \epsilon P \\ \overline{T}_g \text{ otherwise} \end{cases} \tag{8.19}$$

where e_{ig}, e_{mg}, λ_{fg} and t_g are the shares of government output allocated to local commodities, direct imports, hired factors, and taxes, respectively.

We also assume that government transfers to households are exogenous:

$$H_{hg} = \overline{H}_{hg}, \text{ all } h \tag{8.20}$$

Government fiscal allocations to different departments are assumed to be proportional to total government revenue, that is:

$$R_g = \mu_g (T + \overline{R}) \tag{8.21}$$

where $\overline{R}$ is the net transfer from state and district governments, and is assumed to be fixed.

Since the expenditures and receipts of each department need not balance, savings (on current accounts) must be specified endogenously:

$$S_g = -[\sum_h H_{hg} + T_g + \sum_i C_{ig} + \sum_f F_{fg} + M_g] + [R_g + \sum_i D_{gi} + \sum_f F_{gf}] \tag{8.22}$$

Savings may be positive or negative, hence S_g must be unconstrained in sign in the model.

FACTORS. We assume that total factor earnings F_f are allocated in fixed proportions to households, governments, and firms. That is:

$$F_{hf} = \lambda_{hf} F_f, \text{ all } h, f \tag{8.23}$$

$$F_{gf} = \lambda_{gf} F_f, \text{ all } g, f \tag{8.24}$$

$$F_{jf} = \lambda_{jf} F_f, \text{ all } j, f \tag{8.25}$$

where λ_{hf}, λ_{gf}, and λ_{jf} are the relevant shares.

INVESTMENT. We assume that regional investment I is exogenous, that is:

$$I = \overline{I} \tag{8.26}$$

The Regional Model

Under assumptions (8.10) and (8.11), it follows that:

$$Y_h - T_h = (1 - t_h)Y_h - \overline{T}_h$$

and that:

$$Y_h - T_h - S_h = (1 - t_h)(1 - s_h)Y_h - (1 - s_h)\overline{T}_h, \text{ all } h$$

This relation, together with assumptions (8.1) to (8.26), can now be substituted into the SAM equations to give a linear, economic model for the region. The new equations are as follows, where terms in square brackets are constants:

Household incomes

$$Y_h = [\sum_{h^*}\overline{H}_{hh^*} + \sum_g \overline{H}_{hg} + \overline{R}_h] + \sum_j \omega_{hj}X_j + \sum_f \lambda_{hf}F_f, \text{ all } h$$

Government income by department

$$G_g = \begin{cases} [\mu_g\overline{R}] + \mu_g T + \sum_i d_{gi}Z_i + \sum_f \lambda_{gf}F_f, \text{ all } g\epsilon P \\ [\mu_g\overline{R} + \sum_i \overline{D}_{gi}] + \mu_g T + \sum_f \lambda_{gf}F_f, \text{ otherwise} \end{cases}$$

Government savings by department

$$S_g = \begin{cases} [-\sum_h \overline{H}_{hg}] + (1 - t_g - \sum_i e_{ig} - \sum_f \lambda_{fg} - e_{mg})G_g, \text{ if } g\epsilon P \\ G_g - \sum_h \overline{H}_{hg} - \overline{T}_g - \sum_i \overline{C}_{ig} - \sum_f \overline{F}_{fg} - \overline{M}_g, \text{ otherwise} \end{cases}$$

Local tax revenues

$$T = [\sum_h \overline{T}_h + \sum_{g\epsilon Q} \overline{T}_g] + \sum_h t_h Y_h + \sum_{g\epsilon P} t_g G_g + \sum_j t_j X_j$$

where Q denotes those government sectors not a member of the set P.

Private sector gross outputs

$$X_j = [-\sum_i d_{ji} \sum_{g\epsilon Q} \overline{D}_{gi}] + \sum_i d_{ji} (1 - \sum_{g\epsilon P} d_{gi})Z_i + \sum_f \lambda_{jf}F_f, \text{ all } j$$

Commodity sales

$$Z_i = [\sum_h \gamma_{ih} + \sum_{g\epsilon Q} \overline{C}_{ig} - \sum_h \beta_{ih}(1 - s_h) \overline{T}_h + \overline{I}_i - \sum_h \beta_{ih}(\sum_f \overline{F}_{fh} + \sum_{h^*} \overline{H}_{h^*h})]$$

$$+ \sum_h \beta_{ih} (1 - t_h)(1 - s_h)Y_h + \sum_{g\epsilon P} e_{ig} G_g + \sum_j a_{ij} X_j + E_i, \text{ all } i$$

Factor payments

$$F_f = [\sum_h \overline{F}_{fh} + \sum_{g\epsilon Q} \overline{F}_{fg} + \overline{I}_f + \overline{R}_f] + \sum_{g\epsilon P} \lambda_{fg} G_g + \sum_j \lambda_{fj} X_j, \text{ all } f$$

Net capital inflow to the region

$$B = [\overline{I} + \sum_h s_h \overline{T}_h] - \sum_g S_g - \sum_h s_h (1 - t_h) Y_h - \sum_j s_j X_j$$

Total imports

$$M = [\sum_{g\epsilon Q} \overline{M}_g - \sum_i d_{mi} \sum_{g\epsilon Q} \overline{D}_{gi} + \overline{I}_m] + \sum_{g\epsilon P} e_{mg} G_g$$

$$+ \sum_j a_{mj}X_j + \sum_i d_{mi} (1 - \sum_{g\epsilon P} d_{gi})Z_i$$

The following variables are endogenous to the model: Y_h, X_j, Z_i, F_f, R_g, G_g, E_i, T, R, B, and M. So there are $h + j + 2i + f + 2g + 4$ variables and $h + j + i + f + 2g + 4$ equations, or i more variables than equations. If i variables are assigned predetermined values (e.g.,

X_i or E_i, all i), then the system can be solved for the values of all the remaining variables.

Since the model is linear, it can be solved by simple matrix inversion. However, we found it more advantageous to work with a linear programming formulation. This enabled us to use an available matrix generator program, and the available linear programming package also provided additional insights into the model solution.

To solve the model by linear programming, a few modifications to the model are required. First, as many as possible of the equalities need to be replaced by inequality constraints. This facilitates the solution procedure, but since the matrix is square, the constraints will be satisfied as equalities in an optimal solution. Second, R_g and B need to be specified as variables that could take on negative or positive values in an optimal solution. Linear programming algorithms require that all the variables be non-negative, but if an activity vector is duplicated in the matrix and then the duplicate column is multiplied by -1, this avoids the non-negativity restrictions.

Last, an objective function has to be created for the model. Since the matrix is square, the same solution will be optimal irrespective of which variables are maximized. We chose to maximize total value added for the region, since the shadow prices on the constraints are then regional value added multipliers. Regional value added is defined here as:

$$VA = \sum_j v_j X_j + \sum_g v_g G_g$$

where v_j and v_g are the ratios of value added to gross output for sector j and government department g, respectively.

Calibration of the Model

The model's coefficients were estimated from two data sources. Division of the 1982/83 SAM entries by their respective column sums provided all the coefficients except γ_{ih}, β_{ih}, $\overline{T}_h$, and t_h. The latter were estimated by regression analysis using the 1982/83 IFPRI-TNAU household survey data.

For reporting purposes, we retain the same account definitions and numbering in this chapter as used for the SAM in Chapter 7. However, some of the production accounts—agricultural wholesale merchants (36), petty shops (75), general provision and grocery shops (77), and dairy, fish, and meat shops (79)—were further disaggregated by major commodities in the model. This was necessary to avoid assuming fixed commodity bundles in their trading activities. We have added these up again in presenting the results.

Of the government departments, the following were assumed to have endogenously determined outputs: agriculture and marketing (13), railways (18), post and telecommunications (19), cooperatives (20), nationalized banks (21), electricity (22), road transport (23), and civil supplies (24).

As noted earlier, *i* (in this case $i = 134$) of the endogenous variables have to be exogenously fixed before the model can be solved. We chose to fix the export level of each commodity at 1982/83 levels (with many of these being zero), and to allow all sectoral gross outputs to be endogenous. This is tantamount to assuming that the supplies of all commodities are perfectly elastic over the range of outputs permitted by demand.

Such an assumption may not be a bad approximation for service sectors producing for local demand; it is demand rather than supply that constrains their gross outputs. But for the region's export sectors, particularly agriculture, gross output is more likely constrained by fixed resource endowments (e.g., land) and the available technology. For these sectors, it may be better to constrain gross output levels rather than exports in the model (as in Bell, Hazell, and Slade 1982). However, since the supplies of commodities such as milk and eggs are probably more elastic than paddy or groundnuts, fixing gross outputs is more satisfactory if agricultural production is disaggregated by commodity in the model. Since our model is not disaggregated in this way, we have chosen to stay with the export constraints, but interpreting these as depicting inelastic supplies for the export market rather than as demand constraints. As agricultural output includes a mix of products in our model, the implicit assumption of elastic supplies for the region's domestic market can be defended on the grounds that these supplies represent a different mix of commodities than the region's exports.

To check the reliability of the model, we tried to duplicate the 1982/83 base year. Comparison of the predicted gross outputs by sector with their 1982/83 SAM counterparts shows a close match (Table 8.2). Total regional gross output is about 0.9 percent too high, but regional value added is correct to within 0.01 percent. The match on government-sector outputs and household incomes was equally good.

Value Added to Gross Output Multipliers

For each sector, a value added to gross output multiplier can be derived that gives the increase in total regional value added resulting from a 1-rupee increase in the demand for the corresponding sector's output. These multipliers are obtained from the shadow prices on the private-sector production accounts in the model solution. Two sets of

TABLE 8.2
Production-Sector Results from the Regional Model (thous Rs)

Account Number	Sector Name	Gross Output: SAM	Gross Output: Model Solution	Value Added in Model Solution	Value Added to Gross Output Multiplier: Income Endogenous	Value Added to Gross Output Multiplier: Income Exogenous	Value Added Multiplier
28	Small farms (rural)	335,166	336,354	260,860	1.95	0.94	2.51
29	Large farms (rural)	806,317	810,339	638,021	1.86	0.93	2.36
30	Other agric. (rural)	52,642	52,569	38,291	2.24	0.98	3.07
31	Agric. (urban)	50,438	50,961	35,273	1.80	0.90	2.60
32	Agric. inputs & machinery service centers	100,160	100,565	49,636	0.98	0.59	1.99
33	Rice mills	302,346	315,924	55,145	1.77	0.90	10.14
34	Other grain mills	17,311	17,765	7,603	1.80	0.97	4.21
35	Oil extraction mills	451,871	454,805	72,369	1.85	0.97	11.62
36	Agric. wholesale merchants	1,162,305	1,186,229	132,742	1.71	0.89	15.15
37	Livestock traders	48,061	48,081	3,582	1.68	0.82	22.55
38	Chemical products mfg.	17,528	17,598	8,160	1.05	0.65	2.26
39	Printing	4,171	4,076	1,920	1.52	0.86	3.23
40	Leather products mfg. & sales	52,707	52,784	18,206	1.65	0.96	4.78
41	Tobacco mfg.	1,914	1,990	1,370	1.40	0.83	2.03
42	Matches & paper products mfg.	12,464	12,366	6,192	1.41	0.83	2.82
43	Plastic & rubber products mfg.	742	619	320	1.15	0.65	2.22
44	Metal products mfg.	10,627	10,472	4,725	1.05	0.61	2.33
45	Handicrafts & *khadi*	8,492	8,089	4,818	1.49	0.82	2.50
46	Pottery	3,772	3,746	2,159	1.62	0.88	2.81
47	Furniture mfg. & sales	4,345	4,388	2,516	1.46	0.88	2.55
48	Engineering works	27,429	27,467	13,868	1.40	0.78	2.77
49	Motor vehicle repairs, service, & sales	4,811	3,349	1,658	1.08	0.62	2.18

50	Blacksmiths	3,083	3,085	2,409	1.66	0.91	2.13
51	Sawmills, carpentry, & timber shops	19,899	19,820	12,807	1.61	0.92	2.49
52	Electrical goods servicing	1,680	1,394	906	1.55	0.92	2.38
53	Soda & ice cream mfg.	2,544	2,617	1,335	1.69	0.89	3.31
54	Jewelry & goldsmith services	14,695	12,199	7,756	1.25	0.77	1.97
55	Silk textiles	224,967	224,515	78,439	0.71	0.38	2.03
56	Cotton textiles	25,031	23,441	9,657	0.84	0.47	2.04
57	Vessel & metal goods sales	8,399	8,059	3,969	1.50	0.90	3.05
58	Hardware & electrical goods sales	60,422	54,949	23,021	0.82	0.56	1.96
59	Firewood & charcoal mfg. & sales	15,023	14,996	8,458	1.55	0.87	2.75
60	Cycle shops	2,209	1,853	926	0.93	0.59	1.86
61	Photo & optical shops	729	729	486	1.26	0.82	1.89
62	Truck transport services	43,523	43,664	25,116	1.42	0.87	2.47
63	Bus & taxi services	18,768	19,565	12,060	1.52	0.95	2.47
64	Pawnbrokers & local financial services	31,128	31,206	30,946	2.24	1.47	2.26
65	Lottery agents	5,574	5,574	1,994	0.69	0.41	1.93
66	Cinemas	14,480	9,981	5,630	1.10	0.67	1.95
67	Restaurants & hotels	17,382	18,194	8,852	1.60	0.91	3.29
68	Personal services	13,104	13,029	12,193	1.88	0.99	2.00
69	Textile shops	98,375	92,019	39,074	1.18	0.72	2.78
70	Handlooms	4,199	3,986	2,528	1.68	0.95	2.65
71	Gasoline, diesel, & kerosene sales	75,651	73,159	25,745	0.68	0.47	1.93
72	Medicine shops & private medical services	27,269	25,742	14,518	1.02	0.59	1.81
73	Liquor sales	21,284	19,713	9,359	0.91	0.57	1.92
74	Commercial godowns & gunny sales	1,514	3,724	1,948	1.48	0.87	2.83
75	Petty shops	38,474	39,111	10,637	0.50	0.36	1.78
76	Tea & snack food shops	11,961	12,138	6,741	1.60	0.90	2.88

TABLE 8.2
Continued

		Gross Output			*Value Added to Gross Output Multiplier*		
Account Number	*Sector Name*	*SAM*	*Model Solution*	*Value Added in Model Solution*	*Income Endogenous*	*Income Exogenous*	*Value Added Multiplier*
77	General provisions & grocery shops	788,245	815,756	115,541	1.30	0.71	9.14
78	Vegetable, fruit, & flower shops	100,216	103,852	18,163	1.11	0.57	6.35
79	Dairy, fish, & meat shops	68,427	65,577	16,158	1.73	0.87	7.05
80	Installment plan shops	2,732	2,143	948	0.91	0.63	2.06
81	Masonry materials mfg. & sales	45,549	45,465	24,775	1.06	0.60	1.95
82	Wholesale importers	24,470	24,591	3,643	0.42	0.25	2.83
83	Commercial banks	4,737	4,749	4,025	1.79	1.02	2.11
84	Professional services	2,922	2,188	1,437	1.53	0.83	2.33
85	Construction contractors	179,673	179,299	97,503	1.53	0.82	2.81
86	Laundry & drycleaning	4,623	4,717	2,734	1.37	0.75	2.36
13–26	Government sectors	567,580	573,134	217,379	1.08	0.75	2.86
	Total gross output	6,066,160	6,120,478	n.a.	n.a.	n.a.	n.a.
	Total value added	2,219,215	2,219,247	2,219,247	n.a.	n.a.	n.a.

multipliers were obtained. The first set corresponds to the basic model in which household incomes, and hence household expenditures, are endogenous to the model. These multipliers capture the combined impact of the interindustry, or production, linkages and the household consumption linkages on the regional economy. The second set of multipliers was derived by solving the model with household incomes fixed exogenously at their base-period values.[1] In this case, the multipliers reflect only the impact of the production linkages. Both sets of multipliers are reported in Table 8.2.

The agricultural sectors (28–31) have relatively large multipliers, ranging from Rs 1.8 to Rs 2.24 when incomes are endogenous. Using 1982/83 value added shares as weights, the average multiplier for the agricultural sectors is Rs 1.9. In other words, if the aggregate demand for agricultural output were increased exogenously by 1 rupee, regional value added would be Rs 1.9 larger.

The multipliers are also relatively large for the agroprocessing sectors, and for a number of the service-oriented sectors, especially agricultural trading, local financial services, commercial banks, and various personal services. The multipliers tend to be smaller for manufacturing, and particularly for those sectors (e.g., silk textiles) that have a high import content (silk yarn) and low ratios of value added to gross output.

The importance of the household expenditure linkages is shown by the much smaller multipliers obtained when incomes are fixed exogenously in the model. The weighted average of the multipliers for the agricultural sectors is only Rs 0.93, or about half of its value when incomes are endogenous. In other words, the production linkages are as important as the household consumption linkages in generating indirect benefits from increased agricultural output. By contrast, in a similar study of the Muda irrigation region of Malaysia, Bell, Hazell, and Slade (1982) found that the household expenditure linkages were about twice as important as the production linkages. The difference is probably a reflection of lower per capita incomes in North Arcot, with a greater share of incremental household income being allocated to foods rather than locally produced nonfood goods and services.

Since the value added content of gross output differs by sector, it is useful to standardize the multipliers in value added terms. Value added multipliers are reported in the last column of Table 8.2; they are defined as the increase in total regional value added resulting from a 1-rupee increase in the corresponding sector's value added. They are

1. In order to allow regional value added to increase in the presence of the household income constraints, a slack activity was introduced to dispose of any "excess" value added.

obtained by dividing the value added to gross output multipliers in Table 8.2 by the value added to gross output ratio (VA/GO) from Table 7.3 of the sector whose output is being exogenously increased.

The value added multipliers range from Rs 2.36 to Rs 3.07 for the agricultural sectors, with a weighted average of Rs 2.44. While these magnitudes are normal for input-output models, they are relatively large compared with the multipliers obtained from semi-input-output models. Haggblade and Hazell (1989), for example, obtain semi-input-output multipliers that are smaller than 2.0 for a wide range of regional economies. Our multipliers are larger because we constrain agricultural exports rather than agricultural output in the model. Given an exogenous increase in agricultural exports, the resultant growth in regional income adds to local demand for agricultural output, and hence generates additional rounds of increases in agricultural output. This cannot happen when agricultural output is constrained. We chose this specification because some agricultural commodities (e.g., milk and eggs) are thought to have more elastic supplies than foodgrains and, in the absence of a more detailed disaggregation of the agricultural sector in the model, we did not want to be too restrictive by assuming an aggregate supply elasticity of zero. The alternative assumption of a perfectly elastic supply bounded only by the export constraint seems preferable, but it may err on the optimistic side in estimating the multiplier.

The value added multipliers lie in the Rs 1.8 to Rs 3.0 range for most nonfarm sectors. Exceptionally large multipliers arise for some agroprocessing and trade sectors that have low VA/GO ratios (e.g., rice mills, oil extraction mills, and general provision shops, which have VA/GO ratios of 17.5 percent, 15.9 percent, and 14.2 percent, respectively). In order to generate one additional rupee of value added, these sectors have to increase their gross output by Rs 6 to Rs 7, and this generates significant levels of regional growth through the demand for production intermediates.

Note that our earlier analysis of the relative importance of the production and consumption linkages would not change if we were to use value added multipliers instead of value added to gross output multipliers. This is because the exogenous income multiplier for each sector is also obtained by dividing the relevant value added to gross output multiplier by the sector's VA/GO ratio, and hence the ratio of the endogenous to exogenous income multipliers remains unchanged.

The Impact of Agricultural Growth

Agricultural production and incomes have increased significantly in the region since the 1960s, largely as a result of increases in paddy and groundnut production. We turn now to an analysis of the multiplier effects these changes have induced in the regional economy.

Our approach to measuring these multipliers is as follows. First, we recognize that since 1982/83 was a severe drought year in the study region, our model needs to be adjusted to reflect a more normal level of agricultural output for that year. The normalized solution for 1982/83 becomes our new base solution. Second, we use the model to predict sectoral outputs and household incomes for 1982/83, given agricultural production levels typical of the mid-1960s. Comparison of these predictions with the new base solution provides the basis for calculating the regional impact of growth in agricultural output.

Adjusting for the Impact of Drought in 1982/83

Paddy production was down sharply in North Arcot in 1980/81, 1981/82, and 1982/83, but by 1983/84 it had recovered to the levels of the late 1970s (Table 2.2). These changes were due to drought rather than any trend decline in paddy production, hence a reasonable measure of 1982/83 output under normal weather conditions is given by the average production for 1977/78 to 1979/80, the three years immediately preceding the drought. This required increasing paddy production by 136 percent over its level in the base-year solution.

Groundnut production, on the other hand, was relatively high during the drought years of the early 1980s (Table 2.2). To be consistent with our treatment of paddy, we normalized the model to the average groundnut production in 1977/78 to 1979/80. This required a 33 percent reduction from its level in the 1982/83 base solution.[2]

We did not change any other export constraints in the model, and the gross outputs of all other sectors, including government sectors 13 and 18–24, were left free to adjust to changes in the region's domestic demands induced by the revised paddy and groundnut exports. Nor did we attempt to change prices or any other exogenous variables in the model. All changes in the model solution are therefore entirely due to the changes in paddy and groundnut production.[3]

2. Given that sectoral gross outputs are only indirectly constrained through export constraints in the model, the normalization was done on a trial and error basis in which the export limits for paddy, rice, groundnuts, and edible oils were varied until the value of paddy and groundnut transactions at farm-gate prices had been changed by the desired percentages. In the absence of suitable data for 1977/78–1979/80, we assumed that the ratios of rice to paddy exports, and of groundnuts to edible oil exports, were the same as in 1982/83.

3. Some prices, e.g., land rents and agricultural wage rates, could reasonably be argued to be endogenously determined within the region, and hence should be allowed to adjust in the model when solving for different levels of agricultural output. This cannot be done without a much more ambitious modeling approach than adopted here, and it seems hardly worthwhile given the small changes in real wages and land values reported in Chapters 3 and 4.

The normalized base solution for 1982/83 appears under the column labeled B in Table 8.3. Column A contains the original base solution for comparison. Differences between the two solutions, which are expressed in ratio form in the column headed A/B, are due to the impact of drought.

The drought reduced total regional value added by 29 percent and reduced the average per capita income of all households by 25 percent. Its impact was of course greatest in agriculture, and hence on agriculturally dependent households. The landless laborers and the small-scale farmers were most adversely affected, with a 30 percent loss in their per capita incomes. However, the effects were pervasive throughout the regional economy. Even the nonagricultural households in the towns suffered income losses of between 17 and 22 percent. Savings and exports were particularly affected, and the capital outflow from the region fell by 70 percent.

The Impact of the Green Revolution

Given the weather-normalized base solution for 1982/83, we can now attempt to measure the multiplier effects of the increase in agricultural output that occurred between the pre– and post–green revolution eras. Table 2.2 shows that paddy production increased sharply in 1970/71 and remained at high levels until the early 1980s. Poor rains in 1967/68 and 1968/69 depressed paddy production in those years, but average production for 1963/64 to 1965/66 would seem to provide a reasonable indication of the pre–green revolution situation. Taking average production in 1977/78 to 1979/80 as indicative of the output levels attainable with the maturing of the green revolution, then the green revolution period corresponded to a 59 percent increase in paddy production and a 14 percent increase in groundnut production. The sources of these production increases are analyzed in detail in Chapter 2.

To simulate the regional economy in the absence of the green revolution, it is also necessary to make some plausible assumptions about the technology for paddy farming. Clearly, paddy farmers would have used less fertilizers and agrochemicals in 1982/83 if there had not been a green revolution, and there would also have been less investment in wells and pumping equipment, and hence less use of fuels and electricity. Real wages would likely have remained stagnant, and there would have been less mechanization of spraying and threshing activities. We used the CCPC cost of cultivation data (see Chapter 3) to adjust the technology coefficients in the model to reflect these assumptions.

The model solution corresponding to 1982/83 with pre–green revolution levels of technology and paddy and groundnut production is given in column C in Table 8.3. Comparison with the post–green revolution situation (column B) is facilitated by expressing the changes in ratio form (column B/C).

Note that changes in the model solution are not to be interpreted as estimates of the actual changes that occurred in the region between 1963/64–1965/66 and 1977/78–1979/80. This is because no attempt has been made to analyze autonomous changes in, among other things, population size, relative prices, government activity, manufacturing (especially silk weaving), and the like. The predicted changes are estimates of the difference between what would have been the situation in 1982/83 given normal rainfall, and with and without the agricultural productivity changes that occurred between 1963/64–1965/66 and 1977/78–1979/80.

The Agricultural Multiplier

Regional value added increased by Rs 766.7 million, of which Rs 408.9 million (53 percent) arose in agriculture, Rs 141.8 million (19 percent) in agrobusiness, Rs 59.2 million (8 percent) in government activities, and Rs 156.8 million (20 percent) in the private nonagricultural sector. In terms of increases, agriculture and agrobusiness both increased by about 40 percent, whereas government and the private nonfarm sector increased by about half as much (26 percent and 21 percent, respectively). Total regional value added increased by 33 percent.

There are two ways to calculate the value added multiplier for agriculture. The first is simply to take the ratio of the increase in regional value added to the increase in agricultural value added, i.e., 766.7/408.9 = 1.87. On this basis, each rupee of additional value added generated in agriculture led to an increase of Rs 0.87 in nonagricultural income. This multiplier does not separate the increase in agricultural income between the part due to the initial exogenous increase in paddy and groundnut output, and the part due to an increase in the output of all agricultural commodities as a result of endogenously driven increases in local demand. It corresponds to the multiplier in a production-constrained model where the entire increase in agricultural value added is exogenously driven, and in this sense it is comparable to the semi-input-output multiplier reported by Bell, Hazell, and Slade (1982, p. 175) for increased agricultural production in the Muda irrigation region of Malaysia. They report a very similar multiplier (1.83), though the composition of their multiplier was rather different, as shown below:

Multiplier component	*Muda*	*North Arcot*
Other agriculture	0.04	Not applicable
Agrobusiness	0.10	0.35
Government[4]	0.06	0.14
Private, nonagriculture	0.63	0.38
Total	0.83	0.87

In Muda, a much larger share of the multiplier was due to value added increases in the private, nonagricultural sector, whereas in North Arcot the agrobusiness sector (processing and trade) was about as important as nonagriculture. As with our earlier multiplier analysis, this confirms that the interindustry, or production, linkages are relatively more important in North Arcot, whereas the Muda economy was more strongly driven by household expenditures.

The second multiplier approach is consistent with the definition of the value added multipliers in Table 8.2, and takes the multiplier as the ratio of the increase in regional value added to the initial, exogenously given increase in agricultural value added. In our model, the export constraints are used to capture rigidities in agricultural supply, and hence the initial increase in agricultural value added is simply the value added content of the permitted increases in paddy and groundnut exports between the pre– and post–green revolution solutions. This is equal to Rs 350.9 million,[5] hence the multiplier is 766.7/350.9 = 2.18. In this case, each rupee increase in agricultural income generates an additional Rs 1.18 of value added in the regional economy. The latter now includes endogenously driven increases in agricultural income, and hence is necessarily larger than the Rs 0.87 multiplier derived from the first approach. Given the contrasting assumptions about the agricultural supply underlying these two multipliers, they provide a range (Rs 0.87 to Rs 1.18) within which the true multiplier might be expected to lie.[6]

Changes in Household Incomes

The per capita incomes are almost identical in columns A and C of Table 8.3. This implies that the income levels realized during the 1982/83 drought were about the same as the incomes that would have materialized that year had rainfall been normal but if the productivity gains of the green revolution had not occurred.

4. To facilitate comparison, government in Muda is taken to include rail transport, electricity, water, and post and telecommunications, as well as the sectors labeled as government in Table 7.6 of Bell, Hazell, and Slade (1982).

5. Calculated as the gross value of the increase in paddy, rice, groundnut, and edible oil exports multiplied by the average VA/GO ratio for agriculture.

6. Smaller multipliers are still possible if the fixed price assumptions of the model do not hold (see Haggblade, Hammer, and Hazell 1991).

Given normal rainfall, the model predicts that per capita incomes increase by 27 percent on average as a result of the green revolution. The agriculturally dependent households enjoy the largest percentage increase in per capita incomes. There are substantial absolute gains to the nonagriculturalists, especially for the self-employed in the towns, but their proportional increases are smaller, and hence the distribution of income between agriculture and nonagriculture, and hence between rural and urban areas, improves. Within the rural villages, the model predicts a relatively modest gain of 19 percent for the nonagricultural households, but a 28–32 percent gain for the landless and small-scale farmers. Large-scale farmers gain almost the same proportionately as small-scale farmers, but the absolute gains are of course larger.

Table 8.4 contrasts the rural household income results from the model with the income changes observed in the resurvey villages between 1973/74 and 1983/84 (see Chapter 3). We should not expect these results to be the same since (1) the model results pertain to the entire study region and not just to a sample of poorer villages, (2) the model results are based on normalized paddy and groundnut production in with– and without–green revolution situations and not on the output for individual years, and (3) the farm households in the model include nonpaddy farms, whereas the survey results reported are only for paddy farms. Nevertheless, there are some important points of agreement between the two sets of results. Both show sizable increases in real incomes for all four rural household groups, though the gains are more moderate in the model results. Further, both show that the landless-laborer households gain favorably compared with the other household groups, and that they improve their position relative to the nonagricultural households.

Table 8.5 shows the composition of the changes in household incomes between the with– and without–green revolution solutions. Not surprisingly, agriculture (own farm plus paid agricultural employment) accounts for the lion's share of the income increase for all agriculturally dependent households, but it accounts for only small shares (less than 13 percent) of the income increase for nonagricultural households. The latter obtain sizable income increases from nonagricultural activity, especially paid employment and own nonfarm businesses.

While the multiplier effects from agricultural growth are clearly critical in spreading the benefits of the green revolution to the region's nonagricultural households, they also benefit the poorer, agriculturally dependent households in the rural villages. Small-scale farmers and landless laborers obtained 31.1 and 17.9 percent, respectively, of their income increase from nonagricultural sources. Agriculturally dependent households in the urban villages and towns (which rank lowest in the income distribution within their respective locations) also received more

TABLE 8.3
Results from the 1982/83 Regional Model with Normalized with– and without–Green Revolution Paddy and Groundnut Production Levels

Variable	*Base Solution (A)*	*With Green Revolution*[a] *(B)*	*Without Green Revolution*[b] *(C)*	*Impact of Drought (A/B)*	*Impact of Agricultural Growth (B/C)*
Value added (thous Rs)					
Agriculture (28–31)	972,445	1,470,008	1,061,149	0.66	1.39
Agrobusiness (32–37)	321,077	470,198	328,405	0.68	1.43
Government (13–26)	217,379	285,803	226,563	0.76	1.26
Private nonagric. (38–86)	708,346	894,434	737,613	0.79	1.21
Total	2,219,247	3,120,443	2,353,730	0.71	1.33
Per capita income (Rs)					
Rural villages					
Small farms	718	1,010	767	0.71	1.32
Large farms	1,546	2,096	1,609	0.74	1.30
Landless laborers	385	551	431	0.70	1.28
Nonagriculture	627	768	646	0.82	1.19

Urban villages					
Agric. dependent	1,009	1,324	1,067	0.76	1.24
Self-employed nonagric.	2,694	3,226	2,756	0.84	1.17
Employed nonagric.	1,286	1,523	1,332	0.84	1.14
Towns					
Agric. dependent	1,141	1,528	1,204	0.75	1.27
Self-employed nonagric.	4,142	5,344	4,197	0.78	1.27
Employed nonagric.	1,349	1,635	1,395	0.83	1.17
All households	998	1,335	1,048	0.75	1.27
Exports (thous Rs)	898,675	1,428,844	978,424	0.63	1.46
Imports (thous Rs)	978,129	1,292,024	1,033,615	0.76	1.25
Capital outflow (thous Rs)	86,667	295,127	110,223	0.30	2.67
Paddy output (thous Rs)	499,392	1,174,551	742,537	0.43	1.58
Groundnut output (thous Rs)	464,334	377,903	321,505	1.23	1.18

[a]1982/83 model with average 1977/78–1979/80 levels of paddy and groundnut production.

[b]1982/83 model with average 1963/64–1965/66 levels of paddy and groundnut production, and with adjusted technology coefficients for paddy farms.

TABLE 8.4
Changes in Household Incomes, Regional Model and Survey Results (1982/83 Rs)

	Small Farms[a]	*Large Farms*[a]	*Landless Laborers*	*Nonagri-cultural*
Model results				
Normalized 1982/83 without green revolution	3,722 (178)[b]	7,805 (374)	2,089 (100)	3,135 (150)
Normalized 1982/83 with green revolution	4,900 (183)	10,164 (380)	2,673 (100)	3,725 (139)
Change (%)	31.6	30.2	28.0	18.8
Resurvey village results				
1973/74 actual	2,210 (128)	5,095 (296)	1,724 (100)	2,188 (127)
1983/84 actual	4,214 (109)	6,024 (155)	3,875 (100)	3,386 (87)
Change (%)	90.6	18.2	124.8	54.8

[a]The survey results are for paddy farms only.
[b]Figures in parentheses are income distribution indices with landless households = 100.

than one-fifth of their income increases from nonagricultural sources. These results confirm the ability of the growth linkages to contribute to the alleviation of absolute poverty in both urban and rural areas.

Changes in Trade and the Balance of Payments

The region's exports increase by 46 percent as a result of the increase in agricultural productivity. Since imports increase by only 25 percent, then the balance of trade moves from a deficit of Rs 55 million to a surplus of Rs 136 million. Savings also increase with household incomes and, given that total investment is fixed at its 1982/83 level in the two solutions, there is a substantial increase in the capital outflow from the region, from Rs 110 million to Rs 295 million. As with Bell, Hazell, and Slade's (1982) findings in Muda, it seems likely that sizable increases in agricultural output do generate substantial savings in rural regions that exceed the capacity for local investment at competitive interest rates.

Conclusions

In this chapter we developed and applied an extended input-output model of the regional economy to measure the impact of agricultural growth on the local nonfarm economy. We found that each rupee of

TABLE 8.5
Components of Change in Household Incomes as a Result of the Green Revolution, Regional Model (percent)

Household Type	*Farm Income*	*Agric. Wages*	*Total Agric.*	*White Collar*	*Other Wages*	*Nonfarm Business*	*Other*	*Total Nonagric.*	*Income Increase (Rs)*
Rural villages									
Small farms	58.5	10.4	68.9	0.9	6.5	21.9	1.8	31.1	1,178
Large farms	84.3	2.6	86.9	2.4	1.1	7.9	1.7	13.1	2,359
Landless laborers	24.5	56.7	81.2	0.1	12.9	3.3	2.5	17.9	584
Nonagriculture	—	12.5	12.5	15.9	20.6	50.9	—	87.4	590
Urban villages									
Agric. dependent	43.3	34.3	77.6	2.7	10.9	3.3	5.6	22.5	1,326
Self-employed nonagric.	—	3.8	3.8	32.7	5.7	56.1	1.7	96.2	2,424
Employed nonagric.	—	6.7	6.7	41.1	38.9	10.2	3.1	93.3	985
Towns									
Agric. dependent	30.9	28.4	59.3	0.4	8.8	19.2	12.3	40.7	1,845
Self-employed nonagric.	—	0.1	0.1	0.3	2.4	91.8	5.4	99.9	6,532
Employed nonagric.	—	2.9	2.9	21.5	41.4	31.2	3.0	97.1	1,371
All households	49.0	11.0	60.0	3.8	7.6	26.1	2.5	40.0	1,424

additional value added in agriculture generated between Rs 0.87 and Rs 1.18 of additional value added in the nonfarm economy. The lower estimate of the multiplier (Rs 0.87) approximates a semi- input-output model specification and is similar to the one derived by Bell, Hazell, and Slade (1982) for the Muda region in Malaysia. It is also consistent with the semi-input-output estimates of Asian multipliers derived by Haggblade and Hazell (1989). However, unlike other studies, the household consumption linkages play a less important role in determining the multiplier in North Arcot; they account for only half the multiplier compared with two-thirds or more in other regions that have been analyzed.

Based on experiments conducted with the model, we calculate that if the drought of 1982/83 had not occurred, then per capita incomes in the region would have been about 25 percent larger that year. Even so, the per capita income levels realized during the 1982/83 drought were about the same as those that would have materialized had rainfall been normal but if the productivity gains achieved in the 1970s through the green revolution and increased investments in irrigation had not occurred.

The productivity gains associated with the green revolution increased average per capita incomes by 27 percent. Farmers and landless agricultural workers obtained the largest proportional increases in their per capita incomes, hence the relative distribution of income between agriculture and nonagriculture (and between rural and urban areas) improved. Within the rural villages, landless laborers and farmers gained about the same proportionally. The model results therefore support the findings from the survey analysis in Chapter 3 that the green revolution did not worsen the distribution of total household incomes.

The benefits from the growth linkage effects of agricultural growth on the region's nonfarm economy accrued largely to nonagricultural households. Still, small-scale farmers and landless laborers obtained 31.1 and 17.9 percent, respectively, of the increase in their incomes from nonfarm sources, and agriculturally dependent households residing in urban areas obtained more than 20 percent of their increased incomes from nonfarm activities. The growth linkages are therefore important both in spreading the benefits of agricultural growth to local, nonagricultural households, and in increasing the incomes of the poorest household groups in rural and urban areas.

CHAPTER 9

The Arni Studies: Changes in the Private Sector of a Market Town, 1973–1983

Barbara Harriss

IN A PREDOMINANTLY agrarian region, development of the nonfarm economy is materially affected by the development of the agricultural sector. Agriculture supplies food, raw materials, and surplus labor for agro-industry. Agriculture also supplies the financial resources necessary to the organization of nonfarm firms. These resources can be mobilized through the terms of trade, through the savings and investments of both farmers and agricultural traders, and through direct and indirect taxation. Furthermore, demand from the agricultural sector stimulates nonfarm activity. Nonfarm economic activity not only is decentralized in villages (see Chapter 10) but is concentrated in market towns, in which northern Tamil Nadu is comparatively rich.

Here we describe economic change in one such town over the decade 1973–83 insofar as it can be established from two snapshot field surveys. Our method is to compare and contrast financial, employment, and commodity flow characteristics of randomly sampled private and cooperative firms, disaggregated according to the classification system used for the construction of the North Arcot social accounting matrix (SAM) (Chapter 7; also see Table 9.1). The market town selected in this case is Arni, which is located in the center of the study region (Harriss 1976a, 1976b). Its population of 38,664 in 1971 had increased by about 27 percent, to 49,284, in 1981. The town had its origins in the bazaar that grew up around a fort constructed in the Vijayanagara period. Arni is still a minor administrative center (a *taluk* headquarters), and at least 14 percent of the work force is estimated to be employed in the public sector. The town is a market center for paddy and for groundnuts, crops that dominate the local cropping system. It is also one of the smaller centers of the handloom silk industry of Tamil Nadu. In this respect Arni is not typical, though we believe that the concept of typicalness is as ill applied to towns as it is to villages. Yet it is quite common for small market towns to have an industrial specialization as

TABLE 9.1
Index of Accounting Heads

Type of Firm	*SAM Account Number (Chapter 7)*	
	Production Activity	*Commodity Transactions*
Rice		
Mills	33	89
Wholesalers	36	88,90
Retailers	91	
Other foods		
Workshops	34,53,67,76	123,124,125,127,128,143,144
Wholesalers	36	94,97,100,106
Retailers	73,75,77,78,79	92,95,98,102,104,107,109,115, 118,126,129
Nonfood agric. products		
Workshops	47,51	171,177,184
Wholesalers	36,74	132
Retailers	40,59,69	169,172,188,190,194,196,197, 199,215,216
Farm inputs		
Retailers	32	130,140
Silk		
Factories	55	189
Workshops	(70)	
Other goods		
Workshops	44,48,50,54,61,68	180,185,201
Wholesalers		
Retailers	72,81	151,176,183,206,208,209,210, 217,219
Durables		
Retailers	57,58,60	136,163,179,184
Transport	62,63	155
Fuel and energy		
Retailers	71	174,175
Transport repairs & services	49	148,149
Other repairs & services	39,46,52,58,60,68,86	146,147,157,159,165,180,220
Financial services	64	

Notes: Many firms in the Arni survey simultaneously carried out production activity and commodity transactions.

A number of account heads in the SAM were not captured in the Arni samples, perhaps the most important being livestock and their products (except for shoes).

The category of agricultural wholesaling (36) appears under three heads according to commodity in our scheme.

The SAM accounts of "engineering" and "vessels and pottery" are disaggregated here under two heads according to whether service or productive activity dominates the particular enterprise.

"Cycles" are also classed as retail or repairing enterprise according to empirical evidence.

well as the type of market functions that Arni shares with other small towns in Tamil Nadu.

This field research was carried out by myself and John Harriss using the same techniques in 1973 and 1983. The population of businesses was ascertained from mapping and listing throughout the built area of the town, a larger territory than the officially defined municipal area. We then drew 6 percent random samples[1] (88 firms in 1973 and 114 firms in 1983) and, with language assistance, proceeded to interview the owners, occasionally the managers, of each of the units sampled. The interviews covered data on the history of the firms and social backgrounds of the owners; sources of capital; the value, geographical sources, and destinations of inputs and outputs; business expansion and investment; credit; and employment. We are well known in this town and have lived there for quite long periods in connection with this and other research, so our data are as reliable as is possible in surveys of small businesses.

Changes in Types of Businesses

Table 9.2 gives census results for businesses over the decade. The problem of classifying commonly occurring multiproduct firms has been dealt with by classifying firms according to the most important product or activity, or both, in value terms. The number of businesses in the town has increased by 61 percent, an average that conceals some unevenness in the performance of different sectors.

Units for the manufacture of silk saris and the milling of paddy are the factory activities that have increased most, relatively and absolutely, over the decade. The highly diverse workshop economy—most notably including blacksmithing, welding, pottery, goldsmithing, beating of metal vessels, printing, baking, and the brewing of tea—accounted for 18 percent of all enterprises in both censuses. We have found the distinction between factory and workshop useful both because of the smaller size of workshop enterprises—whether defined in terms of capital, technological capacity, or labor—and because relatively more household labor is deployed in workshop enterprises. Workshop activity in Arni is different from factory activity because it is unspecialized, being generally combined with commerce, both wholesaling and retailing, and in certain cases with repair services, in a way that would make it misleading to classify it as pure production.

The service sector—transport, financial, and a large category of

1. The sampling fraction was dictated by our research resources in 1973.

TABLE 9.2
Private Firms, Arni

Type of Firm	*1973*	*1983*	*Percent Change*
Rice			
Mills	23	46	100
Wholesalers	17	45	165
Retailers	22	30	36
Groundnuts			
Mills	5	3	−40
Wholesalers	16	5	−69
Retailers	10	10	—
Other foods			
Factories	9	7	−22
Workshops	150	262	75
Wholesalers	9	22	144
Retailers	271	273	1
Nonfood agric. products			
Workshops	4	4	—
Wholesalers	1	3	200
Retailers	60	114	90
Farm inputs			
Retailers	13	28	115
Silk			
Factories	62	243	286
Other goods			
Factories	—	1	—
Workshops	53	77	45
Wholesalers	25	31	24
Retailers	52	86	65
Durables			
Retailers	20	37	85
Fuel and energy			
Retailers	12	18	50
Transport	16	38	138
Transport repairs & services	68	98	44
Other repairs & services	191	321	68
Financial services	87	121	39
Total	1,196	1,923	61

Source: Census by author of entire town (built area exceeding municipal limits).

other miscellaneous services—is numerically large but, like workshop production, with which it overlaps, it accounts for 28 percent of firms at both points in time. Within the service sector financial, medical, and legal services are most important in terms of value, whereas tailoring, hairdressing, cobbling, and laundering are most important numerically. Over the decade a notable expansion has taken place in cycle repair and service shops, in cycle rickshaws plying for hire, and in finance corporations and pawnbroking, while by contrast the numbers of barbers, electrical goods and radio repair shops, truck firms, and bullock carters have declined. Interestingly, although the number of general engineering firms has increased from 8 to 20—for the repair of pumpsets and mechanized grain threshers—there has been no development of production of agricultural machinery or equipment. Even the service and repair of tractors, trailers, and power tillers is carried out elsewhere than in Arni.

With respect to trade, units for the wholesaling of paddy and rice, gunny bags, and other food, especially jaggery, have expanded most rapidly, yet agricultural wholesaling has remained constant at 5 percent of all firms, largely because of a decline in groundnut milling and wholesaling firms. Given a local expansion of groundnut production of 15 percent over the decade (66 percent faster than the state's average rate of increase [Government of Tamil Nadu 1974, 1985]), this apparent atrophy in local production linkages needs some explanation. Groundnuts are the only commodity to be successfully regulated under the Regulated Markets Act (Harriss 1984). Groundnut transactions take place in the regulated market yard under supervision of market officials. This is said to be because the production of this rainfed crop does not require traders' credit, nor is it considered creditworthy. Regulated market data show that sales in the yard are predominantly to merchants from southern Tamil Nadu who are motivated to scour far afield because of excess installed capacity in new technologies for decortication and oil expelling. Their capture of the local regulated market has apparently been the cause for the decline observed in local agroprocessing and mercantile activity based on groundnuts.

Specialized retailing firms increased by only 27 percent over the decade and declined in relative importance from 38 percent of firms in 1973 to 31 percent in 1983, consistent with Wanmali's finding (Chapter 10) that retailing is decentralizing to village locations. This trend conceals a strong expansion in cloth and provision shops. Also, a number of enterprises for goods never or rarely traded in 1973 have emerged; for example, in the workshop sector the manufacture of stainless steel furniture and bottled cold drinks; in the financial services sector 24 "finance corporations" have appeared since 1980 alone; and in the purely retailing sector firms trading eggs—which, somewhat surprisingly, are not goods local to Arni's region but are traded from Chittoor in Andhra Pradesh, which has specialized in intensive production—and selling fancy goods and ready-made clothes, plastic goods, and trinkets, produced under factory conditions in metropolitan locations. But we jump ahead. The main conclusion to draw from our analysis of numbers of firms is that with the exception of striking expansion in the silk industry, decline in the groundnut sector, and a probable decentralization in retailing, there is a strong continuity in the relative contribution of different types of firms to the total number of enterprises in the growing urban economy.

Financial Characteristics of Arni's Firms

We now proceed to our two samples, details of which are furnished in Tables 9.3 and 9.4. Randomly selected, these samples are also satisfactorily representative of the relative frequencies of firms as classified in Table 9.2. Differences in the composition of the samples at two points in time are small; major changes reflect changes discussed earlier.[2] From data on the age of firms in our sample, it would seem that the oldest firms in 1983 come from the same sectors as the oldest firms in 1973. These long-established surviving firms tend to deal in the wholesaling of foods other than paddy and groundnuts, in workshops for nonfood agricultural products, and in the silk industry. Urban sectors dominated by young firms are "other food workshops" (the food industries) and "wholesaling of nonfood agricultural products" (cloth, shoes, gunnies). Whereas farm inputs and fuel retailing were new, young firms in 1973, they have not continued as such and the new, young firms in 1983 feature the workshop (as opposed to factory) production of silk, the wholesaling of other (nonagricultural) goods (consistent perhaps with the move of much retailing to rural locations), and general services and repairs.

2. Silk factories accounted for 4.5 percent of the 1973 sample and 7 percent of the 1983 sample, comparing with 5 and 13 percent, respectively, in the populations. "Other repairs and services" rose from 14 percent of the 1973 sample to 17 percent of the 1983 sample while rising from 16 to 17 percent of the population. The main anomaly is the random overrepresentation of "other (nonagricultural) workshops" in 1973; these formed 10 percent of the 1973 sample but 4 percent of the 1983 sample and of the 1973 and 1983 populations. A problem of our project is that a disaggregated classification consistent with the SAM means that some of our cell sizes are extremely small: in 1973 rice retailing, wholesaling of nonfood agricultural products, and retailing of fuel and energy have each one firm; in 1983 this is true for "other foods wholesaling," "nonfood agricultural products wholesaling," "other goods wholesaling," and transport firms. Given what we have to say later about polarization and concentration of economic activity, it cannot be assumed that small cells contain data representative of the categories to which they refer.

Starting Capital

Tables 9.3 and 9.4 give starting capital in current prices rather than the more useful constant prices, for want of inflators for 1973 going back to the turn of the century. All we can ascertain is that in 1973 activities with the largest financial barriers to entry were rice milling, the manufacture of silk, the retailing of farm inputs, the wholesaling of paddy, and pawnbroking. The first three on this list top that for 1983 too, together with the wholesaling of nonagricultural goods. By contrast, types of enterprises with the smallest financial barriers to entry in 1973 appear to be miscellaneous services and repairs and workshops for nonagricultural products. There is continuity in these last characteristics for 1983, with the addition of ancillary workshop silk production under master weavers.

Gross Output

As in Chapter 7, gross output is defined as total sales, and we do not follow the convention for trading establishments of excluding the value of commodities that are simply purchased and resold without any intermediate processing or production activity.

By and large, firms with large amounts of starting capital also have high gross outputs (Tables 9.3 and 9.4). In 1973 the types of firms with the largest gross output were paddy and rice wholesale firms (averaging Rs 500,000), firms wholesaling other foods (Rs 481,000), and a group that included rice milling and retailing of food and farm inputs (all hovering around Rs 300,000). Firms that had low gross outputs were general repairs and services (Rs 8,800) and nonagricultural workshops (Rs 12,500). The concentration of gross output, however, is far greater than indicated in this classification. The top decile of firms by gross output in our 1973 sample included two silk factories, two rice mills, and four enterprises trading, one each, in provisions, milk, electricals, and hardware. This top decile had a combined gross output of Rs 6.2 million, which was 13 times the combined gross output of the lowest 50 percent of firms. The largest single firm had a gross output 4.5 times the total for the bottom 50 percent of firms.

The largest sectors in 1983 are different from those in 1973. It is now rice milling and wholesaling (Rs 7.495 million and Rs 4.827 million, respectively, in current prices), silk manufacturing (Rs 5.061 million), and fuel and energy retailing (Rs 5.080 million) that are the biggest firms in terms of gross output. The smallest types of firms have not

TABLE 9.3
Financial Characteristics of Sectors of Arni Business Economy, 1973 (thous Rs)

Type of Firm	Sample Size		Average Date of Start	Average Starting Capital (Current prices)	Average Gross Output (Current Prices)	Total Sample Gross Output		Average Value Added (Current prices)	Total Sample Value Added		Value Added to Gross Output Ratio (Percent)	Average Labor Costs (Current prices)	Total Sample Labor Costs	
	Number	Percent				(1973 prices)	(Percent)		(1973 prices)	(Percent)			(1973 prices)	(Percent)
Rice														
Mills	3	3.4	1958	24.0	298	894	7.3	43.4	130	8.2	14.6	7.4	22.2	4.1
Wholesalers	2	2.3	1962	16.0	500	1,000	8.2	15.7	31	2.0	3.1	5.5	11.0	2.1
Retailers	1	1.1	1967	5.0	26	26	0.2	1.7	2	0.1	6.5	—	—	—
Other Foods														
Workshops	8	9.1	1967	5.5	69	552	4.5	19.3	154	9.7	28.0	7.7	61.6	11.5
Wholesalers	3	3.4	1929	5.0	481	1,443	11.8	50.0	150	9.5	10.4	31.0	93.0	17.4
Retailers	11	12.5	1959	6.6	297	3,267	26.7	9.6	106	6.7	3.2	1.5	16.5	3.1
Nonfood agric. products														

Workshops	2	2.3	1946	6.2	50	100	0.8	8.8	18	1.1	17.6	0.6	1.2	0.2
Wholesalers	1	1.1	1970	5.0	36	36	0.3	8.5	9	0.6	23.6	—	—	—
Retailers	7	8.0	1955	5.9	71	497	4.1	6.9	48	3.0	9.7	1.5	10.5	2.0
Farm inputs														
Retailers	3	3.4	1964	15.3	330	990	8.1	21.0	63	4.0	6.4	5.8	17.4	3.2
Silk														
Factories	4	4.5	1952	62.0	376	1,504	12.3	139.0	555	35.0	37.0	67.0	268.0	50.0
Other goods														
Workshops	9	10.2	1959	1.5	13	113	0.9	4.3	39	2.5	33.1	1.0	9.0	1.7
Wholesalers	2	2.3	1954	1.0	45	90	0.7	3.0	6	0.4	6.7	0.5	1.0	0.2
Retailers	11	12.5	1949	8.0	115	1,265	10.3	13.6	150	9.5	11.8	2.5	5.8	1.1
Fuel & energy														
Retailers	1	1.1	1969	1.0	108	108	0.9	2.0	2	0.1	1.9	0.8	0.8	0.1
Transport	2	2.3	1955	7.5	9	18	0.1	6.3	13	0.8	70.0	3.1	6.2	1.2
Other repairs														
& services	12	13.6	1954	2.0	9	107	0.9	5.6	68	4.3	62.2	0.7	8.4	1.6
Financial														
services	6	6.8	1958	11.0	39	234	1.9	7.4	44	2.8	19.0	0.5	3.0	0.6
Total	88	100.0			139	12,243	100.0	18.0	1,587	100.0	13.0	6.1	536.0	100.0

TABLE 9.4
Financial Characteristics of Sectors of Arni Business Economy, 1983 (thous Rs)

Type of Firm	Sample Size		Average Date of Start	Average Starting Capital (Current prices)	Average Gross Output (Current prices)	Total Sample Gross Output		Average Value Added (Current prices)	Total Sample Value Added		Value Added to Gross Output Ratio (Percent)	Average Value of Assets (Current prices)	Rate of Return on Assets (Percent)	Average Labor Costs (Current prices)	Total Sample Labor Costs	
	Number	Percent				(1973 prices)	(Percent)		(1973 prices)	(Percent)					(1973 prices)	(Percent)
Rice																
Mills	4	3.5	1968	46.0	7,495	16,264	20.5	584.2	1,268	10.3	7.8	613	75.9	63.5	138.5	3.1
Wholesalers	4	3.5	1957	18.0	4,827	10,476	13.2	134.1	291	2.4	2.8	98	120.7	9.0	19.6	0.4
Other foods																
Workshops	10	8.8	1970	15.0	210	1,139	1.4	60.8	330	2.7	28.9	40	115.2	109.8	596.0	13.4
Wholesalers	1	0.9	1946	20.0	1,410	765	1.0	73.7	40	0.3	5.2	700	9.2	21.9	11.9	0.3
Retailers	15	13.2	1970	10.7	535	4,350	5.5	56.5	460	3.7	10.6	87	50.8	7.7	63.0	1.4
Nonfood agricultural products																
Workshops	2	1.8	1958	20.0	222	240	0.3	51.6	55	0.4	22.8	207	18.8	10.0	10.8	0.2

Wholesalers	1	0.9	1978	3.0	28	15	—	12.9	7	0.1	46.1	4	122.7	7.0	3.8	0.1
Retailers	9	7.9	1969	16.4	1,359	6,633	8.4	60.8	293	2.4	4.4	188	18.6	13.8	67.5	1.5
Farm inputs																
Retailers	3	2.6	1969	40.0	919	1,494	1.9	46.0	75	0.6	5.0	919	2.1	3.5	5.7	0.1
Silk																
Factories	8	7.0	1954	21.0	5,061	21,968	27.7	1,763.4	7,655	62.2	34.8	5,061	22.9	760.0	3,299.0	74.3
Workshops	3	2.6	1975	2.2	55	90	0.1	22.1	36	0.3	40.2	55	18.3	7.7	12.6	0.3
Other goods																
Workshops	6	5.3	1967	2.2	36	117	0.1	14.1	46	0.4	39.2	7	117.5	3.9	12.6	0.3
Wholesalers	1	0.9	1981	60.0	479	260	0.3	97.6	53	0.4	20.4	70	47.1	53.0	28.8	0.6
Retailers	15	13.2	1973	11.0	645	5,249	6.6	56.5	460	3.7	8.8	74	45.8	4.8	39.0	0.9
Fuel and energy																
Retailers	3	2.6	1951	17.5	5,080	8,268	10.4	116.1	189	1.5	2.3	317	14.1	54.7	89.0	2.0
Transport	1	0.9	1948	6.0	166	90	0.1	82.9	45	0.4	49.9	800	7.4	3.7	2.0	—
Transport repairs																
& services	2	1.8	1945	5.5	24	26	—	12.0	13	0.1	50.0	3	327.8	0.4	0.4	—
Other repairs																
& services	19	16.7	1965	2.2	35	361	0.5	11.8	122	1.0	33.7	15	48.2	2.4	24.7	0.6
Financial																
services	7	6.1	1961	18.0	371	1,409	1.8	228.5	868	7.1	61.6	170	131.2	3.5	13.3	0.3
Total	114	100.0			1,281	79,214	100.0	198.9	12,306	100.0	15.5			71.7	4,437.7	100.0

changed over the decade—general repair and services (Rs 35,000) and nonagricultural workshops (Rs 36,000).

However, our 1983 sample shows a staggering increase in the concentration of gross output. Now the top decile includes four silk factories, three rice mills, a grain wholesaling firm, a petrol station, and two provisions firms. The combined gross output of the top decile (at Rs 119.762 million) is now 66 times the total output of the bottom 50 percent of firms. The largest single firm (at Rs 17 million) has a gross output 9 times that of the bottom half of firms. This is one of the most important results to emerge from this historical case study.

Whether or not the biggest types of firm are the biggest sectors of the urban economy depends on the numbers of firms per sector. In 1973 the sectors having the biggest types of firm as listed above accounted for 62 percent of total turnover. In 1983 such sectors had increased their domination to 77 percent of total gross output.

A comparison of the composition of gross output in constant prices allows further changes to be perceived[3] (Tables 9.3 and 9.4). Total gross output for the samples increased by a factor of 6.5 over the decade and was mostly dominated by the expansion of the silk industry by a factor of 14.6. Our data may exaggerate the growth trajectory of this sector, because our first survey was at a time of slump for silk while 1983 was during a boom; however, there is no doubt about the importance of its secular growth. Other sectors of the economy that expanded real gross output at a rate greater than average were rice milling, rice wholesaling, the retailing of nonfood agricultural products, and the retailing of fuels and energy (by factors of 18, 11, 13, and 76, respectively). By contrast, sectors where gross output increased at a rate less than average included the retailing of farm inputs and food, workshops manufacturing nonagricultural goods (by factors of less than 1.5), and pawnbroking (by a factor of 6).

Value Added

Value added measures the return to all factors and includes wages, profits or dividends, interest, depreciation, rent and taxes, and licenses (see Chapter 7). As might be expected, workshop activity, services, and repairs show the highest ratios of value added to gross output

3. The deflator to convert 1983 prices to 1973 constants is the standard one of the IFPRI-TNAU project: 0.5426, derived from the Tamil Nadu state government cost-of-living index for a village in North Arcot district (see Chapter 3). It must be noted that it is a lower deflator than one arguably more relevant to the urban economy. The general consumer price index for industrial workers in Tamil Nadu yields a deflator of 0.455.

(Tables 9.3 and 9.4). Retailing has the lowest, while wholesaling enterprises have a comparatively high ratio of value added to gross output. The total value added for our 1973 sample amounted to Rs 1.587 million, of which 35 percent was contributed by silk. Rice milling and wholesaling combined and each sector of the rest of the food industry contributed roughly a further 10 percent each. Remaining sectors of significance were pawnbroking (2.8 percent), farm inputs (4 percent), and the retailing of nonagricultural products (9.5 percent).

By 1983 the total value added in Arni had increased in real terms by a factor of 7.8 (to Rs 12.306 million). Silk factories increased their contribution from 35 to 62 percent, rice milling increased its share from 8.2 to 10.3 percent, and pawnbroking increased from 2.8 to 7.1 percent. Other activities generally declined in relative significance. While there is no reason to expect the share of these sectors in total regional value added to be similar, because of Arni's particularities, it is interesting to note that silk contributes only 3.8 percent to total regional value added as computed for the SAM, and rice milling and wholesaling appear to contribute three times more to total value added in Arni's economy than they do to that of the region. Pawnbroking is over four times more important in Arni's total value added than it is in that of the region as a whole. Provisions and groceries are two-thirds as important in this respect (compare Chapter 7, Table 7.3).

Capital Assets

The value of capital assets gives an alternative indication of the size of firms. We did not ask for assets in 1973, but in 1983 we asked for the value of land, buildings, machines, stocks, own working capital, and money lent or goods sold on credit or both. When circumstances did not permit detailed questioning, we accepted respondents' statements for the total value of their businesses.

The majority of individual firms in the sectors of workshop fabrication of nongrain food and other nonfood products are characterized by individual average assets of under Rs 10,000; general repairs and services have average assets of some Rs 15,000 (Table 9.4). Firms with assets under Rs 15,000, which make up one-third of our sample, account for just 1.6 percent of the total sample's assets. By contrast, the types of firms with average assets in excess of Rs 500,000 are familiar (rice mills and silk factories) and unfamiliar ones (truck companies and retailing of agricultural inputs). Together they account for 84 percent of the combined assets of the sample. The silk industry alone accounts for 73 percent of the assets in Arni.

The top decile in terms of the value of assets—all individually in

TABLE 9.5
Frequency of Investments by Type of Firm, Arni

	Sample Size		*Number of Firms with Investments in:*							
			Finance		*Commercial Property*		*Industry*		*Agro-ind Workshops*	
Type of Firm	*1973*	*1983*	*1973*	*1983*	*1973*	*1983*	*1973*	*1983*	*1973*	*1983*
Rice										
Mills	3	4	—	3	1	3	—	—	—	5
Wholesalers	2	4	—	2	2	2	—	—	2	3
Retailers	1	—	—	—	—	—	—	—	—	—
Other foods										
Workshops	8	10	3	2	1	4	—	1	2	—
Wholesalers	3	1	—	1	2	1	—	1	1	—
Retailers	11	15	—	3	1	4	—	—	2	2
Nonfood agric. products										
Workshops	2	2	—	—	—	1	—	—	1	1
Wholesalers	1	1	—	—	—	—	—	—	—	—
Retailers	7	9	—	5	1	4	—	—	—	3
Farm inputs										
Retailers	3	3	—	3	—	—	—	—	1	1
Silk										
Factories	4	8	—	4	1	3	—	—	2	6
Workshops	0	3	—	—	—	—	—	—	—	—
Other goods										
Workshops	9	6	—	2	—	—	—	—	—	—
Wholesalers	2	1	—	1	—	1	—	—	1	—
Retailers	11	15	—	5	2	5	1	2	1	6
Fuel and energy										
Retailers	1	3	—	2	1	1	1	1	—	1
Transport	2	1	—	1	—	—	—	—	—	—
Transport repairs & services	—	2	—	—	—	—	—	—	—	—
Other repairs & services	12	19	—	3	—	1	—	—	—	—
Financial services	6	7	—	6	5	6	—	—	1	3
Total	88	114	3	43	17	36	2	6	15	31
Top decile of gross output distribution	8	11	—	7	3	9	—	—	3	10
Bottom decile of gross output distribution	9	11	—	1	1	—	—	—	—	1

[a]Cars and trucks.
[b]Bicycles.

TABLE 9.5
Continued

	Number of Firms with Investments in:									
	Nonagric Trade		*Agricultural Trade*		*Agriculture/ Land*		*Services*		*Vehicles*	
Type of Firm	*1973*	*1983*	*1973*	*1983*	*1973*	*1983*	*1973*	*1983*	*1973*	*1983*
Rice										
Mills	—	1	1	4	1	2	1	1	—	4
Wholesalers	—	—	—	—	—	2	—	—	—	4
Retailers	—	—	—	—	—	—	—	—	—	—
Other foods										
Workshops	—	—	2	2	3	1	1	1	—	8
Wholesalers	1	1	—	1	1	1	1	—	—	1
Retailers	—	1	6	3	5	4	—	—	—	11
Nonfood agric. products										
Workshops	—	—	—	—	1	1	—	—	—	2
Wholesalers	—	—	1	1	—	—	—	—	—	1
Retailers	—	1	3	—	3	2	—	—	—	7
Farm inputs										
Retailers	—	2	1	—	2	—	—	—	—	3
Silk										
Factories	1	—	—	—	2	2	—	1	—	3
Workshops	—	—	—	—	—	1	—	—	—	—
Other goods										
Workshops	—	3	1	—	2	—	—	—	—	3
Wholesalers	1	—	1	—	7	—	—	—	—	1
Retailers	1	11	—	—	2	3	—	—	—	11
Fuel and energy										
Retailers	—	3	—	2	—	1	—	1	—	3
Transport	—	—	—	—	—	—	—	—	1	1
Transport repairs & services	—	1	—	—	—	—	—	—	—	1
Other repairs & services	1	2	2	—	—	—	—	—	—	14
Financial services	—	1	—	—	2	—	—	—	—	6
Total	5	27	18	13	31	20	3	4	1	84
Top decile of gross output distribution	2	3	3	5	4	4	—	2	4	9[a]
Bottom decile of gross output distribution	—	1	—	—	2	1	—	—	—	5[b]

[a]Cars and trucks.
[b]Bicycles

excess of Rs 600,000 in current prices—is a mixed bag: four silk factories, three rice mills, one vegetable wholesaler, one cloth trading company, a trucking firm, and a pawnbroker. Their combined assets are 70 times greater than those of the bottom half of firms, all of which had individual assets of under Rs 20,000.

Rates of Return to Capital

Profits—the difference between gross output and total operating costs plus raw materials costs—have been expressed as a proportion of capital assets in Table 9.4. Great variation is shown, and a large number of firms have high rates of return on capital. In the case of small workshops operated largely with family labor, this will be because assets are small in relation to gross output and because profits are gross rather than net of household expenditure. The ranking is as follows: wholesaling (with an average rate of return to capital assets of 95 percent), services (87 percent), workshop enterprises (63 percent), factories (42 percent), retailing (38 percent), silk factories (23 percent), and silk workshops (18 percent).

Portfolios of Investments

Finally, we turn to the uses to which the accumulations of businesses are put. At the outset we must note that not all businesses accumulate. Many fail, but we cannot obtain quantitative evidence for the frequency and reasons for this. Table 9.5 shows that small businesses in the bottom gross output decile had no investment portfolios as such in 1973, and few were landed. A decade later such firms are only slightly more complex and have grown very little in scope.

The largest decile in terms of gross output in 1973 had investments in shops, mills, land, and a few bikes. By 1983 its portfolio is far more elaborate, instances of investment having increased by a factor of 2.75. The top decile includes firms individually different but collectively as old as those in the top decile in 1973. The urban economy is being developed by such firms, and among them they own large tracts of the town (at least 201 houses and shops for rent out) and almost all have vehicles (9 cars, 7 trucks, and 6 motorbikes or scooters). Almost all have interests in finance companies, and collectively this group has over 95 acres of land, 12 agroprocessing firms, 5 other agricultural wholesaling enterprises, and 2 cinemas. The silk industries in this group have holdings of urban property, rice mills, twisting factories and power looms, and finance companies, but only a modest interest in agriculture.

Taking the samples as wholes, the most common investment of

mercantile profits in 1973 was in agriculture (energizing lift irrigation), in agricultural trade, and in urban shops for renting out. Money lending, nonagricultural trade and industry, and the purchase of vehicles were unimportant. By 1983, however, the most common investments are in vehicles (bicycles, bullock carts, motorcycles, cars, and trucks), education, dowries, and an urban house for own use (the latter so common as to be untabulated). Money lending increases from 3 percent of instances of investment to 16 percent. Pawnbrokers who branched out into urban property in 1973 added finance corporations to their portfolios over the decade. Money lending is now carried out by almost all other sectors as well—notably by rice and silk factory owners and all types of retailers. Nonagricultural goods trading has doubled in its proportion of instances, though nonagricultural industry is still uncommon. The proportion of instances of investment in agriculture has halved.

Changes in Employment

Types of firms in Arni are characterized by sizable internal variation not only in size as defined by assets and turnover but also in employment. Family businesses, enterprises with a combination of household and wage labor, and those with absolutely large wage labor forces can be found within many of the individual sectors of the urban economy. Further, the category of wage labor that we use here for simplicity masks a variety of forms of production, trade, and services that may embrace labor gangs on contract, casual labor on piece or daily wages (in combinations of cash and kind), monthly salaried labor, apprenticeships, and forms of illegal child labor with a variety of levels and kinds of remuneration. This variety is outside the scope of this chapter to analyze. However, it is relevant to any attempt to characterize nonfarm employment generated by growth from agriculture. Our crude data on how the various sectors of the urban economy have contributed to jobs are found in Table 9.6.

Household and Wage Labor

In 1973 the types of firms employing most household labor—more than two family members per firm—were the silk factories and pawnbrokers, together with the wholesaling and retailing of nonfood and nonagricultural products. Those employing the least wage labor were pawnbroking (in order to control money lending tightly), general services, and repairing enterprises (too small to generate jobs for em-

TABLE 9.6
Labor and Employment Details in Arni Business Economy

Type of Firm	*Sample Size*	*Average Number of Family Laborers per Firm*[a]	*Average Number of Wage Laborers per Firm*	*Total Number of Jobs in Sample*	*Percent Female Workers*	*Assets/ Job Ratio (1973 prices)*	*Wages/ Profit Ratio*
1973							
Rice							
Mills	3	1.0	10.0	33	52		0.22
Wholesalers	2	1.5	6.5	16	—		0.60
Retailers	1	1.0	—	1	—		—
Other foods							
Workshops	8	1.4	6.3	62	—		0.52
Wholesalers	3	1.3	19.6	63	—		1.72
Retailers	11	1.3	4.0	58	—		0.26
Nonfood agric. products							
Workshops	2	1.5	1.0	5	—		0.08
Wholesalers	1	1.0	—	1	—		—
Retailers	7	2.3	1.5	27	—		0.33
Farm inputs							
Retailers	3	1.0	5.7	20	—		0.41
Silk							
Factories	4	2.0	49.0	204	24		0.95
Other goods							
Workshops	9	1.0	2.0	32	—		0.40
Wholesalers	2	2.0	0.5	5	20		—
Retailers	11	2.4	2.0	48	—		0.08
Fuel & energy							
Retailers	1	1.0	1.0	2	—		0.44
Transport	2	1.0	4.5	11	—		1.14
Other repairs & services	12	1.5	0.6	25	—		0.14
Financial services	6	2.2	0.5	16	—		0.06
Total	88			629	10		
1983							
Rice							
Mills	4	1.5	30.0	126	60	10.5	0.14
Wholesalers	4	1.5	3.5	20	—	10.6	0.01
Other foods							
Workshops	10	2.0	5.2	72	—	3.0	2.40
Wholesalers	1	1.0	6.0	7	—	54.3	0.34
Retailers	15	2.0	2.1	62	—	11.4	1.05
Nonfood agric. products							
Workshops	2	1.0	3.5	9	—	25.0	0.26
Wholesalers	1	1.0	3.0	4	—	0.5	1.40
Retailers	9	1.8	4.1	53	—	17.3	0.08
Farm inputs							
Retailers	3	1.0	1.6	8	—	187.0	0.18
Silk							
Factories	8	2.4	216.0	1,747	8	12.6	0.74
Workshops	3	1.0	5.0	18	55	4.9	1.16

TABLE 9.6
Continued

Type of Firm	*Sample Size*	*Average Number of Family Laborers per Firm*[a]	*Average Number of Wage Laborers per Firm*	*Total Number of Jobs in Sample*	*Percent Female Workers*	*Assets/ Job Ratio (1973 prices)*	*Wages/ Profit Ratio*
Other goods							
Workshops	6	2.0	1.2	19	—	6.2	0.44
Wholesalers	1	1.0	5.0	6	17	6.3	1.61
Retailers	15	2.0	0.9	44	—	13.6	0.14
Fuel & energy							
Retailers	3	1.0	5.0	18	—	28.7	1.30
Transport	1	8.0	2.0	10	—	43.0	0.06
Transport repairs & services	2	1.3	1.0	5	—	0.7	0.03
Other repairs & services	19	1.5	1.5	57	—	2.8	1.40
Financial services	7	1.3	0.5	13	—	49.7	0.03
Total	114			2,298	10		

[a]All male labor.

ployees). Those with the largest wage labor forces were the silk factories (average 49 wage workers per firm), food wholesaling (average 19 wage workers, although this result is distorted by one exceptionally large firm), rice milling (10 per firm), and rice wholesaling and farm inputs retailing (6 workers per firm each). Combining family and wage workers together, we see that in 1973 food processing and marketing provided 37 percent of all jobs, while silk provided a further third.

Changes, 1973–1983

Over the decade the total number of jobs in our samples increased from 629 to 2,298, a factor of 3.6, compared with the almost sevenfold real increase in gross output. Most of this increase is accounted for by the growth of the silk industry—which doubled its share of urban jobs, employing 62 percent of all female and 77 percent of all male wage workers in 1983—and to a lesser extent by the expansion in rice-milling capacity in the town. Rice milling increased its share of jobs from a quarter to a third of all female employees while continuing to employ under 3 percent of all male workers. In several sectors characterized by small firms (e.g., general services and repairs and nonfood and nonagricultural workshop activity), an expansion in real gross output has not been accompanied by an increase in employment. Women were

10 percent of the work force at both times, confined with few exceptions to the rice and silk mills. But if we exclude the silk industry, total employment increased by 25 percent (108 jobs), male employment increased by 10 percent (42 jobs), and female employment increased by 471 percent (66 jobs).

Over the decade there has been little change in the types of firms that use absolutely most family labor and absolutely least wage work, although it appears that family workers are being replaced by wage workers in pawnbroking firms. The average size of the wage labor force in rice mills has trebled and in silk factories has quadrupled. From our sample it would appear that food processing and marketing generate only 16.5 percent of all jobs, while silk manufacture generates two-thirds of all jobs. A considerable proportion of the employment created by the expanding silk industry is not located in Arni itself but in surrounding villages (see also Harriss and Harriss 1984, pp. 94–95).

Labor Intensity

Ratios of assets to jobs have been calculated for 1983 (Table 9.6). Workshops and services tend to be the least capital intensive per job; trade in farm inputs is the most. Significantly, capital invested in large types of firms as defined earlier generates high employment—in silk, in rice milling and wholesaling, and in provisions and general goods shops. The silk industry demonstrates a combination of high capital barriers to entry, large scale of operation, and relatively high labor intensity defined in terms of assets to job ratios.

Trends in Wages

Wages in the urban economy vary by gender, women earning 25 to 33 percent less than men for comparable sorts of work. They vary according to the age, experience, loyalty, indebtedness, and skills of the worker. Wages also vary according to caste. Being a member of a scheduled caste is still a barrier to entry into the urban labor force. The data on wages appearing in Tables 9.7 and 9.8 must be viewed as a very condensed summary of these complex relations.

Table 9.7 shows time trends in wages. Although rural, agricultural labor incomes have increased over the decade (see Chapter 3), it seems that the real value of wages in Arni has remained constant or has even declined, although this depends crucially on whether rural or urban wage deflators are used. At any rate the exceptions to this trend are to be found in the silk and rice-milling industries, precisely those that have expanded the most during this time.

TABLE 9.7
Average Urban Wages, Arni (Rs/month)

Type of Wage	*1973*	*1983*	*1983 Wages Deflated to 1973 Prices* (a)	(b)
Weavers (male)	120–150	230–250	125–135	105–114
Twisting factory workers (male)	65	160	87	73
Twisting factory workers (female)	50	140	75	64
Rice mill clerks (male)	100	225	122	103
Provisions shop clerks (male)	45–100	100–200	54–108	45–90
Cloth shop clerks (male)	50–70	150–210	81–114	68–95
Average all employees	116	222	120	101

Source: Averages calculated from the author's 6 percent sample of firms.
Note: (a) = IFPRI-TNAU rural deflator (see note 3); (b) = deflator derived from general consumer price index for urban industrial workers in Tamil Nadu.

TABLE 9.8
Rural and Urban Wages, Arni and Region, 1983

Type of Wage	*Rs/day*
Rural wages	
Agricultural labor (male)	3.0–5.0
Agricultural labor (female)	2.0–3.0
Rural/urban wages	
Weavers	9.2
Urban wages	
Rice mill and *mundy* coolies (male)	7.0
Rice mill and *mundy* coolies (female)	4.5–5.5
Twisting factory workers (male)	6.4
Twisting factory workers (female)	5.4
Provisions shop clerks (male)	5.5
Cloth shop clerks (male)	7.5

Despite the probably different trends between agricultural and non-agricultural wages, Table 9.8 shows that both urban and rural non-agricultural labor is more highly remunerated than is agricultural labor, so the expansion of the local urban economy is associated with higher wage payments and with increasing flows of wages from the town to the surrounding countryside (Harriss 1986).

The aggregate wages for the samples (Tables 9.3 and 9.4) were Rs 536,000 in 1973 and Rs 4.438 million in constant prices in 1983, a more than eightfold increase. In 1973 the most important sectors of the urban economy with respect to the generation of wages were silk (50 percent of the sample total) and workshop and wholesaling activity for foods other than rice (12 and 17 percent, respectively). These sectors remain the most important in 1983. In both periods rice milling and pawnbroking made contributions to total urban wages incommensurate with their contributions to total value added and profits.

Distributive Shares

The distributive shares, or wages/profit ratios, are shown in Table 9.6. In 1973 profits stood at a total of Rs 944,000; that is three-quarters as much again as the total bill to labor. Thirty percent of all profits accrued to the silk industry, 11 percent to rice milling, and 8 percent to agricultural wholesaling. The share of total profits exceeds that of total value added in the following sectors: rice milling, general repairs and services, retailing, and pawnbroking. Wages approach parity with profits or exceed them only for agricultural wholesaling and transport. In 1983 sample profits (in 1973 prices) stood at Rs 8.336 million, two-thirds as much again as the total bill to labor, so that over the decade the distributive share of labor appears to have increased slightly. Fifty-three percent of all profits now accrue to the silk industry and 12 percent to rice milling. Wages approach parity or exceed it in more sectors of the urban economy than earlier: in workshops and retailing for other foods, in wholesaling for nonfood agricultural products and other goods, in retailing for fuel and energy, and in workshops for miscellaneous goods and services. The silk industry has a high distributive share, with ratios of wages to profits of 0.74 for factories and 1.16 for workshops. By contrast, that of rice milling is low and has declined, from 0.22 to 0.14.

Incomes

In Table 9.9 annual profits for firm-owning households in 1983 have been expressed as multiples of Dandekar and Rath's (1971) poverty line—Rs 48 per capita per month in 1973 prices. These can be contrasted with estimates of poverty in the urban labor force, among rural paddy producers, and among the agricultural labor force. There is considerable inequality in per capita income within the town, reduced to some

TABLE 9.9
Per Capita Income as Multiple of Poverty Line, Arni and Region, 1983

Type of Firm/Household	*Average Income per Capita as Multiple of Poverty Line*[a]	*Household Size*
Silk—factories	95.0	13.0
Rice—mills	36.0	8.5
Rice—wholesalers	20.0	6.5
Other foods—retailers	10.0	6.0
Fuel & energy—retailers	5.6	9.0
Nonfood agric. products—workshops	5.3	6.5
Farm inputs—retailers	4.6	7.3
Other goods—wholesalers (1 firm)	4.4	7.0
Other goods—retailers	4.5	6.5
(Other goods—retailers: exceptional firm)	15.7	6.0
Other foods—retailers	3.0	6.8
Nonfood agric. products—retailers	2.4	7.9
Transport repairs & services	2.4	4.5
Financial services	2.2	8.5
(Financial services: exceptional firm)	226.0	6.0
Other foods—workshops	2.0	7.0
Other goods—workshops	1.6	6.0
(Other goods—workshops: exceptional firm)	85.0	4.0
Other repairs & services	1.4	6.4
Rice mill labor (male)	0.49	4.0[b]
Rice mill labor (female)	0.35	4.0
Twisting factory labor (male)	0.45	4.0
Twisting factory labor (female)	0.38	4.0
Paddy farms[c] > 1 ha	1.85	n.a.
Paddy farms < 1 ha	0.92	n.a.
Agricultural labor[c] (male)	0.28	4.0[b]
Agricultural labor[c] (female)	0.18	4.0[b]

[a]Rs 48/capita/month (Dandekar and Rath, 1971), all data deflated to 1973 prices.
[b]Simulated household size, not real averages.
[c]Data for this calculation from J. Harriss 1986.

extent by the fact that the richest sectors have the largest families. If we ignore a few exceptional firms, then silk factory, rice milling, and rice wholesaling firms are richest, with per capita incomes of 95, 36, and 20 times the poverty line, respectively, for their owners and their households.

By contrast, general repairs and services and workshop activity in other foods and in nonagricultural goods generate average incomes for their household members that put them at around twice the poverty line. Twenty percent of the firms we sampled in 1983 brought in insufficient income to raise their households above the poverty line, if unsupplemented by other activities. Over a third of the firms in three sectors—workshops and retail firms for foods other than grain, and general repairs and services—were apparently in this position. The firm-owning households in these poorest sectors of the urban economy are on a par with farming households having over 1 hectare of land—per capita incomes averaging 1.85 times the poverty line. Unsupplemented male wage work in the urban economy, from wages in rice milling and twisting factories, would keep a family of four at about half the poverty line. The equivalent for unsupplemented female urban wage work is 0.35 to 0.38 of the poverty line. Even this is higher than the per capita income for a family of four for a male agricultural laborer working 25 days a month and unsupplemented by any other earnings (0.28). For a female agricultural laborer in such a situation, the per capita income is 0.18 of the poverty line. Such comparisons show that the rural inequality that has been the focus of so much academic analysis and policy advocacy is dwarfed by rural-urban differentials in this particular region. The per capita income in a silk manufacturing household is some 200 times that of the household of a male laborer in a silk factory, 240 times that of the household of a female worker, and 530 times the income of members of a household of four forced to depend on female agricultural labor.

Changes in Commodity Flows

Data in Tables 9.10 (for 1973) and 9.11 (for 1983) show flows for purchased raw and intermediate materials and for gross outputs. These data exceed those of the samples in small ways outlined in the notes accompanying the tables, particularly because they include appropriate estimates of the groundnut trade in both 1973 and 1983, and trade through weekly markets and the activity of professional services in 1973. The purpose of the regional classification is to distinguish rural and urban flows in the most disaggregated way feasible. Thus, "other districts" in 1973 could be disaggregated between Madras, Coimbatore, and rural and urban origins in other districts within Tamil Nadu state in 1983.

The Geography of Commodity Flows

Within the set of commodity sectors, food accounted for about two-thirds of total commodity flows in 1973, within which sector rice and groundnuts made up 42 percent. Foodgrain flows originated in local villages, passed through wholesalers or processors located in Arni to radiate out to wholesale destinations through the state but predominantly in Vellore, Madras, Coimbatore, and the deep south. The provisions trade was characterized by diverse origins, wholesaling through Vellore and Arni to destinations within the town and in local villages. By 1983 food flows had decreased to 44 percent of all flows, though rice and groundnuts increased their domination to 82 percent of all food flows.

The origins of foodgrains, however, are now much more diversified, 24 percent coming from South Arcot, Thanjavur, and Trichy districts far to the south, and 30 percent coming from rice-surplus districts in Andhra Pradesh to the north. This trend toward geographical diversification is in part due to the reduction in local supplies of paddy during drought. If merchants themselves are to be believed, this is also to be considered a secular trend deriving from Arni's emerging role as a specialist center for the marketing of fine rice to urban wholesalers all over the state and even for export to adjacent states. The pattern of trade in general provisions has also changed over the decade, with local villages growing in importance as centers of origin from 5 percent of all provisions flows to 49 percent, perhaps evincing diversification in the local agricultural economy, certainly evincing a deepening commercialization. Whereas in 1973 18 percent of provisions sales from Arni were wholesale, this had also increased to 34 percent in 1983.

Nonfood agricultural products is a catchall category for land-based goods. In 1973 these came from cities: Bangalore (a wholesale center for flowers) and Madras and Coimbatore (centers for trading in shoes and cotton textiles). Only timber hailed directly from rural areas, but these were located at long distances within the forests of Kerala state. The destinations of such trade were entirely local, though 22 percent of such sales were to wholesalers. By 1983 wholesale centers in states other than Tamil Nadu were the most important single source, testifying to the "metropolitanization" of mercantile activity. Silk flows rose from 10 to 26 percent of total gross output in the town over the decade, yarn originating at both points of time from wholesalers in Bangalore who control sericulture in its environs (Charsley 1982). Silk textiles are not retailed from Arni in any significant amounts. They are exported, now as then, either directly to wholesalers in metropolitan cities or increasingly through intermediaries in Madras.

Agricultural inputs (fertilizer and pesticides) declined from 7 to 2 percent of total gross output. In 1973 they were purchased from Madras and sold to local villages. In 1983 their origins had diversified to include urban factories in other states.

Industrial consumer goods constituted about 7 percent of flows at

TABLE 9.10
Commodity Flow Accounts, Arni, 1973 (thous Rs)

Sector	Percent Firms in Sample	Gross Output	Gross Operating Margin[a]	Origin of Purchased Raw and Intermediate Materials[b]					Intermediate Destination of Output					Final Destination of Output			
				A	*V*	*OT*	*OD*	*OS*	*A*	*V*	*OT*	*OD*	*OS*	*A*	*V*	*OT*	*OD*
Rice																	
Mills	3.5	895	148	301	446				370		89	436					
Wholesalers	2.3	1,000	34		966				345			565		90			
Retailers	1.1	26	2	16	8									18	8		
Groundnut mills and wholesalers[c]	n.a.	2,109	8		2,100							1,582	527				
Other foods																	
Workshops	9.0	553	218	97	8	200	3	27						320	233		
Wholesalers	3.0	1,444	185	552	274		433		80	200				1,091	73		
Retailers[d]	13.0	3,524	245	217	179	2,524	271	82	311	267	20			1,919	988	18	
Nonfood agric. products																	
Workshops	2.0	100	20		4		34	43		16				51	33		
Wholesalers	1.0	36	10	8	4	7	8	1	7					5	24		
Retailers	8.0	497	68	5	6	42	352	28	25	86				69	318		
Farm inputs																	
Retailers	3.4	990	65	47	46		831							43	948		

Silk																	
Factories	4.5	1,547	608	37		5	13	877	47		90	660	750				
Other goods																	
Workshops	10.0	113	45	20	11	31	7		14	1				31	67		
Wholesalers	2.0	90	7			12	71		42	33				1	14		
Retailers	13.0	1,264	183	11		310	458	298	241	49				445	530		
Fuel and energy																	
Retailers	1.0	108	2				106		6	10				75	17		
Transport	2.0	18	14			3								7		9	1
Misc. repairs																	
& services[e]	13.6	107	82	12	1	11	2		3	1				33	71		
Financial																	
services	6.8	234	77	38	116	2								51	183		
Total[f]		14,653	2,019	1,359	4,168	3,146	2,590	1,354	1,489	662	199	3,243	1,277	4,248	3,507	28	1

Source: 6 percent sample of firms.

[a] The operating margin includes rent, depreciation, electricity, fuel, post, telephone, entertainments, donations, taxes and licenses, travel, handling, transport, interest on money borrowed, wages, and profits. Locational information on these services and purchased items was not collected.

[b] A = Arni.
V = surrounding villages.
OT = other *taluks* within North Arcot district (predominantly Vellore).
OD = other districts within Tamil Nadu, including Madras and Coimbatore.
OS = other states.

[c] Data on groundnuts were taken from Arni Regulated Market Statistics and multiplied by 0.06 for comparability with sample.

[d] This sector includes commodity flow data from a 6 percent sample of the weekly market stalls (vegetables, fruits, meats, and fish) made in 1973.

[e] This sector includes professional services (doctors and lawyers).

[f] Total will not exactly match equivalents in Table 9.3 because of inclusions explained above in notes [c], [d], and [e], where commodity data were obtained but useful data about finance and labor were not obtained. Such firms are included here to improve the precision of the account.

TABLE 9.11
Commodity Flow Accounts, Arni, 1983 (thous Rs, 1973 prices)

Sector	Percent Firms in Sample	Gross Output	Gross Operating Margin[a]	Origin of Purchased Raw and Intermediate Materials[b]								
				A	V	Ve	Ms	Cbe	ODR	ODU	OSR	OSU
Rice												
Mills	3.5	16,268	4,672	292	5,092		3		2,736		3,476	
Wholesalers	3.5	10,475	476		4,107				4,084		1,807	
Groundnut mills and wholesalers[c]	n.a.	2,134	220		1,914							
Other food												
Workshops	9.0	1,141	474	576	50	81	20					
Wholesalers	0.8	766	114		33				218			403
Retailers[d]	13.0	4,355	480	136	2,152	1,077	259		111	11	59	63
Nonfood agric. products												
Workshops	1.7	240	68	2		6			49		114	
Wholesalers	0.8	15	9		7							
Retailers	7.8	6,638	527	8	17		429	2,281		144		3,237
Farm inputs												
Retailers	2.6	1,496	81	107		426	538	37				306
Silk												
Factories	7.0	20,863	9,608	7	9		48			2		11,190
Wholesalers	2.6	220	73	21	1		102			2		20
Other goods												
Workshops	5.2	116	56	3	7	39	11					
Wholesalers	0.9	260	64		98		98					
Retailers	13.0	5,253	480	7	137	1,554	1,339	751	210	213		557
Fuel and energy												
Retailers	2.6	8,269	183				7,009	41	76			958
Transport	0.9	90	58		29				3			
Transport repairs & services	1.7	26	15	2		3	7					
Other repairs & services[e]	17.0	361	122	86	47	54	51					
Financial services	6.0	1,411	1,166	107	100	17	16					
Total[f]		80,396	18,945	1,293	13,799	3,257	9,929	3,110	7,487	371	5,456	16,735

Source: 6 percent sample of firms.

[a]The operating margin includes rent, depreciation, electricity, fuel, post, telephone, entertainments, donations, taxes and licenses, travel, handling, transport, interest on money borrowed, wages, and profits. Precise locational information on these services and purchased items was not collected. Whether the latter are local, imported, or exported is, unfortunately, not known.

[b]A = Arni.
V = surrounding villages.
Ve = Vellore.
Ms = Madras.
Cbe = Coimbatore.
ODR = rural areas in other districts within Tamil Nadu state.
ODU = urban areas in other districts within Tamil Nadu state.
OSR = rural areas in other states.
OSU = urban areas in other states.

TABLE 9.11
Continued

	Intermediate Destination of Output									*Final Destination of Output*					
Sector	*A*	*V*	*Ve*	*Ms*	*Cbe*	*ODR*	*ODU*	*OSR*	*OSU*	*A*	*V*	*Ve*	*Ms*	*Cbe*	*ODR*
Rice															
Mills	274	182	464	2,317	12,366			464		97	38			45	27
Wholesalers	6,416				2,668	1,392									
Groundnut mills & wholesalers[c]					2,134										
Other foods															
Workshops										748	391	2			
Wholesalers	526	225								1,232	2,092	16		2	1
Retailers[d]	575	437													
Nonfood agric. products															
Workshops	58	167								7	9				
Wholesalers	15														
Retailers	336	845				543				1,120	3,251				543
Farm inputs															
Retailers		27								47	1,422				
Silk															
Factories	2,306			8,919	543		3,918		5,155						22
Wholesalers	220														
Other goods															
Workshops										54	62				
Wholesalers	33	71		130							26				
Retailers	1,361	104		130						2,092	1,563				
Fuel & energy															
Retailers	332	422								4,062	2,826		32	32	
Transport													32	59	
Transport repairs & services										7	19				
Other repairs & services[e]	4									185	170	1	2		
Financial services										636	782				
Total[f]	12,456	2,480	464	11,496	17,711	1,935	3,918	464	5,155	10,287	12,651	19	66	138	593

[c]Data on groundnuts were taken from Arni Regulated Market Statistics on transactions for 1982–83, multiplied by 0.06 and deflated to give values comparable to those in the rest of the table. The gross value added was unknown. This has been estimated using the weighted average of "groundnut oil extraction" and "agricultural wholesaling" from the North Arcot SAM (Table 9.3).

[d]This does not include estimates from subsample of weekly market stalls.

[e]This does not include professional and legal services, which were not selected in the random sample in 1983.

[f]Discrepancies between totals here and those in Table 9.4 derive from the inclusion of groundnut estimates, plus differences due to rounding up. Differences between the accounts here and those presented in Harriss and Harriss 1984 (where the constant price total for 1983 is 15 percent less than it is here) are explained by the use of different deflators, and by differences in the inclusiveness of accounts, maximized here.

both times. Over the decade their origins have grown more dispersed, the domination of Madras and Coimbatore over the value of purchases having declined from 42 to 36 percent, with a compensating increase in the share of local villages from nil to 6 percent. Fuel and energy (kerosene, gasoline, and diesel) have increased their share from 0.6 to 10 percent of total gross output. They originate in Madras and Bombay and are locally sold, disproportionately to urban consumers.

Miscellaneous repairs and services, the updated jobs of the service castes (laundering and barbering, etc.), electrical repairs, and tailoring are insignificant in terms of commodity flows, though they generate jobs. Arni itself has become more important as the origin, through wholesalers or retailers, of raw materials for such services, at the expense of Vellore and Madras. These services are catering increasingly in both absolute and relative terms to an urban clientele. Exactly the same is true for pawnbroking.

The Role of Regions

With respect to the origins of purchased raw and intermediate materials flowing into Arni, the share of the local region (town plus village hinterland) has dropped from 43 percent of flows to 25 percent. That of Vellore has dropped even more sharply, from 25 to 5 percent. By contrast, "other districts" within Tamil Nadu (we know this means Madras and Coimbatore) increased their share from 20 to 34 percent; other states (Bangalore, Bombay, and Calcutta cities) from 10 to 35 percent. Over the decade the relative importance of goods produced in metropolitan factories or wholesaled through big cities has increased strikingly.

The proportion of goods flowing to destinations within the town or the village hinterland dropped from 68 percent to 47 percent over the decade, and the share of goods exported from Arni to other states also declined, from 10 to 7 percent. The proportion of goods flowing to Vellore fell from 1.5 to 0.6 percent, but goods going to Madras, Coimbatore, and other rural destinations outside the locality increased from 22 to 45 percent. So Arni's long-distance export role has been consolidated.

Changes in Arni's Functional Role

Wholesale transactions have increased by a factor of 8 compared with a threefold increase in retail sales. Most shops that had retail licenses in 1973 now combine both retailing and wholesaling. The commodity flow accounts depict Arni increasingly as a wholesale center.

Whereas in 1973 47 percent of sales were wholesale flows to nonfinal destinations, by 1983 this had increased to 67 percent. This trend is not to be understood as increased wholesaling of consumer goods for retail sale in local villages, although we saw earlier that this is indeed happening. The relative importance of such trade has actually decreased from 10 to 5 percent. The more important component of this trend is the increase in wholesale flows of rice and silk to Madras and Coimbatore. Wholesale flows within Arni have not altered in relative terms.

Retail Sales

If the geography of Arni's wholesale trade has changed, so also has its retail geography. Whereas in 1973 less than half (45 percent) of all retail flows were to consumers from the village hinterland, by 1983 more than half (55 percent) were. Clearly, real rural purchasing power has been increasing. Retail traders of the town can each identify their market hinterland. In 1973 the town's modal hinterland was estimated to contain about 191,000 rural people to the town's 39,000. In 1983 a (low) estimate for the hinterland was 200,000, while the town had some 49,000 people. Thus, while retail sales per capita were only about Rs 18 for rural dwellers in 1973, they had increased in real terms by 250 percent to an estimated Rs 63 by 1983. Agrarian change must have contributed to this upward trend in average purchasing power; however, the expansion of the weaving industry on a rural putting-out basis must also have contributed. Urban purchases have increased, but not at this rate—from Rs 109 per capita in 1973 to Rs 207 per capita in 1983. On the other hand, although the differential between rural and urban purchasing power has halved, urban purchases are still three times those of rural purchases. However, only part of the expenditures of rural people are captured in Arni because they buy many low-order goods in smaller settlements (see Chapter 10). The urban dwellers, on the other hand, probably do nearly all their shopping in Arni.

Conclusions

Commodity flow data show five major developments over the decade. First, every commodity group has components involving exchange outside the locality, and increasingly so as time goes on. Second, just as the urban economy appears to be diversifying if we examine business units, so it appears to be increasingly specialized, if we examine the value of commodity flows. Such diversification as has undoubtedly occurred is thus not yet of great quantitative importance to commodity flows. Third, rural demand is increasing in relative importance for Arni, although there is still a large discrepancy between rural and urban purchases per capita. Fourth, Arni's wholesale role is increasing, as are the imports of goods produced in, or wholesaled through, metropolitan or big provincial cities. Fifth, we must note a much smaller countervailing trend with the emergence of the village hinterland as a supplier of general provisions and nonagricultural consumer goods, testifying to the existence of rural diversification or deepening commercialization, or both.

There are two more final points to be reiterated from earlier in the chapter. One is that whereas in 1973 the economic base of Arni was agricultural marketing, now Arni is also the location of an important agro-industry (silk) that is based both historically and contemporaneously neither on local raw materials nor on local markets, but rather on local finance capital (derived from trade and money lending) and on local labor. The development of the silk industry is not per se responsible for a concentration of control over gross output. However, it is the most striking feature of urban growth over the past decade. It is occurring in all major sectors of the urban economy and must considerably exceed the concentration of control over rural gross output. In this sense the local economy seems to be characterized by urban bias (Lipton 1977). Its implications for local politics are, however, unknown.

CHAPTER 10

Changes in the Provision and Use of Services in the North Arcot Region

Sudhir Wanmali

SUCCESSFUL AGRICULTURAL DEVELOPMENT requires not only the development of physical infrastructure such as irrigation, electrification, and roads but also the increased provision of key services such as credit, transport, agroprocessing, marketing, and the delivery of farm inputs. Agricultural growth also stimulates increased demands by rural people for consumer-oriented services, such as improved health and education, transport, communication, and retail and personal services. If these consumer services are not adequately provided, then the potential growth multipliers emanating from agricultural growth will not be fully realized by the regional economy.

This chapter is concerned with the development of the service sector in the North Arcot study region and its contributions to the growth of the local economy. Because many of the services that are essential for agricultural growth are also increasingly demanded to meet consumer needs as rural incomes rise (e.g., electricity, transport, credit, and wholesale and retail services), it is difficult to attribute strict cause-and-effect relations between service provision and agricultural and regional growth. Such causal analysis is not attempted here; rather, we focus on a description of the patterns of provision and use of services in the study region and how they changed during the period 1973–83. Given that the region's economy grew successfully during this period, largely as a result of technological change in agriculture, our descriptive analysis provides useful insights into the nature and extent of improvements in the service sector that accompany successful regional development. Such insights may be particularly useful to planners and policymakers dealing with less successfully developed regions.

A useful description of the development of the service sector requires information on not only changes in the number and types of services available but also their spatial configuration. Convenient physical access to services is at least as important as their existence and cost to rural people. To this end, this chapter uses Christaller's (1966) principles of central place theory to analyze the spatial patterns of development in services.

The data used in this analysis were obtained from two sources. All the 350 households participating in the 1982/83 IFPRI-TNAU rural household survey (see Chapter 2) were administered an additional questionnaire about the types of services they use, how frequently they use them, and how far they travel to obtain them.

In addition, a special village survey was undertaken in 1983 to obtain information on the types of services available in each village and where the villagers went to obtain services not available locally. This survey was conducted in all the rural villages in the study region that had a population of at least 750 persons in the 1971 census. There were 535 such villages, and in each case the interviews were conducted with a group of village leaders that included a primary school teacher, the postmaster, a village-level worker, and three to four representatives of the farming population. Information was also elicited on the availability of services in 1973.

The Regional Pattern of Service Provision

The Situation in 1983

Table 10.1 lists all the services used in the 535 villages surveyed. There are 134 altogether, and these include public as well as privately provided services. Also noted against these services in the table is the number of villages in the study region having that particular service.

There is a considerable disparity in the availability of individual services within villages. Some services that might be considered more basic are available in a large number of villages (e.g., primary schools, post offices, and petty shops). Others, however, are available in only a few villages or have to be obtained from larger, urban settlements (e.g., colleges, banks, and liquor shops).

Further analysis shows definite clustering patterns in the availability of different types of services within the villages.[1] There is a group of services, hereinafter called *low-order services*, that are widely available in villages with population sizes of 1,000 or less. Another group of

1. Such clustering occurs in all settlement systems, though the exact location of the clustering varies from one region to another (see, for example, Sen et al. 1971; Wanmali and Khan 1970). The location of the clustering also changes over time within a settlement system (Wanmali 1983a, 1983b).

TABLE 10.1
Occurrence, Ranking, Thresholds, and Weights of Services, 1983

Service	*Number of Villages with Service*	*Order of Service*	*Threshold*	*Weight*[a]
Education services				
Primary school	522	Low	806	1.00
Middle school	272	Low	918	1.14
High school	96	Middle	1,021	1.27
Higher secondary school	28	Middle	1,334	1.66
College	3	High	19,274	23.91
Health services				
Allopathic clinic	246	Low	806	1.00
Family planning camp	22	Middle	1,075	1.33
Family planning clinic	30	Middle	1,084	1.34
Primary health center	27	Middle	1,084	1.34
Private hospital	33	Middle	1,480	1.84
Government hospital	26	Middle	1,505	1.87
Pathological & radiological tests	8	High	5,583	6.93
Postal services				
Postage	457	Low	860	1.07
Money order	387	Low	860	1.07
Registration	384	Low	860	1.07
Postal order	66	Low	860	1.07
Telegrams	44	Low	860	1.07
Radio license	131	Low	918	1.14
Telephone	149	Low	918	1.14
Banking services				
Primary cooperative credit society	135	Low	860	1.07
Land development bank	10	Low	918	1.14
Agriculture/cooperative bank	18	Middle	1,075	1.33
Commercial bank	17	Middle	1,440	1.79
Nationalized bank	15	Middle	1,440	1.79
Lead bank	22	Middle	1,508	1.87
Transport services				
To board a bus	354	Low	806	1.00
To book goods by road	17	Middle	1,327	1.65
To board a train	16	Middle	1,327	1.65
To book goods by train	15	Middle	1,961	2.43
Agricultural Input Services (purchase)				
Tools	368	Low	806	1.00
Implements	49	Middle	1,072	1.33
Electric motors	4	Middle	2,443	3.03
Electric pumpsets	5	Middle	1,829	2.27
Oil engines	4	Middle	1,829	2.27
Sugarcane crushers	3	Middle	1,829	2.27
Sprayers	4	Middle	1,829	2.27
Dusters	4	Middle	1,829	2.27
Threshers	1	Middle	1,829	2.27
Purchase of seeds	63	Middle	1,012	1.26
Purchase of fertilizer & pesticides	82	Middle	1,012	1.26

TABLE 10.1
Continued

Service	*Number of Villages with Service*	*Order of Service*	*Threshold*	*Weight*[a]
Agricultural input services (hiring)				
Tools	443	Low	806	1.00
Implements	448	Low	806	1.00
Oil engines	299	Low	806	1.00
Sugarcane crushers	103	Middle	1,002	1.24
Sprayers	352	Low	806	1.00
Dusters	282	Middle	1,002	1.24
Threshers	100	Middle	1,023	1.27
Tractors	153	Low	860	1.07
Cage wheel	122	Middle	1,015	1.26
Agricultural input services (servicing)				
Tools	466	Low	806	1.00
Implements	422	Low	806	1.00
Electric motors	90	Middle	1,012	1.26
Electric pumpsets	81	Middle	1,012	1.26
Oil engines	57	Middle	1,012	1.26
Sugarcane crushers	18	Middle	1,254	1.56
Sprayers	95	Low	918	1.14
Dusters	83	Middle	1,012	1.26
Threshers	6	Middle	1,012	1.26
Tractors	3	Middle	1,380	1.71
Cage wheel	3	Middle	1,380	1.71
Animal husbandry services				
Key village centers	806	Low	806	1.00
Veterinary dispensaries	42	Middle	1,035	1.28
Marketing services				
Sale of vegetables	100	Middle	1,012	1.26
Sale of fruits & coconuts	52	Middle	1,012	1.26
Sale of paddy	34	Middle	1,119	1.39
Sale of *bajra*	155	Middle	1,030	1.28
Sale of *jowar*	163	Middle	1,028	1.28
Sale of pulses	98	Middle	1,015	1.26
Sale of castor	85	Middle	1,042	1.29
Sale of groundnuts	34	Middle	1,133	1.41
Sale of other oil seeds	91	Middle	1,002	1.24
Sale of sugarcane	22	Middle	1,050	1.30
Sale of jaggery	27	Middle	1,042	1.30
Sale of chilies	110	Middle	1,012	1.26
Sale of turmeric	11	Middle	1,119	1.39
Sale of tamarind	34	Middle	1,021	1.27
Sale of poultry products	425	Low	806	1.00
Sale of dairy products	519	Low	806	1.00
Sale of firewood	89	Middle	1,021	1.27
Retail services				
Blacksmith	494	Low	806	1.00
Carpenter	492	Low	806	1.00

TABLE 10.1
Continued

Service	*Number of Villages with Service*	*Order of Service*	*Threshold*	*Weight*[a]
Cobbler	495	Low	806	1.00
Retail petty shop	524	Low	806	1.00
Retail cloth shop	58	Low	806	1.00
Tea & coffee	483	Low	806	1.00
Laundry	497	Low	806	1.00
Barber	510	Low	806	1.00
Bakery	395	Low	806	1.00
General provisions	382	Low	860	1.07
Ready-made garments	33	Middle	1,075	1.33
Household utensils	17	Middle	1,395	1.73
Medical shops	15	Middle	1,395	1.73
Glassware	5	Middle	3,426	4.25
Pottery	457	Low	860	1.07
Electrical goods	32	Middle	1,352	1.68
Footwear	17	Middle	1,924	2.39
Bicycle purchase	6	High	16,083	19.95
Bicycle repair	410	Low	806	1.00
Timber	15	Middle	1,164	1.44
Fuel	404	Low	918	1.14
Bricks & tile	406	Low	806	1.00
Cement	32	Low	806	1.00
Stone	348	Low	806	1.00
Lime	35	Low	860	1.07
Hardware	17	Middle	1,036	1.29
Wooden furniture	273	Middle	1,015	1.26
Steel furniture	8	Middle	2,540	3.15
Opticals	2	High	38,664	47.97
Stationery	76	Middle	1,012	1.26
Watch purchase	6	High	16,083	19.95
Watch repair	23	Middle	1,075	1.33
Radio purchase	4	High	16,083	19.95
Radio repair	24	Middle	1,075	1.33
Transistor purchase	4	High	16,083	19.95
Transistor repair	21	Middle	1,075	1.33
Scooter repair	7	High	7,889	9.79
Automobile repair	7	High	7,889	9.79
Gasoline, diesel, & lubricants	8	High	5,583	6.93
Jewelry	11	Middle	2,443	3.03
Furnishings (bed mattresses)	23	Middle	1,270	1.58
Arrack shops	463	Low	806	1.00
Foreign liquor	10	Middle	1,075	1.33
Bookbinding	17	Middle	1,075	1.33
Printing	17	Middle	2,540	3.15
Sweetshops	27	Middle	1,075	1.33
Leather goods	11	High	5,026	6.24
Photography	16	Middle	1,924	2.39
Purchase of vegetables	281	Low	806	1.00
Purchase of fruits	347	Low	806	1.00

TABLE 10.1
Continued

Service	*Number of Villages with Service*	*Order of Service*	*Threshold*	*Weight*[a]
Purchase of poultry products	485	Low	806	1.00
Purchase of meat products	405	Low	806	1.00
Purchase of dairy products	501	Low	806	1.00
Cold drinks	503	Low	806	1.00
Restaurant	291	Low	860	1.07

[a]See note 2 for a definition of the weights.

services, hereinafter called *middle-order services*, are to be found in villages with population sizes of between 1,000 and 3,500 people. Finally, a group of services that we shall call *high-order services* are to be found only in villages and towns having at least 5,000 people. The classification of each service into these three groups is also shown in Table 10.1.

A *service threshold* can be defined for each service as the minimum population size of a village at which that service first occurs (also shown in Table 10.1). Obviously, low-order services tend to have the smallest threshold values, and high-order services have the largest.

Individual services can be ranked on the basis of their threshold values and each can be assigned a weight.[2] By summing the weights of all the services provided in a given settlement, one arrives at a *centrality score* for that settlement. The centrality scores for each of the 535 villages were calculated, and the results are summarized in Table 10.2.

There is a high and statistically significant correlation (0.557) between the population of a settlement and its centrality score. This should not come as a surprise, since any concentration of population should constitute a center of demand for, and supply of, services.

The availability of services is not uniform among the settlements of the study region, nor are all the services used by a settlement located in that settlement. This means that people need to travel in order to avail themselves of some services. We turn now to the task of identifying

2. The low-order service with the lowest threshold is given a weight of 1.00. Other weights are calculated from this base. For example, in Table 10.1 a primary school has the lowest population threshold at 806. A middle school with a population threshold of 918 therefore has a weight of 918/806 = 1.14. A primary cooperative credit society has a population threshold of 860, and therefore its weight is 1.07. If there are two primary schools in a settlement, then primary education will get a total weight of 2 × 1.14 = 2.28.

TABLE 10.2
Centrality of Service Provision and Distribution of Settlements, 1983

Centrality Score	*Number of Settlements*	*Sum of Centrality Scores*	*Percent of Total Score*
10.00–40.00	334	10,686.96	46.52
40.01–70.00	169	7,976.84	34.69
70.01–100.00	15	1,230.24	5.35
100.01–130.00	9	1,085.68	4.73
130.01–3,999.99	8	2,000.80	8.71
Total	535	22,980.52	100.00

the range of services provided by different settlements and the service (market) areas they serve. For this purpose it is useful to distinguish between settlements that provide more than half of the services used by their inhabitants and those that do not. Settlements that provide at least half their own services are called *service centers*, whereas settlements that depend on other settlements for more than half of the services they use are called *dependent settlements*. The same classification of settlements can also be applied separately to the provision of low-, middle-, and high-order services.

Taking the low-order services first, there are 473 villages in the study area that can be classified as service centers. Of these, 12 villages also serve at least one other village in addition to their own inhabitants, while 461 villages are self-sufficient in the sense that they do not depend on any other settlement for low-order services. Given the rather basic nature of the services provided, it is not surprising that so many settlements classify as service centers at this level of the service hierarchy.

There are 22 settlements that classify as service centers for middle-order services. Of these, 17 are located within the study region and 5 lie beyond its boundaries. These settlements, together with some of their service characteristics, are shown in Table 10.3. Their service areas are mapped in Figure 10.1.

Of the 17 service centers located within the study region, 10 are small and serve an average of 2.1 villages each. However, the other 7 are quite large and serve an average of 44.4 villages each. Six of the 17 service centers are *taluk* headquarters (Arkonam, Thiruvathipuram, Wandiwash, Tiruvannamalai, Polur, and Arni); eight are community development block headquarters (Nemili, Peranamallur, Thellar, Desur, Kilpennathur, Kalasapakkam, Chetpet, and Kaveripakkam); and three are without any revenue and development administrative function (Panapakkam, Vettavalam, and Kannamangalam). The six *taluk* headquarters have functioned as such at least since the turn of the century, if not also from an earlier time, whereas the block headquarters were created in the early 1950s. The "older" centers have a greater number of services, they serve larger areas and more people, and they have higher centrality scores than the "younger" centers (Table 10.3).

There are 12 settlements that classify as service centers for high-order services, of which 7 are located in the study region (Table 10.4 and Figure 10.2). Six of the seven service centers located within the study region are *taluk* headquarters and thus are important revenue and development administrative centers.

The region's dependence on outside service centers increases as one moves from low-order to high-order services. The region is largely self-

TABLE 10.3
Spatial Features of Middle-Order Service Centers, 1983

Region	*Centrality Score*	*Service Population*	*Service Area (sq km)*	*Number of Services*	*Settlements Served*[a]
Inside study region					
Chetpet	919.47	35,226	87.37	92	17
Desur	110.70	4,301	6.59	90	1
Kalasapakkam	109.99	2,443	2.08	85	1
Kannamangalam	129.44	5,026	9.98	94	1
Kilpennathur	166.70	10,471	24.60	96	2
Nemili	170.67	6,498	14.77	96	3
Peranamallur	126.74	4,256	14.97	96	1
Thellar	122.43	6,513	14.70	74	2
Arkonam	3,314.67	108,085	201.87	117	33
Arni	5,160.26	154,661	420.18	116	59
Polur	1,228.76	32,318	57.55	102	11
Thiruvathipuram	1,281.55	35,821	61.78	103	14
Tiruvannamalai	8,245.30	267,490	650.83	109	108
Wandiwash	2,081.55	71,656	212.86	103	35
Kaveripakkam	709.27	14,141	32.68	99	5
Panapakkam	149.10	8,748	9.94	88	2
Vettavalam	196.50	12,121	23.46	92	3
Outside study region[b]					
Kancheepuram	887.71	40,599	140.78	n.a.	21
Solingar	262.76	12,846	42.73	n.a.	7
Tirukovilur	40.93	1,482	2.89	n.a.	1
Tirutani	159.77	12,376	34.32	n.a.	4
Uthramerur	39.63	1,061	6.25	n.a.	1

[a]Number of villages dependent on the service center for at least half of their middle-order services.

[b]Information about the service centers outside the study region is not complete.

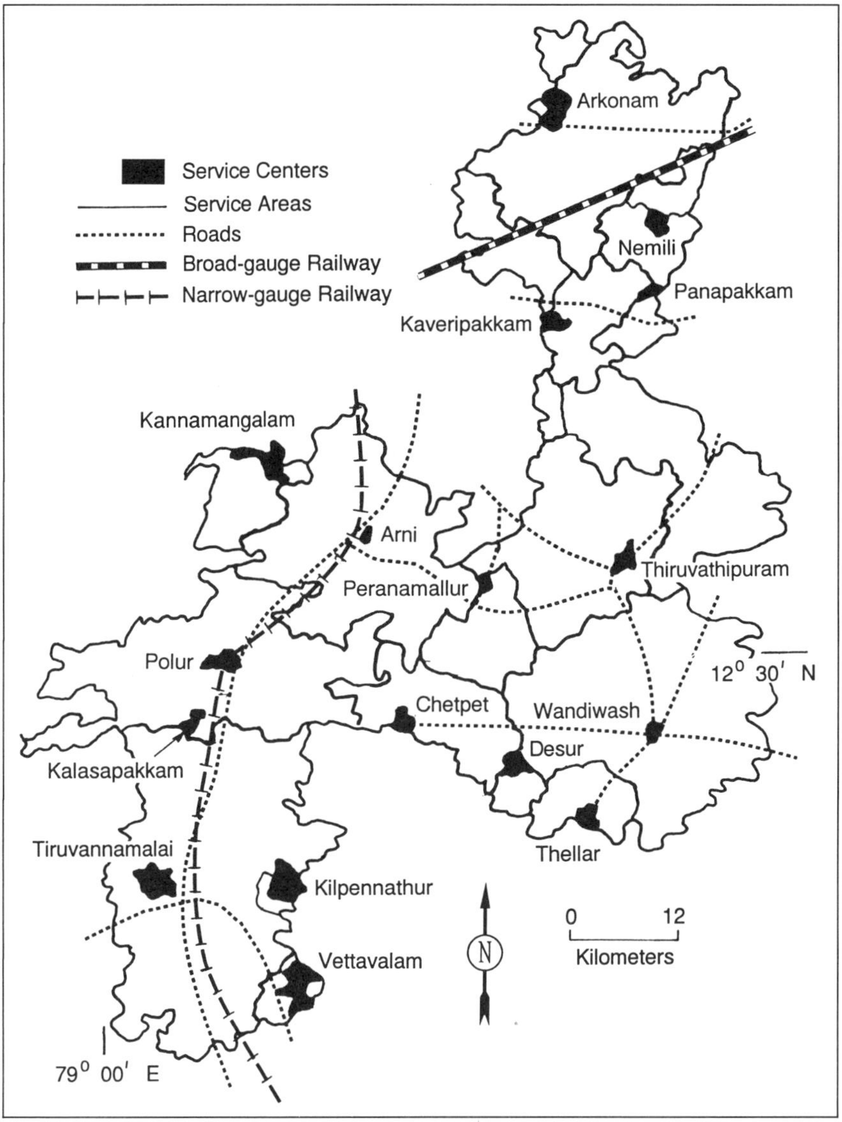

Fig. 10.1 North Arcot study region, middle-order service centers.

sufficient for low- and middle-order services, which together account for 123 of the 134 services used. However, many settlements use service centers located outside the region for high-order services (Table 10.4). Interestingly, the district headquarters town, Vellore, is used only for high-order services, of which there are 11, and then only by 61 of the

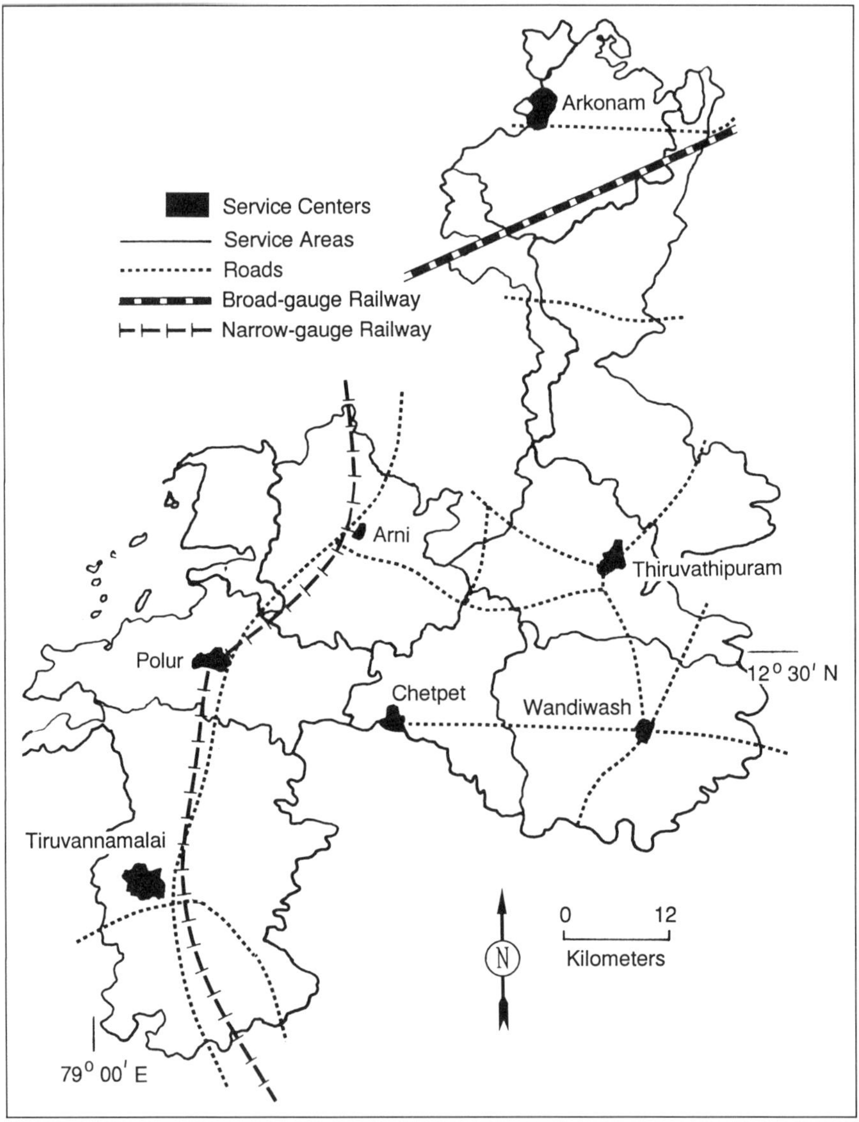

Fig. 10.2 North Arcot study region, high-order service centers.

TABLE 10.4
Spatial Features of High-Order Service Centers, 1983

Region	*Centrality Score*	*Service Population*	*Service Area (sq km)*	*Number of Services*	*Settlements Served*[a]
Inside study region					
Chetpet	457.56	9,375	15.96	92	4
Arkonam	3,384.25	111,398	222.11	117	34
Arni	4,664.82	129,879	325.11	116	44
Polur	1,228.76	32,318	57.55	102	11
Thiruvathipuram	1,281.55	35,821	61.78	103	14
Tiruvannamalai	8,245.30	267,490	650.83	109	108
Wandiwash	2,081.55	71,656	212.86	103	35
Outside study region[b]					
Kancheepuram	2,322.89	101,753	328.50	n.a.	53
Madras	1,030.49	54,728	138.36	n.a.	21
Tindivanam	41.57	1,257	2.93	n.a.	1
Tirutani	202.93	13,672	36.88	n.a.	5
Vellore	2,328.29	145,701	417.92	n.a.	61

[a]Number of villages dependent on the service center for at least half of their high-order services.
[b]Information about the service centers outside the study region is not complete.

study region's settlements (Table 10.4). These facts provide strong justification for omitting Vellore in the definition of the study region (see Chapter 2).

Changes since 1973

The region's population increased by 1.6 percent per year between 1971 and 1981 (see Chapter 2). This increase was accompanied by a general increase in the size of the settlements, and this, together with rising incomes, facilitated an expansion in the range of services provided by individual settlements. Table 10.5 shows a sharp increase between 1973 and 1983 in the centrality scores of the 535 villages surveyed, particularly at the lower and middle levels of the spectrum. The number of settlements with centrality scores between 40 and 70 almost doubled between 1973 and 1983. At the same time the larger villages and towns declined in relative importance as major providers of services.

The number of service centers for low-order services increased substantially between 1973 and 1983—from 75 to 474. The increase was more modest for middle-order service centers (from 16 to 22), and there was no change at all in the number of high-order service centers.

TABLE 10.5
Centrality Scores of Service Provision, 1973 and 1983

	1973				*1983*			
Centrality Score	*No. of Settlements*	*Percent of Settlements*	*Total Score*	*Percent of Total Score*	*No. of Settlements*	*Percent of Settlements*	*Total Score*	*Percent of Total Score*
Less than 10.00	1	0.19	7.14	0.03	0	0.00	0.00	0.00
10.00–40.00	420	78.50	12,490.42	59.75	334	62.43	10,686.96	46.52
40.01–70.00	89	16.64	4,204.35	20.11	169	31.59	7,976.84	34.69
70.01–100.00	15	2.80	1,216.98	5.82	15	2.80	1,230.24	5.35
100.01–130.00	2	0.37	212.76	1.02	9	1.68	1,085.68	4.73
130.01 or more	8	1.50	2,774.72	13.27	8	1.50	2,000.80	8.71
Total	535	100.00	20,906.37	100.00	535	100.00	22,980.52	100.00

Table 10.6 shows the changes between 1973 and 1983 in the service centers providing middle-order services. Of the original 16 centers in 1973, two, namely Tindivanam and Vellore, had become high-order service centers for the region by 1983. Eight new service centers had emerged by 1983, and their emergence, together with a strengthening of the older centers, led to a decline in the number of villages served by each center and in the average size of the areas they served.

In general, the provision of services became more decentralized between 1973 and 1983. A growing economy and an increasing population facilitated the emergence of a greater number of service centers, as well as increasing complexity in the types of services they provided.

Service Use in the Eleven Sample Villages

The Regional Context, 1983

The 11 sample villages surveyed in 1973/74 and 1982/83 (see Chapter 2) all qualify as service centers for low-order services, but they vary in their degree of access to middle- and high-order services (Table 10.7). Duli and Nesal are the most favorably located villages, being close (5.0 and 6.5 kilometers, respectively) to major service centers that offer a complete range of middle- and high-order services. Meppathurai, followed closely by Amudhur, are the least favored villages, being 17 and 15 kilometers, respectively, from a major service center.

The sample households use less than the full range of 134 services available in the region (Table 10.8). On average, they use 95 services, of which 43 are available within the village and 52 are obtained elsewhere. Four villages (Amudhur, Kalpattu, Veerasambanur, and Vengodu) provide more than half of the services they use and hence qualify as service centers. However, the other seven villages are dependent settlements in terms of their use of services.

Patterns of Use of Consumer Services

In an earlier study, Wanmali (1985) hypothesized that the frequency of service use is influenced not only by the socioeconomic status of households but also by the distance they must travel to obtain them. He also noted that expenditure rather than frequency of use would be a better measure of service use to examine these relationships. The availability of household expenditure data from the 1982/83 IFPRI-TNAU survey for the same households and villages studied here pro-

TABLE 10.6
Spatial Features of Middle-Order Service Centers, 1973 and 1983

Service Center	1973 Service Area (sq km)	1973 Service Population	1973 Settlements Served	1983 Service Area (sq km)	1983 Service Population	1983 Settlements Served
Inside the study region						
Chetpet	85.23	31,134	17	87.37	35,226	17
Nemili	12.28	5,279	3	14.77	6,498	3
Arkonam	316.23	111,953	48	201.87	108,085	33
Arni	505.79	183,251	70	420.18	154,661	59
Polur	232.59	77,961	44	57.55	32,318	11
Thiruvathipuram	198.46	67,046	38	61.78	35,821	14
Tiruvannamalai	616.45	222,202	104	650.83	267,490	108
Wandiwash	396.32	118,144	66	212.86	71,656	35
Kaveripakkam	21.08	9,732	3	32.68	14,141	5
Desur	—	—	—	6.59	4,301	1
Kalasapakkam	—	—	—	2.08	2,443	1
Kannamangalam	—	—	—	9.98	5,026	1
Kilpennathur	—	—	—	24.66	10,471	2
Peranamallur	—	—	—	14.96	4,256	1
Thellar	—	—	—	14.70	6,513	1
Panapakkam	—	—	—	9.94	8,748	2
Vettavalam	—	—	—	23.46	12,121	3
Outside the study region						
Solingar	49.58	11,849	8	42.73	12,846	7
Tirukovilur	2.89	1,265	1	2.89	1,482	1
Tirutani	34.32	10,301	4	34.32	12,376	4
Uthramerur	6.25	1,069	1	6.25	1,061	1
Tindivanam	2.93	1,130	1	—	—	—
Vellore	55.12	26,882	8	—	—	—
Kancheepuram	—	—	—	140.78	40,599	21

Note: Dashes indicate center was not a middle-order service center that year.

TABLE 10.7
Sample Villages and Their Service Centers

Village	*Middle-Order Services*	*High-Order Services*
Kalpattu	Kannamangalam (8.6 km)	Vellore (15.0 km)
Meppathurai	Polur or Tiruvannamalai (17.0 km)	Polur or Tiruvannamalai (17.0 km)
Vayalur	Kilpennathur (6.4 km)	Tiruvannamalai (17.0 km)
Veerasambanur	Chetpet (7.0 km)	Arni (15.0 km)
Vinayagapuram	Arni (13.0 km)	Arni (13.0 km)
Nesal	Arni (6.5 km)	Arni (6.5 km)
Amudhur	Wandiwash (15.0 km)	Wandiwash (15.0 km)
Vengodu	Uthramerur (10.0 km)	Wandiwash (17.0 km)
Duli	Thiruvathipuram (5.0 km)	Thiruvathipuram (5.0 km)
Sirungathur	Thiruvathipuram (7.0 km)	Thiruvathipuram (7.0 km)
Vegamangalam	Kaveripakkam (6.0 km)	Kancheepuram (18.0 km)

Note: Villages are their own low-order service centers.

TABLE 10.8
Number of Services Used within and outside of Sample Villages

Village	*Number Used Within*	*Number Used Outside*	*Percent Used Outside*
Amudhur	45	42	48.3
Duli	31	67	68.4
Kalpattu	54	45	45.5
Meppathurai	39	52	57.1
Nesal	54	63	53.9
Sirungathur	34	59	63.4
Vayalur	34	65	65.7
Veerasambanur	43	33	43.4
Vegamangalam	47	59	55.7
Vengodu	51	34	40.0
Vinayagapuram	37	56	60.2

vides a unique opportunity to examine the determinants of service use in more detail.

The household expenditure survey included usable data on 35 of the consumer services delineated in Table 10.1. Although information on expenditures for other consumer services was collected by the IFPRI-TNAU team, it was not sufficiently disaggregated to identify the places where individual services were obtained, and hence it could not be used here. The omitted services account for about 20 percent of total household expenditure.

For the purposes of this analysis, the services were aggregated in three different ways (Table 10.9). One grouping corresponds to the hierarchy of low-, middle-, and high-order services used earlier in this chapter. It is hypothesized that distance will have a negative influence on low-order services but will be less important for middle- and high-order services. The second grouping distinguishes among services that are used with low, middle, and high frequency. It is expected that distance will be negatively related to high frequency of use. The final grouping sorts the services according to more conventional demand groups: food and personal services, consumer durables, health services, and transportation. The three classification schemes encompass the same 35 consumer-oriented services, but the groups within each scheme are mutually exclusive.

To estimate the impact of distance on expenditure patterns and hence service use, a system of expenditure equations was estimated. The dependent variable in each equation is the budget share for the

TABLE 10.9
Definition of Service Groups

Service Group	*Component Services*	
Low order	Allopathic clinic	Fuel
	Bus stop	Arrack shop
	Retail petty shop	Purchase of vegetables
	Tea & coffee	Purchase of fruits
	Laundry	Purchase of poultry
	Barber	Purchase of meat
	Bakery	Cold drinks
	General provisions	Restaurant
Middle order	Board a train	Hardware
	Retail cloth shop	Wooden furniture
	Ready-made garments	Steel furniture
	Household utensils	Stationery
	Medical shop	Jewelry
	Electrical goods	Furnishings (mattresses)
	Footwear	Sweet-shop

TABLE 10.9
Continued

Service Group	*Component Services*	
High order	Bicycle purchase	Transistor purchase
	Watch purchase	Petrol, diesel, & lubricants
	Radio purchase	
Low frequency (less than 6 uses/year)	Allopathic clinic	Steel furniture
	Board a train	Stationery
	Retail cloth shop	Watch purchase
	Ready-made garments	Radio purchase
	Household utensils	Transistor purchase
	Medical shop	Gasoline, diesel, & lubricants
	Electrical goods	Jewelry
	Footwear	Sweet-shop
	Bicycle purchase	Purchase of poultry
	Hardware	
	Wooden furniture	
Middle frequency (6–12 uses/year)	Bakery	Furnishings (mattresses)
	Fuel	Purchase of meat
High frequency (more than 12 uses/year)	Bus stop	Arrack shop
	Retail petty shop	Purchase of vegetables
	Tea & coffee	Purchase of fruit
	Laundry	Cold drinks
	Barber	Restaurant
	General provisions	
Food & personal	Retail petty shop	Arrack shop
	Tea & coffee	Sweet-shop
	Laundry	Purchase of vegetables
	Barber	Purchase of fruits
	Bakery	Purchase of poultry
	General provisions	Purchase of meat
	Medical shop	Cold drinks
	Fuel	Restaurant
Consumer durables	Retail cloth shop	Stationery
	Ready-made garments	Watch purchase
	Household utensils	Radio purchase
	Electrical goods	Transistor purchase
	Footwear	Gasoline, diesel, & lubricants
	Bicycle purchase	Jewelry
	Hardware	Furnishings (mattresses)
	Wooden furniture	
	Steel furniture	
Health	Allopathic clinic	
Transport	Bus stop	Board a train

relevant group of services, and the explanatory variables are total household expenditure, average distance traveled to procure the relevant services, and several socioeconomic variables describing the household's characteristics (Table 10.10). The choice of variables and functional form were taken from Hazell and Röell (1983), and the equations were estimated by ordinary least squares regression.

The value of the distance variable for each group of services was calculated as the sum of the distance for each service in the group multiplied by its expenditure share within that group. The distances used were those reported as actually traveled to procure each service; they were not necessarily the distance to the nearest source for each service.

Table 10.11 summarizes the expenditure behavior of the average household in the 11 villages. The marginal budget shares were evaluated from the regression equations at the sample means. Note that neither the average nor the marginal budget shares sum to unity because not all the services in total expenditure were included in the model's dependent variables.

Foods and personal services account for 71 percent of the average household's budget and 65 percent of incremental expenditure. Because foods and personal services are also the predominant members of the low-order and high-frequency service groups, the average and marginal budget shares for these groups are also large.

TABLE 10.10
Independent Variables in Regression

INVERSEE	=	1/E
LOGE	=	LOG (E) where E = total expenditure per capita
LOGN	=	LOG (N) where N = household size
LOGNPERE	=	LOG (N)/E
FARM	=	Per capita operated land
FARMPERE	=	FARM/E
CHILDREN	=	Proportion of household members under 5 years old
CPERE	=	CHILDREN/E
YOUTH	=	Proportion of household members between 6 and 14 years
YPERE	=	YOUTH/E
WOMEN	=	Proportion of household members that are female and 15 years old or more
WPERE	=	WOMEN/E
SEX	=	Sex of household head (1 = male; 2 = female)
ED	=	Education of household head (6 levels)
EDPERE	=	ED/E
CREDIT	=	Loans received for food and clothing expenditures
CREDPERE	=	CREDIT/E
DISTANCE	=	The weighted-average distance to obtain each group of services

TABLE 10.11
Average and Marginal Budget Shares for Sample Households (percent)

Service Group	*Average Budget Share*	*Marginal Budget Share*
Low order	73.27	68.77
Middle order	6.81	16.20
High order	0.30	0.99
Low frequency	7.97	18.98
Middle frequency	3.92	5.03
High frequency	68.46	61.60
Food & personal	70.79	65.02
Consumer durables	6.67	16.97
Health	0.82	1.76
Transport	2.08	2.20

High-order services account for a mere 0.3 percent of the average budget, and only 1.0 percent of incremental expenditure is allocated to their purchase. Again, the unimportance of Vellore as a service center for the study region is confirmed. Not only is its role in relation to the study region restricted to providing high-order services to a mere 61 settlements, but the value of the total expenditures involved is clearly very small.

About two-thirds of incremental expenditure is allocated to low-order and high-frequency services. These services are primarily foods and personal services that are produced and distributed locally. As a result, increases in household incomes can be expected to generate additional incomes and employment in the study region, and particularly in the larger villages and small towns providing low-order and high-frequency services.

Table 10.12 summarizes the effect of distance and the household characteristic variables on expenditure behavior. Rather than report all the estimated coefficients from the model, it is more useful to summarize the effect of each exogenous variable by calculating the change in the average household's expenditure given an incremental change in the variable of interest.

As expected, distance has a negative and statistically significant effect on household expenditures on foods and personal services, and on low-order and high-frequency services. A 1 percent reduction in the distance traveled to procure these types of services would increase household expenditure by 3.2 percent for foods and personal services, 2.4 percent for low-order services, and 2.3 percent for high-frequency services.

TABLE 10.12
Effects of Household Characteristics and Distance on Average Expenditures by Service Group

Service Group	*LOGN*	*FARM*	*CHILDREN*	*YOUTH*	*WOMEN*	*SEX*	*ED*	*CREDIT*	*DISTANCE*	R^2
Low order	−104.25*	−150.62*	201.18*	42.62	3.01	30.96	3.10	−79.60*	−3.84*	0.52*
	(6.44)	(10.29)	(3.39)	(0.81)	(0.07)	(1.25)	(0.19)	(2.73)	(1.87)	
Middle order	56.47*	−4.48	−59.27*	−2.40	23.30	3.24	−6.08	7.09	0.52	0.44*
	(7.16)	(0.62)	(2.04)	(0.09)	(1.03)	(0.27)	(0.77)	(0.50)	(1.41)	
High order	3.42*	−2.52	1.79	−1.94	1.28	1.18	−0.97	6.11*	−0.08	0.07
	(1.81)	(1.46)	(0.26)	(0.31)	(0.24)	(0.41)	(0.51)	(1.79)	(0.84)	
Low frequency	60.57*	−2.19	−33.43	−0.79	24.35	5.74	−6.32	16.43	0.01	0.48*
	(7.55)	(0.30)	(1.13)	(0.03)	(1.06)	(0.47)	(0.79)	(1.13)	(0.03)	
Middle frequency	−3.45	−11.42*	40.88*	22.38*	2.45	6.66	−2.96	−9.43*	2.01*	0.20*
	(1.20)	(4.39)	(3.85)	(2.39)	(0.30)	(1.51)	(1.04)	(1.82)	(2.79)	
High frequency	−102.12*	−143.44*	130.81*	19.59	1.99	22.62	5.70	−71.86*	−3.28*	0.55*
	(6.71)	(10.43)	(2.34)	(0.40)	(0.05)	(0.97)	(0.38)	(2.62)	(1.80)	
Food & personal	−105.50*	−154.44*	176.50*	50.87	6.29	29.56	−4.25	−89.80*	−4.73*	0.56*
	(6.62)	(10.66)	(3.02)	(0.98)	(0.14)	(1.21)	(0.27)	(3.12)	(2.47)	
Consumer durables	62.13*	−8.33	−57.23*	−12.73	25.01	2.07	−9.10	11.57	0.48	0.47*
	(7.92)	(1.16)	(1.98)	(0.50)	(1.11)	(0.17)	(1.16)	(0.82)	(1.26)	
Health	0.18	3.67*	27.10*	4.02	2.61	2.93	−0.49	3.60	−0.46	0.20*
	(0.12)	(2.75)	(4.99)	(0.83)	(0.62)	(1.29)	(0.34)	(1.35)	(1.53)	
Transport	−0.35	3.32	−4.17	−3.28	−7.99	0.46	11.19*	7.06*	0.00	0.19*
	(0.15)	(1.57)	(0.49)	(0.43)	(1.20)	(0.13)	(4.83)	(1.67)	(0.02)	

Notes: Asterisk indicates significance at the 0.95 level. Figures in parentheses are t-statistics.

Other things being equal, an increase in household size reduces household expenditure on foods and personal services, low-order services, and high-frequency services. But it is positively associated with the demand for durables, and for high-order and low-frequency services. Increased access to consumer credit has a similar effect, as does farm size.

The age composition of the household, particularly the proportion of children, is also an important factor determining expenditure patterns. An increase in the proportion of children would increase expenditures on foods and personal services, and on low-order and high-frequency services, but it would reduce expenditures on middle-order services and consumer durables.

The variables for youths, women, sex, and education of the household head did not generally have significant effects on household expenditures. However, an addition to the proportion of youths in the household would increase the share for middle-order services, and an increase in the educational level of the household head would have a similar effect on the expenditure for transportation.

Patterns of Use of Production Services

Complete service use data (including expenditure and distance) were available by household for two production inputs—fertilizer and credit. These data were used to estimate the input demand equations shown in Table 10.13. Credit was defined as loans received during the year for the purchase of farmland, livestock, machinery, or variable inputs such as seeds and fertilizers. Fertilizer is disaggregated into kilograms of nitrogen, phosphorus, and potassium purchased during the year.

Four independent variables were included in the model: the proportion of the cultivated area under high-yielding varieties (HYVs), the total cultivated area, a household-specific index of the availability of agroservices,[3] and distance. For the three fertilizer equations, the distance variable is the number of kilometers actually traveled to a fertilizer and pesticide shop. In the case of credit, distance is measured as the number of kilometers traveled to a land development bank, nationalized bank, or agriculture cooperative bank. If more than one supplier of an input was involved, the distances traveled were simply averaged. Note that input prices are not included in the equations. This

3. The index of agricultural infrastructure is equal to the sum of centrality scores for each of the agroservices that the household uses. The agroservices considered for this exercise are communications, credit and banking, transport, agricultural inputs, animal husbandry, and marketing.

TABLE 10.13
Estimated Input Demand Equations

Dependent Variable	*Proportion of Land under High-Yielding Varieties*	*Cultivated Area (ha)*	*Index of Agroservice Availability*	*Distance (km)*	R^2
Nitrogen	42.201*	7.910*	1.286*	0.481	0.4747*
	(3.649)	(9.529)	(1.808)	(0.801)	
Phosphorus	14.776*	4.908*	0.575	−0.262	0.4136*
	(1.943)	(8.992)	(1.230)	(0.663)	
Potassium	10.297*	2.893*	0.545	−0.002	0.2987*
	(1.705)	(6.675)	(1.469)	(0.007)	
Credit	565.301	183.237*	21.847	−34.357*	0.2967*
	(1.487)	(7.058)	(0.946)	(2.182)	

Notes: Asterisk indicates significance at the 0.95 level. Figures in parentheses are t-statistics.

is because they were estimated using cross-sectional data for one year, and there was virtually no difference in the costs of fertilizers and institutional credit across households.

As should be expected, the proportion of HYVs and the total cultivated area are positively and significantly (except in one case) associated with the demand for fertilizers and credit. The availability of agroservices is only weakly related to demand, though the signs are at least positive, as we would expect.

Distance is negatively and significantly associated with the use of farm credit, but not with the use of fertilizers. On average, credit is not obtained at a greater distance than fertilizer—they are both middle-order services in Table 10.1—but it is possible that the sources from which credit is obtained for purchases of farmland, livestock, and agricultural machinery are diverse and are located in different settlements. Therefore, the need for repeated visits to obtain and service credit may accentuate the importance of distance.

Changes in Service Provision, 1973–1983

The accessibility of services generally improved between 1973 and 1983 in the 11 sample villages (Table 10.14). Our regression equations suggest that the reduction in distances will have contributed to an increase in household expenditure over this period, particularly on low-order and frequently used services. This will have reinforced the effects of agricultural growth on incomes and employment in the local nonfarm economy, particularly in the larger villages and smaller towns that provide these kinds of services.

TABLE 10.14
Mean Distances by Service Category

	Distance (km)	
Service Category	*1973*	*1983*
Education	8.88	4.47
Health	15.62	12.61
Communication	5.18	4.24
Banking	7.56	8.34
Transport	10.80	10.15
Agricultural inputs	10.21	7.33
Animal husbandry	4.69	4.90
Marketing	16.75	9.22
Retail	11.90	7.59

Conclusions

The analysis in this chapter has shown that the study region is largely self-sufficient in providing services for its rural households. Some middle- and high-order services are procured from larger urban centers located outside the region, but these services are few in number and amount to only a small share of the average rural household's total expenditure. These findings confirm that the study region is a well-defined unit of analysis, embracing a number of central towns (the *taluk* headquarters) and all their second-tier towns and dependent villages. The region encompasses most of the places where rural households do their shopping and where they spend nearly all of their money. This is not to deny that there are important trade linkages between the region's towns and larger urban centers located elsewhere (see Chapter 9), but these are primarily trade flows of intermediate goods that form the usual grist of interregional trade. The important feature preserved by the study region's boundaries is that by capturing the household expenditure linkages, a meaningful growth linkage analysis can be undertaken (see Chapter 8).

It has also been shown that low-order services account for 70 percent of the average rural household's budget and for two-thirds of its incremental expenditure. These services are mostly foods and personal services that are locally produced, and increases in their demand can be expected to have significant income and employment multipliers in the larger villages and small towns that supply them. The demand for these services is also negatively related to the distance traveled to procure them, hence the improvement in access to low-order services that occurred between 1973 and 1983 will have reinforced the increases in demand generated by the contemporaneous increases in rural incomes.

Services became more accessible in the study region during a period of significant agricultural growth. More services became available in more places, and households had to travel shorter distances to avail themselves of these services. Part of these changes in the service sector were supply induced—for example, the government's provision of services to agriculture—and they were undoubtedly important in contributing to the agricultural growth. The growth in other services were demand induced—for example, foods and personal services, health, and transportation—and were a direct consequence of increases in incomes, population, and improved access to these services. The expansion in both types of services was important in fostering the growth of the region's economy, and particularly in allowing the growth multipliers arising from agricultural growth to be realized in the local nonfarm economy.

The state government is also active in the North Arcot region in providing a range of producer and consumer services, for example, foods and general provisions through civil supply shops, bus services, agricultural marketing, and financial services, often in competition with the private sector. An important issue, not addressed in this study, is whether this government involvement is justified. Is the private sector being actively hampered by subsidies, licensing, and other regulations that favor government enterprises? Or, as Wanmali (1983a) observes, is the government simply filling a void until the private sector expands to meet the region's demand for services? If it is the former and a potentially more efficient private sector is being held back, then the agricultural growth multipliers will not have realized their full potential. These are important issues for further research that need to be looked into for a full understanding of the development of the service sector and its contribution to the growth of the local economy.

CHAPTER 11

Conclusions and Policy Implications

Peter B. R. Hazell and C. Ramasamy

IN THIS STUDY we set out to quantify the effects of the green revolution on the North Arcot region, in both the villages and the towns. For this task we had available a unique set of data obtained from household surveys undertaken in 1973/74, 1982/83, and 1983/84, which together span an era of change in the region's paddy technology.

Our task was complicated by the severe drought of 1982/83, the incomplete village coverage of the 1983/84 survey, and the lack of a regionally representative survey of urban households in 1973/74. Comparisons between 1973/74 and 1982/83 grossly underestimate the impact in the villages of the intervening changes in irrigation and paddy technology. On the other hand, comparisons between 1973/74 and 1983/84, while more acceptable in terms of available water for irrigation, are limited to a sample of the poorer villages in the region. Despite these limitations of the data set, our qualitative results are generally supported by independent longitudinal data collected by John Harriss, and by the results from a regional model that is used to simulate the impact of the green revolution after normalizing for rainfall conditions.

The green revolution in North Arcot was much more modest than the dramatic technological changes observed in areas like Punjab and Haryana. Yields have increased as a result of the high-yielding varieties (HYVs), and there have been accompanying increases in the irrigated area, together with some displacement of competing crops in the cropping pattern. But limited tank and groundwater reserves, together with the fact that several key features of the HYVs had already been embodied in locally improved rice varieties prior to their release, prevented dramatic productivity increases. Nevertheless, regional paddy output increased by 57 percent between 1963/64–1965/66 and 1977/78–1979/80, and this growth had a significant economic impact on the region's villages and towns.

Since the details of our findings are summarized in the conclusions to individual chapters, we focus here on some of the more important issues that follow from our work. We first marshal our results to address explicitly the more important criticisms of the green revolution promulgated by earlier writers. Then follows a discussion of our growth linkage results for the region, the impact of the 1982/83 drought, and the prospects for future agricultural growth in the North Arcot region. Throughout we seek to draw out the important implications for agricultural research and policy.

Questions and Answers about the Green Revolution

As we saw in Chapter 1, early writers on the green revolution were apprehensive about its likely impact on the rural poor. In this section we summarize those concerns in four key questions and marshal our evidence to answer them for the case of North Arcot.

Did small farms adopt the new technology and obtain levels of productivity comparable to the large farms?

The evidence from the Cambridge and Madras universities study shows that the early adopters of HYVs were typically the larger farmers. Chinnappa (1977) reports that the average size of the operational holding for HYV adopters was about 2 hectares, compared with 1 hectare for nonadopters. Also, the percentage of HYV adopters increased across farm size groups, as did the percentage of the paddy area planted to HYVs. Only 15 percent of the farmers operating less than 0.4 hectare planted HYVs in 1972/73, compared with 67 percent of the farmers operating more than 4 hectares. The proportion of paddy area planted to HYVs increased from 10 to 23 percent between the same groups.

By the time of John Harriss' return visit to North Arcot in 1976, adoption of HYVs was much more widespread (Harriss 1977). And by the time of the IFPRI-TNAU surveys in the early 1980s, over 90 percent of the paddy area was consistently planted to HYVs, with no systematic differences by farm size group.

There are a number of reasons why adoption by small farms may have lagged. Chinnappa (1977) identifies greater problems in obtaining credit and fertilizers for small farmers, and John Harriss (1977) emphasizes the need for reliable water supplies over a relatively long growing period for early HYVs such as IR5 and IR8.

The provision of formal credit and farm inputs did improve (see Chapters 4 and 10), in part because of a crash program mounted by the government to increase rice production in Tamil Nadu. The release of locally developed HYVs in the mid–1970s that were better adapted to the growing conditions of small farms with their less reliable water supplies also helped. Both developments highlight the importance of government action in preventing the development of serious inequities when green revolution–type technologies are first released. Necessary inputs should be made readily available to all farmers, and local research institutions have an important and timely role to play in adapting genetic material from external sources to local conditions. In North Arcot, plant breeders at TNAU were very successful in adapting International Rice Research Institute (IRRI) genetic material to local conditions.

Turning now to the productivity issue, our analysis of paddy yields in Chapter 3 (Table 3.1) shows that while large-scale farmers obtained higher yields than small-scale farmers in 1973/74, this difference had disappeared by the early 1980s. This finding again reflects the later adoption of HYVs by small farmers. In North Arcot the potential "scale neutrality" of the new technology, therefore, appears to have been realized.

Did the employment and earnings of agricultural workers increase as a result of the new technology?

Although Cost of Cultivation of Principal Crops (CCPC) data show that HYVs require a little more labor per hectare than the available local varieties (about 5 to 10 percent more, depending on the year—Tables 2.4 and 2.5), total employment in crop production declined by 4 percent per paddy farm in the resurvey villages between 1973/74 and 1983/84. This decline is attributable to a downward trend in labor use per hectare for both HYVs and local varieties during the 1970s, a reflection of the increased mechanization of irrigation pumping and paddy threshing. The loss in per hectare paddy employment was sufficiently large, in fact, to offset the employment gains from an increase in the paddy crop area on both small and large farms.

The use of family labor increased on both small and large farms between 1973/74 and 1983/84 (Table 3.4), hence the brunt of the decline in total employment fell on the hired workers. On average, their employment fell by 25 percent per paddy farm, or by 11 percent per farm if attached labor is also included.

Yet despite this loss in the use of hired labor, real wage rates increased modestly for some tasks—though not consistently in all the sample villages or for all tasks (Tables 3.5, 4.1, and 6.6). Moreover, agricultural employment earnings virtually doubled in the resurvey villages for small-paddy-farm, landless-labor, and nonagricultural households (Tables 3.8, 3.11, and 3.12) and increased by 40 percent for nonpaddy-farm households (Table 3.10). These increases were possible because of a decline in the amount of hired labor supplied by farms operating more than 1 hectare of land (Table 3.6), and because of competing employment opportunities in dairying and nonfarm activities.

Additionally, there were two key features of the transition to the new technology in North Arcot that facilitated these favorable results. First, the incidence of landlessness changed little. Most farmers were able to retain access to their land, and migration to urban areas reduced the impact of demographic pressures on the agricultural labor market (Chapter 4).

Second, despite an initial and worrying increase in the number of tractors (Harriss 1977), there has been little mechanization of land preparation in the region. Water pumping for irrigation is now almost exclusively mechanized, and some farmers rent threshing machines, but these activities have not displaced large amounts of hired labor. That tractors did not make greater inroads is probably a consequence of the small size of the farms in the region and the prohibitive per hectare costs of private ownership. However, it remains a puzzle as to why a rental market emerged for threshing machines but not for tractor services.

Did the distribution of land become less concentrated?

Neither the available survey data nor John Harriss' own field data (Chapter 4) provide evidence of any general increase in the concentration of land, or of the loss of land by small landholders.

As a result of population growth and the partitioning of some holdings, the average farm size declined marginally from 1.23 to 1.18 hectares in the sample villages between 1973 and 1983. This decline was nearly all concentrated in the rich villages—that is, the ones with better irrigation resources (Table 3.19). The average farm size also declined in all four quartiles of the size distribution in the rich villages. The farms in the first and second quartiles lost relatively more land than average, but the farms in the top quartile lost the most land in absolute terms.

Average farm sizes also declined in the first three quartiles of the poor villages, but the average farm size of the top quartile increased by about 8 percent. Thus, the only evidence for a (modest) worsening of land distribution comes from the villages that, having the poorest irrigation resources, benefited the least from the green revolution.

Duli is the only village in which the distribution of land became substantially worse. Table 3.17 shows that the average farm size in the bottom quartile declined by 15.5 percent, whereas it increased by 30.8 percent, 61.5 percent, and 57.2 percent in the second, third, and fourth quartiles, respectively. John Harriss' data show a similar increase in concentration (Table 4.6). Based on an in-depth field investigation, Harriss attributes the change to larger farmers buying back land owned by moneylenders and silk weavers in the town of Cheyyar who acquired the land in the 1930s, rather than to any significant transfer of land from smaller to larger landholders.

Harriss (Table 4.6) also provides evidence that, of his sample of households that initially inherited land and still owned it in 1973, virtually none of them were dispossessed between 1973 and 1984.

Land leasing is relatively rare in North Arcot, and over 90 percent of the farms are now owner occupied. Moreover, the farms are typically small, and there are virtually no farms larger than 30 hectares. Within this context, the risk that with the advent of the green revolution landlords would dispossess tenant farmers, or that large farmers would buy up small farms, seems to have been small. The implications for regions with least equitably distributed land resources are obvious.

Was there a decrease in the inequality of income and a reduction of absolute poverty?

The available evidence from the resurvey villages shows that small paddy farmers and landless laborers gained the largest proportional increases in family income between 1973/74 and 1983/84—90 and 125 percent, respectively (Table 3.7). Large paddy farmers (because of sharp cost increases, especially for fertilizer and labor), nonpaddy farmers (who do not have access to irrigated land), and nonagricultural households did less well, but the real value of their family incomes still increased by 18, 17, and 55 percent, respectively.

These changes are corroborated by measured changes in the real value of household consumption expenditure (Table 3.13), by a sharp improvement in calorie and protein intake (Table 5.5), and by the growing importance of higher-quality foods and nonfoods in total household expenditure (Table 3.15). Moreover, the regional model in Chapter 8, which normalizes to average rainfall conditions, also predicts that the green revolution increased the incomes of farmers and landless laborers by about 30 percent and of nonagricultural households by 20 percent (Table 8.4).

We conclude, therefore, that there were sizable absolute gains for all household groups, and that absolute poverty declined. The relative distribution of household incomes improved in that the small paddy farmers and the landless workers gained relative to other groups (Table 3.16). On the other hand, households that did not gain directly from the green revolution because they do not participate in paddy farming lost in their relative standing. In particular, the nonagricultural households became the poorest income group, whereas previously they had been about as well off as the small paddy farmers.

There are a number of factors that explain these favorable income changes. First, because the distribution of land did not become noticeably more concentrated, there was little increase in the size or number of large farms, and hence there was limited scope for a greater concentration of income at the top end of the distribution.

Second, agricultural wage earnings increased significantly and these translated into higher incomes for landless laborers, nonagriculturalists, and small farmers. This process was facilitated by rural-urban migration and a low incidence of increased landlessness, both of which helped to curtail any increase in the number of hired workers in agriculture (Chapter 6).

Third, the per hectare net returns to paddy farming, and especially to HYVs, declined after the initial gains of the early 1970s (Figure 2.3). This was partly because of sharp increases in the costs of labor and fertilizers, but also because the real price of paddy stagnated and perhaps declined. The net result was that farm incomes did not increase in direct proportion to the area of HYVs grown, but the gain depended, among other things, on a farmer's dependence on hired labor, his skill in managing fertilizers and irrigation, and his choice of crops and livestock to rear. Within this context, the larger farmers were not always the most successful in increasing incomes, and the new technology may have contributed more to an improvement in the distribution of income than its initial scale-neutral features would have suggested. This is supported by the survey evidence. In 1982/83 small farms realized Rs 2,020 of net farm income per hectare of operated land, compared with Rs 1,090 for large-sized farms. Almost identical results emerged in the resurvey villages in 1983/84.

Fourth, there were significant increases in nonfarm sources of income. These were not only crucial to the specialized nonagricultural households, but were also an important component of the increase in incomes for the small paddy farmers, the nonpaddy farmers, and the landless laborers (Chapter 3). Some of this income was due to government employment programs and, in the case of Nesal, Veerasambanur, and Vinayagapuram, to increased silk weaving (Chapter 4). But more generally, the importance of the increase in nonfarm incomes provides support for the argument that the growth linkages emanating from agricultural growth do benefit the poorer households in the rural villages.

Since the increase in family incomes was reasonably equitable, the green revolution does not seem to have increased antagonisms between classes within the villages. On the contrary, John Harriss (Chapter 4) finds that because the government is now a more important economic factor in village life through its involvement in providing credit, electricity, and transport, as well as its employment programs and subsidized food and school meals schemes, then political alliances are emerging to make demands on the state that cut across existing class antagonisms.

The Downstream Benefits from the Green Revolution

So far we have focused on the research findings in the rural villages, but an important part of the analysis in this study concerns the impact of the green revolution on the larger regional economy, especially that of the local towns and urban villages.

The regional analysis in Chapter 8 led to the conclusion that each rupee increase of value added in agriculture stimulated an additional Rs 0.87 of additional value added in the region's nonfarm economy. About half of this indirect income gain is due to agriculture's demands for inputs and marketing and processing services, and the rest is due to increased consumer demands as a consequence of higher incomes.

This semi-input-output estimate of the multiplier is almost identical to the one obtained by Bell, Hazell, and Slade (1982) for the Muda River region in Malaysia. It is also consistent with the range of semi-input-output multipliers derived for Asia by Haggblade and Hazell (1989). A distinctive feature of all these estimates is that they are based on the strong assumption that agriculture has a highly inelastic supply, with output increasing only as the result of some exogenous change, such as an increase in irrigation investment or the adoption of improved varieties. In contrast, most nonagricultural commodities, and especially services, are treated as nontradables and are assumed to have highly elastic supplies. Within these assumptions, increases in demand generated by increases in agricultural output have a Keynesian impact on the nonfarm economy; supply expands to meet the increase in demand at existing prices.

While this approach offers important methodological advantages (Bell, Hazell, and Slade 1982) and the assumptions are not unreasonable for a labor-surplus economy like North Arcot, there is a possibility that it may overestimate the size of the multiplier. If the supplies of some nonagricultural commodities are less than perfectly elastic, then part of any increase in demand will be dissipated through price increases and the increase in nonagricultural output, and value added, will be smaller. Haggblade, Hammer, and Hazell (1991) suggest that the true multipliers may be 10 to 30 percent smaller than the estimates obtained from semi-input-output models in labor-surplus regions. Even so, this would still leave the minimum North Arcot multiplier at Rs 60 to Rs 75. There are also other good reasons to believe that the indirect impact of agricultural growth in the North Arcot region has been substantial.

We have already reviewed the importance of increases in nonagricultural income in increasing incomes for the poorer household groups in the rural villages, and this suggests strong growth linkage effects. Additional evidence can be obtained by examining the data on the impact of drought. In 1982/83 North Arcot district's aggregate rice production was only 290,000 tonnes compared with 693,000 tonnes in 1983/84, the immediate postdrought year (Table 2.2). As a result, agricultural incomes (defined here as the sum of farm income and agricultural wage earnings) were also lower in 1982/83 than in 1983/84, by 33, 25, 65, and 90 percent, respectively, for small-farm, large-farm, landless-labor, and nonagricultural households in the resurvey villages (Tables 3.8, 3.9, 3.11, and 3.12). Nonagricultural wage earnings were actually higher during the drought, but much of this was employment in construction projects and government employment programs undertaken outside the surveyed villages. In contrast, nonfarm business earnings plummeted—by 98 percent for nonagricultural households (Table 3.12). Since most nonfarm businesses serve local village demand, the drop in income was a direct consequence of the shortfall in agricultural output and incomes. Moreover, the magnitude of the decline in nonfarm business income relative to the decline in farm income is sufficiently large to add credence to our estimated regional multiplier.

Additional evidence is available from Barbara Harriss' analysis of the changes in the private sector of Arni between 1973 and 1983 (Chapter 9). Unlike the larger regional economy, Arni's economy is dominated by silk manufacturing (62 percent of total value added in 1983), hence only part of the changes in income and employment can be attributed to agricultural growth. But if we net out the silk industry, her data show that value added increased by 347 percent over the decade, and employment increased by 25 percent. Part of these increases must be attributed to multiplier effects arising from the growth of the silk industry itself, but part is undoubtedly due to agricultural growth in the Arni hinterland. It must also be remembered that Barbara Harriss collected her data during the 1982/83 drought, and just as nonfarm activity contracted sharply in the sample villages that year, in all likelihood it was also below normal in Arni.

Finally, there is independent evidence from the Census of India. Table 11.1 shows relevant data on the number of workers from the 1971 and 1981 censuses for the study region. The nonagricultural work

TABLE 11.1
Changes in the Structure of Regional Employment (number of full-time workers)

	Farmers	*Agricultural Workers*	*Nonagricultural Workers*			*All Workers*
			Rural	*Urban*	*Total*	
1971	252,893	196,081	85,552	48,204	133,756	582,730
1981	306,986	262,291	114,962	71,065	186,027	755,304
Change (%)	21.4	33.8	34.4	47.4	39.1	29.6

Source: Census of the Government of India.

force increased by 39.1 percent over the decade. Relating this to the 41 percent increase in agricultural value added when normalized for rainfall (Table 8.3), each 1 percent increase in agricultural value added was associated with a 0.95 percent increase in nonagricultural employment. Of course, not all the increase in nonagricultural employment can be attributed to agricultural growth; some is due to other autonomous sources of growth such as the silk industry in Arni. But given the structure of the region's exports as revealed by the social accounting matrix (SAM) in Chapter 7, it is reasonable to suppose that agriculture is the primary engine of growth in the region, and hence the employment multiplier of 0.95 is a useful upper-bound estimate.

Two additional features of the region's nonfarm growth deserve mention. First, although increases in nonagricultural income helped achieve greater equality of income in the rural villages because they accrued largely to the poor, this was not so in the urban areas. Incomes were much less equitably distributed in the towns than in the villages in the early 1980s; compare the range of per capita incomes across household groups in the SAM (Table 7.5) or across sectors in Arni (Table 9.9). Further, the growth experiments conducted with the regional model in Chapter 8 show that in the urban villages and towns, the gains from nonagricultural income exacerbate inequalities in household incomes. For example, in the local towns the household gains of nonagricultural income are Rs 751 for the agriculturally dependent households, Rs 6,525 for the self-employed nonagricultural households, and Rs 1,331 for the employed nonagricultural households (Table 8.5). In ratio form these gains are 1:8.7:1.8, which compare with an initial pre–green revolution distribution of household income of 1:2.6:1.3. Similar calculations for the urban villages give ratios of incremental gains in nonagricultural income of 1:7.8:3.1, compared with an initial income distribution of 1:3.6:1.2.

Second, there was a broad, spatial pattern of development in the growth of the region's nonfarm economy. Wanmali (Chapter 10) reports a sharp increase in the number of villages that became service centers for low-order services (mostly retail and personal services) between 1973 and 1983. The number and range of services available in the towns also increased, with the net result that more services became available in more places, and rural households had to travel shorter distances to avail themselves of these services. By 1983 the region was largely self-sufficient in providing all the production and consumer services demanded by its rural households.

Barbara Harriss' data in Chapter 9 also show a sharp (61 percent) increase between 1973 and 1983 in the number of private businesses in Arni. She also confirms the increasing decentralization of retail services to the villages observed by Wanmali; this sector declined in relative importance in Arni.

The rapid and geographically dispersed growth of the nonfarm economy suggests an elastic supply structure, which is of course essential if the agricultural growth multipliers are to realize their full potential. Government policy has been generally conducive to this pattern of growth. The government actively supports small businesses through an array of direct assistance programs. It has also invested heavily in basic infrastructure over the years, and there is now a well-developed transport, telecommunication, postal, banking, water, and electricity system throughout the region, as well as a legal and institutional setting that encourages the private sector. Government has also been active in providing a range of producer and consumer services itself, for example, foods and general provisions through ration shops, agricultural marketing, and bus and financial services. These activities compete directly with the private sector, and this may help to keep costs down. The government may also have played a lead role in providing these services in the more remote areas where provision by the private sector was less adequate.

The Impact of Drought

An unplanned but useful output of our study is the measurement of the impact of the 1982/83 drought, particularly in the resurvey villages. Paddy production was less than half its level in the immediate post-drought year in the resurvey villages, farm incomes were down 15 percent, agricultural employment halved, and nonfarm business earnings in the villages virtually disappeared. The impact of these changes on rural households was reflected by a roughly 50 percent reduction in the value of total consumption expenditure and a marked deterioration in the quality of the diet.

In terms of family incomes, many households were actually worse off in 1982/83 than in 1973/74, despite the intervening changes in irrigation and paddy technology (Table 3.7). However, the income losses were distributed in approximate proportion to more normal incomes, and relative incomes were the same during the drought as in 1983/84 (Table 3.16).

These findings may overstate the impact of the drought because they are taken from the resurvey villages. These villages were deliberately selected for resurvey in 1983/84 because, having the least reliable supplies of irrigation water, they were thought to have been most adversely affected by the drought. However, at the regional level paddy production was also down about 60 percent (Table 2.2), and real incomes averaged over all 11 sample villages were lower in 1982/83 than in 1973/74 for all the agriculturally dependent household groups (Table 3.7). While the drought had little visible effect on some of the more fortunate villages (e.g., Kalpattu and Vegamangalam with their unusually reliable sources of water), it does seem to have had a generally devastating effect on the region.

The green revolution has not had a stabilizing effect in North Arcot. When there is adequate water paddy production is much higher than it used to be, but in drought years production is no higher than it was during drought years in the 1950s or 1960s (Table 2.2). The basic problem is that the region obtains nearly all its irrigation water from groundwater reserves and storage tanks (reservoirs), which depend on rainfall for their recharge. They are a useful way of redistributing the monsoon rains to obtain multiple crops each year, but they provide limited capacity for carrying water from good to bad rainfall years. Consequently, when the monsoons fail there is inadequate water to maintain a normal paddy area, and farmers drastically reduce the planted area. Interestingly, yields are not that much affected, so farmers are clearly astute in estimating the area of paddy for which they have adequate water each season.

The resultant instability in employment and incomes does pose difficult problems for the region. While per capita incomes are higher on average as a result of the green revolution, they are still low and provide only a basic existence. It is not at all clear that many households can acquire adequate financial reserves to cope with droughts, particularly when low rainfall years tend to be bunched together (e.g., 1967/68 and 1968/69, 1973/74 and 1974/75, and 1980/81 and 1982/83—Table 2.2). The government already plays an active role in drought years by providing relief employment and subsidized food through its ration shops, but judging from our survey results, these efforts are not successful in protecting incomes and consumption for most households. Given the high cost of such public interventions, it is unfortunate that the green revolution has not been more successful in stabilizing production and incomes. There remains a clear need for additional research to identify ways in which government and private institutions can more effectively deal with the instability problem in North Arcot and other similar regions.

The Future of North Arcot

Since the North Arcot economy is highly dependent on agriculture, agricultural growth has, and will continue to be, the *sine qua non* for the economic development of the region. Now that the green revolution in rice has run its course, what are the prospects for future agricultural growth?

Increases in rice production will continue to be the cutting edge for regional growth, and with average yields of less than 3,000 kg/ha, there is still considerable scope for improvements. Plant breeding will undoubtedly lead to further improvements in yield, especially by improving disease resistance and drought tolerance. Further reductions in the growing period of rice varieties would also facilitate an increase in cropping intensity, as well as help to reduce water requirements per crop. Production costs might also be reduced by exploiting biofertilizers such as azolla and blue-green algae, and through improved pest and disease management systems. The region is fortunate to have a first-rate Rice Research Institute at TNAU that is actively pursuing many of these options.

Irrigation water will increasingly become the binding constraint on rice farming. Past increases in the number of irrigation wells, coupled with the mechanization of water pumping, have already tapped most of the groundwater potential in the region. The geological formation of this hard rock area offers little scope for deeper drilling and exploitation of water in deeper layers. Indeed, some evidence suggests that there is already a net mining of groundwater reserves. Nonagricultural demands for water by industries and households will also continue to grow.

Additional supplies of irrigation water can be obtained from increasing the catchment of surface runoff during the monsoons. This requires additional investments in percolation tanks and check dams, and the desilting and deepening of many existing tanks. Greater emphasis will also have to be given to using water more efficiently through improved irrigation practices, and to developing rice varieties that require less water (presumably by reducing their growing period).

The increasing scarcity of irrigation water, together with a stagnant rice price, will provide an increasing incentive for farmers to diversify into other crops besides rice. Groundnuts are already the second most important crop in the region, and they are widely grown on irrigated as well as rainfed land. The real price of groundnuts has also increased in recent years, adding to the attractiveness of this crop. This is a crop deserving of increased research attention; there has not been a major new variety in the region for about 20 years.

There may also be potential for increasing the production of vegetables, flowers, and fruits. North Arcot already exports mangos and bananas to other states, and there are suitable markets for other horticultural products in Madras and Bangalore. Since these crops typically require less water than paddy, they may also offer some scope for stabilizing farm incomes in drought years.

In addition to crop diversification, there is scope for increasing farm incomes through additional milk and livestock production, and through the expansion of sericulture. "Operation Flood," which among other things involves subsidized credit and the formation of milk societies at the village level, has already successfully increased milk production in the region, particularly by small-farm and landless-labor households. Future improvements will require more intensive management practices and expansion of the forage crop area. The potential for sericulture seems particularly attractive, given a ready market for silk yarn among the silk-weaving units at Arni.

Conclusions

In undertaking this study, we have become acutely aware of the difficulties of measuring changes within villages between two points in time. Despite close collaboration with researchers from the earlier Cambridge-Madras universities team, we encountered vexing problems in trying to identify the same village boundaries, and in matching concepts and definitions in the design of the survey instruments. Part of the problem was undoubtedly attributable to having different field personnel, but a larger part was probably due to changes that occurred in the real world—for example, village boundaries did move, and there were changes in farm technologies, in the seasonality of paddy growing, in local units of measurement, and in the terms of labor and rental contracts and other institutional arrangements. In the absence of assured irrigation water supplies, surveys undertaken at specific points in time are also subject to the vagaries of weather, and this makes comparisons between individual years especially fragile. There are no easy answers to these difficulties, and we have had to use more judgment in interpreting our data that we had initially foreseen.

Despite these limitations, this study has shown that the green revolution had a favorable impact in North Arcot. In addition to increasing aggregate paddy output, there were sizable across-the-board gains in income, employment, and the quality of diet for the rural households, and these were not accompanied by any worsening of the interhousehold distribution of income. Nor is there any evidence that the distribution of land deteriorated, except perhaps in some of the villages that had benefited the least from the new technology because of their limited irrigation resources. There were also sizable growth linkage effects that bolstered the nonfarm income of the poorer household groups within the rural villages and stimulated the expansion and decentralization of economic activity in the local towns and urban villages.

These results contrast with the negative findings of the earlier study undertaken by Cambridge and Madras universities and thereby highlight the dangers of reading too much into the adjustment problems that often emerge during the early stages of technology adoption. The small-scale farmers did lag behind their larger brethren during the initial phases of the green revolution, but they subsequently caught up, thereby preventing the undesirable inequity effects that were initially feared.

North Arcot is not a particularly favored rice-growing region by Indian standards. Its average paddy yield of about 3,000 kg/ha is not especially high, and its 2 to 3 percent annual growth in regional production barely matches the all-India average for recent decades. Moreover, unlike many rice-growing areas, North Arcot depends for irrigation largely on the catchment and storage of surface water, and hence production is very sensitive to variations in annual rainfall.

On the other hand, there were clearly a number of key features of the North Arcot region that were instrumental in realizing favorable equity effects from the green revolution. First, the region was, and continues to be, dominated by small-scale, owner-occupied farms. The absence of significant numbers of large-scale farmers and landlords reduced the likelihood that small farmers would be bought out or evicted from their land as it became more valuable. Moreover, only a very small share of the increase in farm incomes accrued to landlords through rental payments.

Second, the region's agricultural labor force did not increase by as much as population growth because of migration from the villages to towns, both within the North Arcot region and to the more distant cities of Madras and Bangalore. This, together with the withdrawal of many farm family workers from the agricultural labor market, and an increase in nonfarm activity, helped prevent real wages from declining over time and enabled small-farm and landless-labor households to increase their total agricultural employment and wage earnings. On the other hand, farm labor costs did not increase to the point at which widespread mechanization of land preparation or harvesting activities proved worthwhile.

Third, the region is fortunate to benefit from a first-rate Rice Research Institute at TNAU, which played a key role in adapting genetic material released by IRRI to local conditions. This was especially important in providing quick-maturing, photoperiod-insensitive, and better-tasting varieties that are better adapted to small farms.

Fourth, local and state governments were committed to equitable agricultural development, and acted to make credit and modern inputs available to small-scale farmers. They also invested heavily over the years in basic infrastructure, expanded the availability of transport and other key services, maintained a legal and institutional setting that encouraged the private sector, and supported small business through an array of direct assistance programs.

While we would be hesitant to claim that these regional attributes are sufficient for equitable growth, they do seem to have been necessary conditions. As such, they provide useful guidelines for public policy in other agricultural regions.

Not all aspects of the change in North Arcot were equitable. Within the rural villages, the households not directly involved in paddy production—the nonpaddy farmers and the nonagriculturalists—increased their incomes by only about half as much as the other household groups. In terms of the relative distribution of per capita income, these households are now emerging as the new rural poor. It also seems that, contrary to the changes in the rural villages, the interhousehold distribution of income became considerably less equitable in the towns and urban villages. While all urban household groups gained in absolute terms, the available rewards to capital and entrepreneurial skills clearly led to much larger relative gains for the better endowed. Moreover, as an inevitable consequence of differences in their irrigation resources, the green revolution led to widening income disparities between villages.

Future growth in paddy production will be more difficult to achieve now that the region's irrigation potential has been almost fully exploited. Indeed, if available evidence on a trend decline in the availability of groundwater reserves is correct, then even current levels of paddy production may prove difficult to sustain with existing technologies. As the emphasis moves toward more efficient use of irrigation water and to the improvement of other, less-water-demanding crops, future rounds of technological change in North Arcot may prove more beneficial to those farmers and villages that, because of their limited access to irrigation resources, have benefited the least from the green revolution in rice.

APPENDIX A

Sources of Growth in the Region's Paddy Production

CHAPTER 2 HIGHLIGHTS the importance of the introduction of high-yielding varieties (HYVs) and increases in the use of water and fertilizers in accounting for the growth in North Arcot's rice production. This appendix attempts a quantitative analysis of the sources of growth in paddy output, both to identify the separate contributions of individual inputs and their interaction effects. It also separates out the effects of changes in prices and annual rainfall.

The analysis is based on time-series data for North Arcot district for the years 1950/51 to 1983/84. The data were provided by the joint director of agriculture and the assistant director of statistics in Vellore.

The Model

Separate area and yield functions were estimated rather than a single paddy output function. This has the advantage of enabling different explanatory variables to be used in each relation, hence enabling the model to capture differences in underlying behavior.

Following Bindlish, Barker, and Mount (1989), area and yield functions were specified as follows:

$$\begin{aligned} \text{AREA}_t = {} & [a_0 + a_1P_{t-1} + a_2NW_t + a_3R_t]\,HYV_t \\ & + [b_0 + b_1P_{t-1} + b_2NW_t + b_3R_t]\,(1 - HYV_t) + u_t \qquad \text{(A.1)} \\ \text{YIELD}_t = {} & [\alpha_0 + \alpha_1N_t + \alpha_2N_t^2 + \alpha_3R_t + \alpha_4R_tN_t]\,HYV_t \\ & + [\beta_0 + \beta_1N_t + \beta_2N_t^2 + \beta_3R_t + \beta_4R_tN_t] \\ & (1 - HYV_t) + v_t \qquad \text{(A.2)} \end{aligned}$$

where

$AREA_t$ = gross cropped area of paddy in year t (ha)
$YIELD_t$ = average district paddy yield in year t (kg/ha)
HYV_t = proportion gross paddy area planted to HYVs in year t
NW_t = number of irrigation wells in the district in year t
R_t = annual rainfall in year t (mm)
P_{t-1} = ratio of paddy to groundnut farm-gate prices in year $t-1$
N_t = total nitrogen use for all crops in the district in year t as a ratio of gross paddy area (kg/ha)
u_t, v_t = error terms.

Area and yield are specified as the weighted sum of the separate areas and yields of HYV and non-HYV varieties. Ideally, the inputs allocated to the different varieties should also be separated out, but this was not possible with the available data. Consequently, the same input variables enter both components of the area and yield functions. In effect, what this specification assumes is that although the same inputs are used for both varieties, in terms of the response these inputs interact differently with each variety.

The gross cropped area of HYV and non-HYV paddy is hypothesized to be determined by annual rainfall, by the number of irrigation wells, and, since groundnuts are the main competing crop on irrigated land, by the lagged price of paddy relative to groundnuts. Once the paddy area is sown, then the ensuing yield is hypothesized to be determined by the amount of nitrogen applied and by rainfall. Unfortunately, the available district data on nitrogen use are not disaggregated by crop, so the total nitrogen use on all crops divided by the paddy area is used instead.

Estimation of equations (A.1) and (A.2) proved difficult because of severe multicollinearity problems. Reasonable results were obtained only after resort to a principal components regression package developed by Mundlak (1981).

The following results were obtained, where figures in parentheses are t-statistics.

$$\begin{aligned} AREA_t = {} & [\underset{(1.44)}{-35{,}330} + \underset{(7.16)}{327{,}547\,P_{t-1}} - \underset{(2.15)}{0.2502\,NW_t} + \underset{(5.16)}{186.7\,R_t}]\,HYV_t \\ & + [\underset{(1.99)}{-66{,}056} + \underset{(14.75)}{38{,}023\,P_{t-1}} + \underset{(0.95)}{0.9503\,NW_t} + \underset{(6.75)}{105.4\,R_t}](1 - HYV_t) \\ & R^2 = 0.976 \end{aligned} \qquad (A.3)$$

$$\text{YIELD}_t = [\underset{(9.61)}{820.5} + \underset{(4.94)}{1767.5}\,N_t - \underset{(1.19)}{5484.9}\,N_t^2 + \underset{(8.51)}{0.8976}\,R_t + \underset{(12.08)}{4.671}\,R_tN_t]\,HYV_t$$

$$+ [\underset{(6.72)}{1362.5} + \underset{(2.75)}{7502.0}\,N_t - \underset{(1.08)}{21{,}643.3}\,N_t^2 + \underset{(0.71)}{0.125}\,R_t$$

$$- \underset{(1.29)}{5.093}R_tN_t](1 - HYV_t)$$

$$R^2 = 0.984 \qquad \text{(A.4)}$$

Production, Area, and Yield Elasticities

Table A.1 shows the elasticities of area, yield, and production with respect to the explanatory variables. The reported elasticities are evaluated at the sample means for a pre-HYV period 1950/51 to 1965/66, a post-HYV period 1966/67 to 1983/84, and the entire period 1950/51

TABLE A.1
Area, Yield, and Production Elasticities for Paddy, North Arcot District

	50/51–65/66	*66/67–83/84*	*50/51–83/84*
Area elasticity with respect to:			
P_{t-1}	0.118	0.360	0.287
HYV	—	0.113	0.032
NW	0.697	0.331	0.552
R	0.496	0.591	0.551
Yield elasticity with respect to:			
HYV	—	0.193	0.086
N	0.011	0.098	0.050
R	0.052	0.269	0.128
Production elasticity with respect to:			
P_{t-1}	0.118	0.360	0.287
HYV	—	0.306	0.082
NW	0.697	0.331	0.552
N	0.011	0.098	0.050
R	0.548	0.860	0.679

Note: See text following equation (A.2) for definitions of variables.

to 1983/84. The production elasticities are derived from the area and yield elasticities using the relation:

$$\xi_x^Q = \xi_x^A + \xi_x^Y$$

where x denotes any explanatory variable of interest.

Paddy production is particularly responsive to changes in annual rainfall, and this responsiveness increased with the introduction of HYVs. The elasticity of production with respect to rainfall increased from 0.548 in 1950/51–1965/66 to 0.860 in 1966/67–1983/84, with much of the increase originating from an increased responsiveness of yields to rainfall (the elasticity of yield with respect to rainfall increased from 0.052 to 0.269 between the two periods).

That regional production has become more sensitive to fluctuations in annual rainfall is also shown by the change in the marginal productivity of water. Evaluated at the period means, the district's marginal productivity of water was 177 tonnes of paddy per millimeter (mm) of rain in 1950/51–1965/66, and it had increased to 419 tonnes per mm of rain in 1966/67–1983/84. These results are consistent with the impact of the drought in 1982/83. Annual rainfall was down 500 mm that year, and the model predicts a loss of 209,400 tonnes, or about 43 percent of normal production. This is close to the actual loss that year (see Table 2.2).

Paddy production is also responsive to the number of irrigation wells in the region, though less so in the post-HYV period; the elasticity declined from 0.697 to 0.331 between the two periods. This response is attributed in the model to changes in the area planted to paddy rather than to any changes in yield. During the period 1950/51–1965/66, each additional well added 1.44 tonnes to the district's annual paddy production. The corresponding figure for 1966/67–1983/84 is 0.64 tonnes per well. Diminishing returns to irrigation wells seem to have set in despite the introduction of HYVs, probably because of an increasing depletion of groundwater reserves.

The elasticity of paddy production with respect to HYVs is 0.306. That is, each percentage increase in the proportion of the paddy area planted to HYVs increases regional production by 0.306 percent. This response arises about equally from an increase in the area planted to paddy and from an increase in average yields.

Paddy production and yield are very inelastic in response to the intensity of nitrogen use, though the elasticities did increase between the two periods. However, these figures may be biased because the nitrogen data used relate to all crops grown rather than just paddy.

Paddy production also became more responsive to price in the post-

HYV period; the elasticity with respect to the lagged price ratio increased from 0.118 to 0.360 between the two periods. This response is entirely due in the model to changes in the area planted to paddy.

Decomposition of the Sources of Growth

Expanding and collecting terms, equations (A.3) and (A.4) can be simplified as follows:

$$\begin{aligned} \text{AREA}_t = {} & 30{,}726\, HYV_t + 289{,}524\, P_{t-1}\, HYV_t - 1.2\, NW_t\, HYV_t \\ & + 81.3\, R_t\, HYV_t + 38{,}023\, \text{P}_{t-1} + 0.95\, NW_t \\ & + 105.4\, R_t - 66{,}056 \end{aligned} \tag{A.5}$$

$$\begin{aligned} \text{YIELD}_t = {} & -542\, HYV_t - 5{,}735\, N_t\, HYV_t + 16{,}158\, N_t^2\, HYV_t \\ & + 0.773\, R_t\, HYV_t + 9.764\, R_t\, N_t\, HYV_t \\ & + 7{,}502\, N_t - 21{,}643\, N_t^2 + 0.125\, R_t \\ & - 5.093\, R_t\, N_t + 1{,}363 \end{aligned} \tag{A.6}$$

Let Δ denote the change in a variable between pre- and post-HYV periods, then the change in area and yield can be derived from the changes in the explanatory variables in equations (A.5) and (A.6) as follows:

$$\begin{aligned} \text{AREA} = {} & 30{,}726\,\Delta HYV + 289{,}524\,(P_0\,\Delta HYV + \Delta P\,\Delta HYV) \\ & - 1.2\,(NW_0\,\Delta HYV + \Delta NW\,\Delta HYV) \\ & + 81.3\,(R_0\,\Delta HYV + \Delta R\,\Delta HYV) \\ & + 38{,}023\,\Delta P + 0.95\,\Delta NW + 105.4\,\Delta R \end{aligned} \tag{A.7}$$

$$\begin{aligned} \text{YIELD} = {} & -542\,\Delta HYV - 5735\,(N_0\,\Delta HYV + \Delta N \Delta HYV) \\ & + 16{,}158\,(N_0^2\,\Delta HYV + \Delta N^2\,\Delta HYV) \\ & + 0.773\,(R_0\,\Delta HYV + \Delta R\,\Delta HYV) \\ & + 7{,}502\,\Delta N - 21{,}643\,\Delta N^2 + 0.125\,\Delta R \\ & - 5.093\,(R_0\,\Delta N + N_0\,\Delta R + \Delta N \Delta R) \\ & + 9.764\,(R_0\,N_0\,\Delta HYV + R_0\,\Delta N\,\Delta HYV + N_0\,\Delta R\,\Delta HYV \\ & + \Delta R\,\Delta N\,\Delta HYV) \end{aligned} \tag{A.8}$$

TABLE A.2
Sources of Change in Area and Yield in Time-Series Model

Source	*Change in Area*	*Change in Yield*
Change in varieties	$(30{,}726 + 289{,}524\ P_0 - 1.2\ NW_0 + 81.3\ R_0)\ \Delta HYV$	$(-542 - 5735\ N_0 + 16{,}158\ N_0^2 + 0.773\ R_0 + 9.764\ R_0\ N_0)\Delta HYV$
Change in nitrogen use		$(7{,}502 - 5.093\ R_0)\ \Delta N - 21{,}643\ \Delta N^2$
Change in lagged price	$38{,}023\ \Delta P$	
Change in number of wells	$0.95\ \Delta NW$	
Change in annual rainfall	$105.4\ \Delta R$	$(0.125 - 5.093\ N_0)\ \Delta R$
Interaction between changes in nitrogen use & varieties		$(-5{,}735 + 9.764\ R_0)\ \Delta N\ \Delta HYV + 16{,}158\ \Delta N^2\ \Delta HYV$
Interaction between changes in rainfall & nitrogen use		$-5.093\ \Delta N\ \Delta R$
Interaction between changes in rainfall & varieties	$81.3\ \Delta R\ \Delta HYV$	$(0.773 + 9.764\ N_0)\ \Delta R\ \Delta HYV$
Interaction between changes in nitrogen use, rainfall, & varieties		$9.764\ \Delta R\ \Delta N\ \Delta HYV$
Interaction between changes in lagged price & varieties	$289{,}524\ \Delta P\ \Delta HYV$	
Interaction between changes in number of wells & varieties	$-1.2\ \Delta NW\ \Delta HYV$	

where a zero subscript denotes the value of a variable in the pre-HYV period, and the fact that no HYVs were grown in the pre-HYV period implies $HYV_0 = 0$. The terms on the right-hand side of equations (A.7) and (A.8) can then be grouped according to the sources of change, as shown in Table A.2.

Using the changes in the period mean values of the variables between 1950/51–1965/66 and 1966/67–1983/84 reported in Table A.3, the results in Table A.4 were obtained. Note that since production Q equals area times yield (i.e.: $Q = A \cdot Y$), then the sources of change in production were derived from the relation:

$$\Delta Q = A_0\, \Delta Y + Y_0\, \Delta A + \Delta Y\, \Delta A \qquad \text{(A.9)}$$

Equation (A.9) was applied to each of the sources of change separately to obtain the decomposition results for production in Table A.4.

The adoption of HYVs and increases in the number of irrigation wells were the predominant sources of growth in paddy production in North Arcot between 1950/51–1965/66 and 1966/67–1983/84. HYVs accounted for 93.0 percent of the increase in production, and additional irrigation wells accounted for another 83.2 percent.

HYVs contributed to increases in area and yields, whereas additional wells had their impact by permitting an expansion of the area planted to paddy. The interaction effect of additional wells and HYVs on production is negative. Since this effect arises from changes in the planted area, it suggests that where additional wells were added along with HYVs, some land was diverted to other crops.

Increased nitrogen use by itself had a small negative impact on paddy production, but there was a positive interaction effect between HYVs

TABLE A.3
Changes in Mean Values of Paddy Variables, North Arcot District

	50/51–65/66	*66/67–83/84*	*Percent Change*
Area (ha)	223,869	249,079	11.3
Yield (kg/ha)	1,517	1,950	28.5
Production (tonnes)	342,666	485,107	41.6
HYV (% planted area)	—	52.0	—
Nitrogen use (kg/ha)	9.74	85.0	772.7
Number of wells	165,465	252,920	52.9
Annual rainfall (mm)	1,053	997	−5.3
Lagged price ratio (paddy to groundnuts)	0.69	0.47	−31.9

TABLE A.4
Decomposition of Sources of Change in Area, Yield, and Production of Paddy, North Arcot District (percent)

Source	*Change in Area*	*Change in Yield*	*Change in Production*
Change in varieties	149.1	47.4	93.0
Change in nitrogen use	—	−12.7	−6.6
Change in lagged price	−19.9	—	−8.2
Change in number of wells	201.1	—	83.2
Change in annual rainfall	−14.0	−1.2	−6.4
Interaction between changes in nitrogen use & varieties	—	73.8	38.2
Interaction between changes in rainfall & nitrogen use	—	6.1	3.2
Interaction between changes in rainfall & varieties	−5.6	−7.2	−6.0
Interaction between changes in nitrogen use, rainfall, & varieties	—	−6.1	−3.2
Interaction between changes in lagged price & varieties	−78.7	—	−32.5
Interaction between changes in number of wells & varieties	−132.1	—	−54.6
Total	100.0	100.0	100.0

Note: All changes measured between the period means for each variable.

and nitrogen that accounted for 38.2 percent of the increase in production and 73.8 percent of the increase in yield.

Price movements had a negative impact on area and production, and this was accentuated by a negative interaction between price and HYVs. The lagged paddy price relative to groundnuts declined from a period mean of 0.69 in 1950/51–1965/66 to 0.47 in 1966/67–1983/84.

APPENDIX B

Survey Design

The 1973/74 Rural Survey

A two-stage sampling design was used. The first stage involved the selection of a representative sample of 11 villages for the study region. The sampling frame used was the 1971 census list of all villages in the study region having a population between 50 and 5,000 people, but excluding villages located in reserved forests or in hilly regions. A twelfth village (Dusi) was also selected, but this village was purposively selected and is not part of the representative sample. Apart from Chapters 4 and 6, the Dusi data were excluded from the analyses reported in this book.

The 11 villages were selected from a population of 989 villages using simple systematic random sampling. That is, every *k*th village (where *k* is the inverse of the sample ratio) was selected from an arranged list, the first selection being at random from the first *k* units in the list. The list was formed by arranging the villages before selection in the following order: (1) by contiguous *taluks*, (2) by distance from towns within the *taluks*, (3) by 1971 population size, (4) by the ratio of agricultural laborers to cultivators, and (5) by spatial proximity (as indicated by village location codes given by the 1971 census).

All the households in the selected villages were listed and, for each household, basic information was collected on the size and composition of the family, their principal means of livelihood, and their landholdings. These data were used to select the second-stage samples.

Several different household samples and questionnaires were used in stage two, and these are fully described in Chambers et al. (1977). The data used in this study were taken almost exclusively from two household surveys.

The first was a sample of 161 paddy-farm households that participated in a detailed farm management survey for the agricultural year ending with the 1974 *sornavari* crop. A paddy farm was defined as a holding of one-fourth acre or larger on which paddy was or could be grown. Prior to selection, the paddy farms in each village were arranged in order according to whether or not they (1) grew high-yielding varieties (HYVs) and (2) had an irrigation pumpset or an iron plow. They were further ranked by farm size and by the maximum area planted to paddy in any one season. Once the farms were ordered in this way, systematic sampling with equal probability was used to select a sample in each village.

The second survey was a household sample of 57 paddy farms, 3 nonpaddy farms, and 77 noncultivator households that participated in a monthly income and expenditure survey between April 1973 and May 1974. The 57 paddy-farm households were selected from the sample of 161 paddy farmers included in the farm management survey. The sampling procedure used was the same as described above.

The sample of 77 noncultivator households was selected by circular systematic sampling, with equal probability, after arranging the noncultivator households in each village by (1) principal means of livelihood, (2) religion and caste, and (3) household size. A noncultivator household was defined as a household operating less than one-fourth acre of land. It includes the landless agricultural-laborer households.

The sample of three nonpaddy farmers was selected by simple systematic sampling with equal probability from the list of households in each village having only dry land. Before sampling, the households were arranged in increasing order of area of operated land, by land tenure classes, and by household size.

The 1982/83 Rural Survey

As in the 1973/74 survey, all the households in the 11 villages were first listed and basic information collected to form a sampling frame. The 1973/74 listing questionnaire was used, and this involved collecting information on the size and composition of the family, occupation, primary source of income, landholding, ownership of irrigation wells and lifting equipment, type and condition of house, and ownership of cycles and radios.

The listing data were used to classify the households into three groups: paddy cultivators, nonpaddy cultivators, and noncultivating households. As in 1973/74, a cultivator was defined as a farmer operating more than one-fourth acre. Different sampling procedures were used to draw a sample within each group.

The paddy cultivators in each village were first sorted into six subgroups according to whether they possessed a pumpset and whether they were tenant farmers, owner-occupiers, or both. Within each group they were then ordered by operated farm size. Preliminary calculations using the 1973/74 survey data showed that a sample size of 160 should provide estimates of aggregate household expenditure that would have a 90 percent chance of falling within plus or minus 10 percent of their true values. Hence, using a predetermined sample size of 160 paddy cultivators for the 11 villages, the sample was allocated among the villages to obtain the same sampling ratio in each village. Systematic random sampling with equal probability was used.

The nonpaddy cultivators in each village were sampled by simple random sampling. Few households fell into this category in 1982/83, hence it was decided to select a total sample size of 25 households from the 11 villages. The sample for each village was determined so as to obtain equal sample ratios across villages.

The noncultivator households were selected by systematic random sampling. A total sample size of 160 households was allocated among the villages to obtain a constant sampling ratio. Within each village, households were sorted into nine groups according to their primary source of income: agricultural labor, other casual labor, trader, village artisan, cottage or village industry, professional service, landlord or rentier, moneylender, and others. Within each group, the households were then arranged by family size.

All the selected rural households were administered inventory questionnaires in February 1982 and June 1983, and from March 1982 to April 1983 they participated in a monthly income and expenditure survey that also included detailed farm management and nonfarm business data where appropriate.

The 1982/83 Urban Survey

The urban survey was designed to provide representative household income and expenditure data for households living in settlements with more than 5,000 people. Table B.1 lists all the villages in the study area that had more than 5,000 people in the 1971 census (these villages are classified as urban in the census), and Table B.2 lists all the towns in the study area, together with pertinent 1971 census data.

Most of the urban villages are predominantly agricultural in that the largest share of workers either are employed as farmers or agricultural workers, or are engaged in related activities such as livestock rearing, forestry, or fishing. Their populations range between 5,028 and 10,644 people, and between 1,044 and 2,333 households. The towns,

TABLE B.1
Urban Villages in Study Region

Taluk/*Village*	*No. of Census Villages*	*1971 Population*	*No. of Households in 1971*	*Percent Workers in Agriculture*
Arkonam				
1. Sembedu	1	7,374	1,527	50.2
2. Minnal	2	5,842	1,180	67.6
3. Takkolam	1	7,996	1,632	68.6
Wandiwash				
4. Marutadu	3	5,662	1,243	83.0
Polur				
5. Kovilur	1	5,360	1,137	95.9
6. Padavedu	1	10,644	2,219	89.0
7. Alliabad	1	10,396	2,333	70.2
8. Kadaladi	3	6,991	1,620	77.0
9. Kannanur	1	6,692	1,436	53.0
10. Chetpet	1	5,583	1,210	58.5
Tiruvannamalai				
11. Mangalam	1	5,414	1,185	89.5
12. Kelpennathur	1	8,871	1,923	74.3
13. Vettavalam	1	9,482	1,907	71.5
Arni				
14. Kattukanallur	1	6,377	1,230	78.1
15. Kannamangalam	4	9,444	1,970	69.6
16. Melnagar	3	5,028	1,044	34.9
17. S. V. Nagaram	3	6,314	1,370	41.0
18. Devikapuram	1	5,684	1,266	51.6
Total	30	129,154	27,432	

however, are typically much larger, with only a small minority of workers engaged directly in agricultural activities. There are two exceptions, Kaveripakkam and Panapakkam in Arkonam *taluk*, which have the same characteristics as the urban villages in Table B.1. For sampling purposes, these two towns were therefore treated as urban villages rather than as towns.

Given the very different economic structure of the towns and urban villages, it was decided to sample them separately. This allowed a larger sampling ratio to be used in the towns, which was desirable given their wider range of occupations, castes, and incomes. A two-stage sampling procedure was used in both the urban villages and the towns.

The 20 urban villages, including the towns of Kaveripakkam and Panapakkam, were sorted by *taluk*, and the *taluks* ordered and numbered from north to south. Within each *taluk*, the villages were then ordered by population size (in decreasing order) and given a serial number. Using systematic random sampling, two villages were selected: Kattukanallur village in Arni *taluk* and Vettavalam in Tiruvannamalai *taluk*. All the households in these two villages were then listed, and information was collected on family members, sources of income, occupation, landholdings, and any nonfarm business.

There are eight towns in the study region (Table B.2), each of which has been partitioned by the National Sample Survey (NSS) into enumeration blocks (EBs) containing about 150 households each. The EBs were taken as the basic sampling unit for drawing the first-stage sample.

To draw a sample of EBs, the towns were listed in the following order: Arkonam, Thiruvathipuram, Wandiwash, Arni, Polur, and Tiruvannamalai. Within each town, the EBs were ordered in a circular fashion, beginning with the EB in the center of the town and then proceeding clockwise. Each EB was assigned a rank number, beginning with the EB in the center of Arkonam as number 1.

There were about 245 EBs altogether, and it was decided to select 16 for the household survey. The 16 EBs were selected using systematic random sampling and the rank numbers described above. Once the 16 EBs were chosen, the same household questionnaire was used as in the urban villages.

Given the selected urban villages and EBs, the same procedures were used within each to select the second-stage sample of households.

All the households were first classified into three groups based on

TABLE B.2
Urban Towns in Study Region

Taluk/*Town*	*1971 Population*	*No. of Households in 1971*	*Percent Workers in Agriculture*
Arkonam			
1. Kaveripakkam	9,683	1,958	59.0
2. Panapakkam	6,589	1,319	39.0
3. Arkonam	43,347	8,343	3.2
Cheyar			
4. Thiruvathipuram	19,274	3,890	16.9
Wandiwash			
5. Wandiwash	16,083	3,094	18.1
Polur			
6. Polur	18,073	3,652	39.0
Tiruvannamalai			
7. Tiruvannamalai	61,370	12,359	13.9
Arni			
8. Arni	38,664	5,514	11.3
Total	213,083	40,129	

their primary source of income: agriculturally dependent, self-employed in nonagriculture, and employed in nonagriculture.

The agriculturally dependent households were sorted into four groups depending on their tenure status: owners, tenants, owners and tenants, and landless. Within each group they were then ordered by household size and assigned a serial number. A sample of households was chosen by systematic random sampling.

Self-employed nonagricultural households were first sorted by primary source of income. Seven groups were used for this purpose: other agriculture, agricultural processing, landlord or rentier, trader, skilled artisan, professional service, and other service. Within these groups, the households were further subdivided, depending on whether or not they hired any workers. This led to at most 14 groups per urban village or EB. The households were then ranked by family size, and systematic random sampling was used to select the sample.

Nonagricultural employee households were sorted in the same way as the self-employed nonagricultural households. Again, systematic random sampling was used to select households.

The total urban sample consisted of 80 households in the urban villages and 240 households in the towns. The sampling ratios were different for the towns and urban villages, but within each the same sampling ratios were used for each household type. Both sampling ratios were considerably higher than the ones used in the rural villages.

The selected households participated in a monthly income and expenditure survey from March 1982 to April 1983 using a questionnaire similar to the rural one. Inventory questionnaires were also administered in February 1982 and June 1983.

The 1983/84 Survey

The drought of 1982/83 had a severe impact on paddy production in most villages, but particularly on those with less assured supplies of irrigation water. Available resources were insufficient to permit mounting a major survey in 1983/84, but some additional information seemed necessary if any meaningful comparisons with 1973/74 were to be attempted. As a compromise solution, a monthly resurvey of about 100 households was undertaken in 1983/84, but this was limited to those villages and urban blocks surveyed in the previous year that had been most affected by the drought.

The rural resurvey was confined to the following villages: Duli, Vayalur, Veerasambanur, Meppathurai, and Amudhur. Within these villages, half of the 1982/83 sample of paddy cultivators and landless

TABLE B.3
Sample Sizes for Usable Monthly Income and Expenditure Data, Rural Surveys

	1973/74			*1982/83*			*1983/84*		
Village	*Paddy Farmers*	*Nonpaddy Farmers*	*Non-farmers*	*Paddy Farmers*	*Nonpaddy Farmers*	*Non-farmers*	*Paddy Farmers*	*Nonpaddy Farmers*	*Non-farmers*
Kalpattu	7	—	11 (8)	11	1	16 (4)	—	—	—
Meppathurai	3	1	4	19	—	10	10	—	5
Vayalur	4	—	6 (2)	7	3	13 (5)	4	3	9 (4)
Veerasambanur	4	—	4	11	1	10	5	1	5
Vinayagapuram	6	—	3	14	3	8 (1)	—	—	—
Nesal	6	—	16 (4)	21	3	33 (13)	—	—	—
Amudhur	5	1	7 (3)	15	1	12 (4)	8	1	8 (4)
Vengodu	7	—	10 (5)	17	4	16 (3)	—	—	—
Duli	4	—	3	11	4	11 (3)	6	4	6 (2)
Sirungathur	5	—	6 (2)	10	5	17 (4)	—	—	—
Vegamangalam	6	1	7 (3)	24	3	7 (2)	—	—	—
Total	57	3	77 (27)	160	28	153 (39)	33	9	33 (10)

Note: Figures in parentheses are the number of nonfarm households not engaged in agricultural labor.

workers were selected at random for resurvey, and all of the 1982/83 sample of nonpaddy cultivators and nonagriculturalists were surveyed.

The urban resurvey was limited to three towns: Vettavalam, Wandiwash, and Tiruvannamalai. Half of the 1982/83 sample of agriculturally dependent and nonfarm, self-employed households were randomly selected for resurvey. However, none of the households employed in nonagriculture were surveyed, because their incomes were thought to be largely unaffected by the drought.

The same monthly questionnaire as used in 1982/83 was administered for the period September 1983 to June 1984. In order to obtain information for the complete agricultural year, households were also asked to recall information for July and August when interviewed in September. The monthly survey was followed by an inventory questionnaire in August 1984.

Sample Sizes

Table B.3 shows the realized sample sizes for the rural surveys in 1973/74, 1982/83, and 1983/84. "Realized" means households for which usable monthly income and expenditure data are available. The realized sample sizes are smaller than planned because of dropouts or because of missing or clearly erroneous data. The comparable sample sizes from the urban surveys are shown in Table B.4.

Nonfarm Business Survey

The nonfarm business survey was conducted to collect additional input-output information for the construction of a social accounting matrix (SAM) (see Chapter 7). Since a representative sample of rural nonfarm businesses was obtained from the monthly income and expenditure

TABLE B.4
Sample Sizes for Monthly Income and Expenditure Data, Urban Survey

	Urban Villages			*Towns*		
	Agric. Dependent	*Self-Employed Nonagric.*	*Employed Nonagric.*	*Agric. Dependent*	*Self-Employed Nonagric.*	*Employed Nonagric.*
1982/83	41	18	21	29	69	142
1983/84	10	4	—	6	15	—

surveys, the business survey was restricted to the urban towns listed in Table B.2 and to large factories located in rural areas.

A sampling frame was compiled using records on the names, addresses, and types of all local businesses kept by the *panchayat* and municipal offices in each town, by the inspector of factories, and by the district industries center. The available data were for 1982/83. A total of 9,883 businesses were listed, and these were classified into 30 groups according to the type of business. These groupings were done for each *taluk* separately, and then a 10 percent random sample was drawn from each *taluk* and type of business. If the sample size in any one cell was less than 10, then a top-up sample was taken. Given the limited information available on each firm, further stratification was not sought. The total sample size was 1,494 businesses.

The business survey questionnaire included information on the type of business, the type of ownership, the history of the firm, sources of finance, family labor involved, use of hired labor, current capital assets, purchased inputs, and details of sales.

References

Ahluwalia, M. S. 1977. "Rural Poverty and Agricultural Performance in India." *Journal of Development Studies* 13 (3): 298–323.

———. 1985. "Rural Poverty, Agricultural Production, and Prices: A Reexamination." In *Agricultural Change and Rural Poverty: Variations on a Theme by Dharm Narain*, pp. 59–75. Ed. by J. W. Mellor and G. M. Desai. Baltimore: Johns Hopkins University Press.

Akino, M., and Hayami, Y. 1975. "Efficiency and Equity in Public Research: Rice Breeding in Japan's Economic Development." *American Journal of Agricultural Economics* 57 (1): 1–10.

Alderman, H. 1986. *The Effects of Food Price and Income Changes on the Acquisition of Food by Low-income Households*. Washington, D.C.: International Food Policy Research Institute.

Athreya, V.; Boklin, G.; Djurfeldt, G.; and Lindberg, S. 1985. "From Usury to Credit? Transformation of Agrarian Credit Markets in Tiruchy District, South India." Unpublished working paper, Department of Sociology, Lund University, Sweden.

Athreya, V.; Djurfeldt, G.; and Lindberg, S. 1990. *Barriers Broken*. New Delhi: Sage.

Attwood, D. 1979. "Why Some of the Rich Get Poorer." *Current Anthropology* 20 (3): 495–516.

Bardhan, P., and Rudra, A. 1986. "Labor Mobility and the Boundaries of the Village Moral Economy." *Journal of Peasant Studies* 13 (3): 91–105.

Barker, R., and Herdt, R. 1978. *Interpretive Analysis of Selected Papers from Changes in Rice Farming in Selected Areas of Asia*. Los Baños, Philippines: International Rice Research Institute.

Bates, R. 1981. *States and Markets in Tropical Africa*. Berkeley: University of California Press.

———. 1983. *Essays on the Political Economy of Rural Africa*. Cambridge: Cambridge University Press.

Bell, C.; Hazell, P. B. R.; and Slade, R. 1982. *Project Evaluation in Regional Perspective*. Baltimore: Johns Hopkins University Press.

Bhaduri, A.; Rahman, Z.; and Arn, A. L. 1986. "Persistence and Polarisation: A Study in the Dynamics of Agrarian Contradiction." *Journal of Peasant Studies* 13 (3): 82–89.

Bhalla, G. S., and Chadha, G. K. 1983. *Green Revolution and the Small Peasant.* New Delhi: Concept.

Bindlish, V.; Barker, R.; and Mount, T. D. 1989. "Can Yield Variability Be Offset by Improved Information? The Case of Rice in India." In *Variability in Grain Yields: Implications for Agricultural Research and Policy in Developing Countries,* pp. 287–300. Ed. J. Anderson and P. Hazell. Baltimore: Johns Hopkins University Press.

Blyn, G. 1983. "The Green Revolution Revisited." *Economic Development and Cultural Change* 31 (4): 705–25.

Byerlee, D., and Harrington, L. 1983. "New Wheat Varieties and the Small Farmer." In *Rural Development: Growth and Equity*, pp. 87–92. Ed. B. L. Greenshield and M. A. Bellamy. Gower for International Association of Agricultural Economists, Aldershot.

Byres, T. 1981. "The New Technology, Class Formation and Class Action in the Indian Countryside." *Journal of Peasant Studies* 8 (4): 405–59.

Cain, M. 1981. "Risk and Insurance: Perspectives on Fertility and Agrarian Change in India and Bangladesh." *Population and Development Review* 7 (3): 435–74.

Caldwell, J. C.; Reddy, P. H.; and Caldwell, P. 1985. "Educational Transition in Rural South India." *Population and Development Review* 11 (1): 29–51.

Chambers, R.; Chinnappa, B. N.; Harriss, B.; and Wickremanayake, B. W. E. 1977. "Research Methodology." In *Green Revolution? Technology and Change in Rice Growing Areas of Tamil Nadu and Sri Lanka*, pp. 37–53. Ed. B. H. Farmer. London: Macmillan.

Chambers, R., and Harriss, J. 1977. "Comparing Twelve South Indian Villages: In Search of Practical Theory." In *Green Revolution? Technology and Change in Rice Growing Areas of Tamil Nadu and Sri Lanka*, pp. 301–22. Ed. B. H. Farmer. London: Macmillan.

Chambers, R; Longhurst, R.; and Pacey, A. 1981. *Seasonal Dimensions of Rural Poverty*. London: Frances Pinter.

Charsley, S. 1982. *Culture and Sericulture*. New York: Academic Press.

Chaudhry, M. G. 1982. "Green Revolution and Redistribution of Rural Incomes: Pakistan's Experience." *Pakistan Development Review* 21 (3): 173–205.

Chinnappa, B. N. 1977. "Adoption of the New Technology in North Arcot District." In *Green Revolution? Technology and Change in Rice Growing Areas of Tamil Nadu and Sri Lanka*, pp. 92–123. Ed. B. H. Farmer. London: Macmillan.

Christaller, Walter. 1966. *Central Places in Southern Germany*. Englewood Cliffs, N.J.: Prentice-Hall.

Cleaver, H. M. 1972. "The Contradictions of the Green Revolution." *American Economic Review* 62:177–88.

Dandekar, V. M., and Rath, N. 1971. *Poverty in India*. Bombay: Indian School of Political Economy.

Evenson, R. E., and Flores, P. M. 1978. "Social Returns to Rice Research." In *Economic Consequences of the New Rice Technology*, pp. 243–65. Los Baños, Philippines: International Rice Research Institute.

Farmer, B. H., ed. 1977. *Green Revolution? Technology and Change in Rice Growing Areas of Tamil Nadu and Sri Lanka*. London: Macmillan.

Farmer, B. H. 1986. "Perspectives on the 'Green Revolution' in South Asia." *Modern Asian Studies* 20 (1): 175–99.

Fertilizer Association of India. Various years. *Fertilizer Statistics*. New Delhi, India.

Frankel, F. R. 1971. *India's Green Revolution: Economic Gains and Political Costs*. Princeton, N.J.: Princeton University Press.

Garcia, M., and Pinstrup-Andersen, P. 1987. *The Pilot Food Subsidy Scheme in the Philippines: Impact on Poverty, Food Consumption, and Nutritional Status*. Washington, D.C.: International Food Policy Research Institute.

Gibb, A., Jr. 1974. "Agricultural Modernization, Non-farm Employment and Low-level Urbanization: A Case Study of a Central Luzon Sub-region." Ph.D. diss., University of Michigan, Ann Arbor.

Glaeser, B. 1987. *The Green Revolution Revisited: Critique and Alternatives*. London: Allen and Unwin.

Government of Tamil Nadu. 1974. *Tamil Nadu—An Economic Appraisal, 1973. Part II: Statistical Tables*. Madras: Evaluation and Applied Economic Research Department.

———. 1985. *Tamil Nadu—An Economic Appraisal, 1984–85*. Madras: Evaluation and Applied Economic Research Department.

Griffin, K. 1972. *The Green Revolution: An Economic Analysis*. Geneva: United Nations Research Institute for Social Development.

———. 1974. *The Political Economy of Agrarian Change*. London: Macmillan.

———. 1988. *Alternative Strategies for Economic Development*. New York: St. Martin's Press.

Griffin, K., and Ghose, A. K. 1979. "Growth and Impoverishment in the Rural Areas of Asia." *World Development* 7 (4/5): 361–83.

Guhan, S., and Bharathan, K. 1984. *Dusi: A Resurvey*. Working Paper no. 52. Madras: Madras Institute of Development Studies.

Guruswamy, P. A. 1985. "Agrarian Structure and Peasant Movements in Coimbatore District." Ph.D. diss., Panjab University.

Haggblade, S.; Hammer, J.; and Hazell, P. 1991. "Modelling Agricultural Growth Multipliers." *American Journal of Agricultural Economics* 73 (2): 361–74.

Haggblade, S., and Hazell, P. 1989. "Agricultural Technology and Farm-Nonfarm Growth Linkages." *Agricultural Economics* 3:345–64.

Haggblade, S.; Hazell, P. B. R.; and Brown, J. 1987. "Farm-Nonfarm Linkages in Rural Sub-Saharan Africa." *World Development* 17 (8): 1173–203.

Harrison, A. 1985. "Some Early Impressions of the Basic Economics of Village Life." Research Report no. 2. Reading University–Tamil Nadu Agricultural University, Project on Credit for Rural Development in Southern Tamil Nadu.

Harriss, B. 1976a. "The Indian Ideology of Growth Centres." *Area* 8 (4): 263–69.

———. 1976b. "An Analysis of Rural Urban Transactions: An Indian and Sri

Lankan Case Study." In *Agriculture in the Peasant Sector of Sri Lanka*, pp. 171–88. Ed. S. W. R. de A. Samarasinghe. Peradeniya: Ceylon Studies Seminar Series.

———. 1981. *Transitional Trade and Rural Development*. Delhi: Vikas.

———. 1984. *State and Market: State Intervention in Agricultural Exchange in a Dry Region of Tamil Nadu*. New Delhi: Concept.

Harriss, B., and Harriss, J. 1984. "Generative or Parasitic Urbanism? A South Indian Market Town 1973–1983." *Journal of Development Studies* 20 (3): 82–101.

Harriss, J. 1977. "The Limitations of HYV Technology in North Arcot District: The View from a Village." In *Green Revolution? Technology and Change in Rice Growing Areas of Tamil Nadu and Sri Lanka*, pp. 124–42. Ed. B. H. Farmer. London: Macmillan.

———. 1982. *Capitalism and Peasant Farming: Agrarian Structure and Ideology in Northern Tamil Nadu*. Bombay: Oxford University Press.

———. 1986. "Agricultural/Non-agricultural Linkages and the Diversification of Economic Activity in Rural Asia." Indo-Dutch Conference on Rural Diversification, New Delhi, mimeo.

Hazell, P. B. R., and Anderson, J. R. 1984. "Public Policy toward Technical Change in Agriculture." *Greek Economic Review* 6:453–82.

Hazell, P.B.R., and Röell, A. 1983. *Rural Growth Linkages: Household Expenditure Patterns in Malaysia and Nigeria*. Research Report no. 41. Washington, D.C.: International Food Policy Research Institute.

Herdt, R. W., and Capule, C. 1983. *Adoption, Spread, and Production Impact of Modern Rice Varieties in Asia*. Los Baños, Philippines: International Rice Research Institute.

Hewitt de Alacantara, C. 1976. "Modernizing Mexican Agriculture." Geneva: United Nations Research Institute for Social Development.

International Labour Organization. 1977. *Poverty and Landlessness in Rural Asia*. Geneva: ILO.

Johnston, B. F., and Kilby, P. 1975. *Agricultural and Structural Transformation: Economic Strategies in Late-developing Countries*. New York: Oxford University Press.

Lipton, M. 1977. *Why Poor People Stay Poor: Urban Bias in World Development*. London: Temple Smith.

——— (with R. Longhurst). 1989. *New Seeds and Poor People*. Baltimore: Johns Hopkins University Press.

Mellor, J. W. 1975. *The Impact of New Agricultural Technology on Employment and Income Distribution—Concepts and Policy*. Occasional Paper no. 2. Washington, D.C.: U.S. Agency for International Development.

———. 1976. *The New Economics of Growth*. Ithaca, N.Y.: Cornell University Press.

Mellor, J. W., and Johnston, B. F. 1984. "The World Food Equation: Interrelations among Development, Employment, and Food Consumption." *Journal of Economic Literature* 22:524–31.

Mundlak, Y. 1981. "On the Concept of Non-significant Functions and Its Implications for Regression Analysis." *Journal of Econometrics* 16:139–49.

Murty, K. N. 1983. "Consumption and Nutritional Patterns of ICRISAT Mandate Crops in India." *ICRISAT's Economic Program Report* 53. Patancheru, India: International Crops Research Institute for the Semi-arid Tropics.

Pandey, S. 1989. "Irrigation and Crop Yield Variability: A Review." In *Variability in Grain Yields: Implications for Agricultural Research and Policy in Developing Countries*, pp. 234–41. Ed. J. Anderson and P. Hazell. Baltimore: Johns Hopkins University Press.

Pearse, A. 1980. *Seeds of Plenty, Seeds of Want.* London: Oxford University Press.

Pinstrup-Andersen, P. 1979. "The Market Price Effect and the Distribution of Economic Benefits from New Technology." *European Review of Agricultural Economics* 6 (1): 17–46.

———. 1982. *Agricultural Research and Technology in Economic Development.* London: Longman.

Pinstrup-Andersen, P., and Hazell, P. B. R. 1985. "The Impact of the Green Revolution and Prospects for the Future." *Food Review International* 1 (1): 1–25.

Pinstrup-Andersen, P., and Jaramillo, M. 1989. "The Impact of Drought and Technological Change in Rice Production on Intrayear Fluctuations in Food Consumption: The Case of North Arcot, India." In *Seasonal Variability in Third World Agriculture: The Consequences for Food Security*, pp. 264–84. Ed. David E. Sahn. Baltimore: Johns Hopkins University Press.

Prahladachar, M. 1983. "Income Distribution Effects of the Green Revolution in India: A Review of the Empirical Evidence." *World Development* 11:927–44.

Pyatt, G., and Round, J. I. 1985. *Social Accounting Matrices: A Basis for Planning.* Washington, D.C.: World Bank.

Rao, B. R. H.; Klontz, C. E.; Rao, P. S. S.; Begum, A.; and Dumm, M. E. 1961. "Nutrition Status Survey of the Rural Population in Sholavaram, Seasonal Dietary Survey." *Indian Journal of Medical Research* 49(2):316–29.

Rao, C. H. H. 1985. "Changes in Rural Poverty in India: Implications for Agricultural Growth." Rajendra Prasad Memorial Lecture, 30th Annual Conference of the Indian Society of Agricultural Statistics, Akola, Dec.

Rudra, A. 1984. "Local Power and Farm Level Decision Making." In *Agrarian Power and Agricultural Productivity in South Asia*, pp. 250–80. Ed. M. Desai et al. Delhi: Oxford University Press.

Scobie, G. M. 1979. *Investment in International Agricultural Research: Some Economic Dimensions*. World Bank Staff Working Paper no. 361. Washington, D.C.: World Bank.

Scobie, G. M., and Posada, R. 1978. "The Impact of Technical Change on Income Distribution: The Case of Rice in Colombia." *American Journal of Agricultural Economics* 60 (1): 85–92.

Sen, L. K.; Wanmali, S.; Bose, S.; Misra, G. K.; and Ramesh, K. S. 1971. *Planning Rural Growth Centres for Integrated Area Development: A Study in Miryalguda Taluka.* Hyderabad: National Institute of Community Development.

Shanin, T. 1972. *The Awkward Class*. London: Oxford University Press.

Shetty, S. L. 1978. "Structural Retrogression in the Indian Economy." *Economic and Political Weekly*. Annual number:185–244.

Steinhoff, M. C.; Hilder, A. S.; Srilathar, V. L.; and Mukarj, D. 1986. "Prevalence of Malnutrition in Indian Pre-school Children: A Survey of Wasting and Stunting in Rural Tamil Nadu, 1983." *WHO Bulletin* 64(3): 457–63.

Sundaraaraj, R., and Pereira, S. M. 1971. "A Diet Survey in a Village of North Arcot." *Indian Journal of Nutrition* 8(1): 9–12.

Walker, T. S., and Ryan, J. G. 1990. *Village and Household Economies in India's Semi-Arid Tropics.* Baltimore and London: Johns Hopkins University Press.

Wanmali, S. 1983a. *Service Provision and Rural Development in India: A Study of Miryalguda Taluka, Andhra Pradesh.* Research Report no. 37. Washington, D.C: International Food Policy Research Institute.

———. 1983b. "Service Provision, Spatial Intervention and Settlement Systems: The Case of Nagpur Metropolitan Region, India." *Annals of the National Association of Geographers of India* 3:27–65.

———. 1985. *Rural Household Use of Services: A Study of Miryalguda Taluka, India.* Research Report no. 48. Washington, D.C.: International Food Policy Research Institute.

Wanmali, S., and Khan, W. 1970. "Role of Location in Regional Planning with Particular Reference to the Provision of Social Facilities." *Behavioural Sciences and Community Development* 4:65–91.

World Bank. 1986. *The World Bank Atlas, 1986.* Washington, D.C.: World Bank.

World Health Organization. 1985. *Energy and Protein Requirements.* Report of a Joint FAO/WHO/UNU Expert Consultation. Geneva: World Health Organization.

Contributors

P. K. Aiyasamy was a professor and head of the Department of Agricultural Economics, Tamil Nadu Agricultural University, Coimbatore, and is now a consultant with Sivanappan Associates, Inc., Coimbatore, Tamil Nadu, India.

Neal Bliven is a research analyst at IFPRI, Washington, D.C.

Barbara Harriss is a lecturer in developmental economics at the International Development Centre, Queen Elizabeth House, Oxford University, Oxford, U.K.

John Harriss was dean of the School of Development Studies, University of East Anglia, Norwich, U.K., and is now with the Development Studies Institute, London School of Economics and Political Science, London.

Peter B. R. Hazell was director of the Agricultural Growth Linkages Program at IFPRI and is now principal economist at the Agriculture and Rural Development Department, World Bank, Washington, D.C.

Mauricio Jaramillo was a research assistant at IFPRI, Washington, D.C.

Per Pinstrup-Andersen was director of the Food Consumption and Nutrition Policy Program at IFPRI. He is now a professor of food economics at Cornell University and director of the Food and Nutrition Policy Program at Cornell, Ithaca, N.Y.

V. Rajagopalan was vice-chancellor of Tamil Nadu Agricultural University, Coimbatore, India, and is now a consultant with the Agricultural Zonal Planning Unit, Planning Commission, Government of India.

C. Ramasamy is a professor of agricultural economics at Tamil Nadu Agricultural University, Coimbatore, India.

Sudhir Wanmali is director of the Agricultural Growth Linkages Program at IFPRI, Washington, D.C.

Index

Designed by Bruce Gore.

Composed by NK Graphics
in Times Roman text and display.

Printed on 50-lb. Glatfelter Offset, Eggshell Finish, B-16,
and bound in Holliston Roxite
by Thomson-Shore, Inc.